The Self AND THE DRAMAS OF HISTORY

Books by Reinhold Niebuhr

CHRISTIAN REALISM AND POLITICAL PROBLEMS

THE IRONY OF AMERICAN HISTORY

FAITH AND HISTORY

DISCERNING THE SIGNS OF THE TIMES

THE CHILDREN OF LIGHT AND THE CHILDREN OF DARKNESS

THE NATURE AND DESTINY OF MAN (ONE VOLUME EDITION)

CHRISTIANITY AND POWER POLITICS

AN INTERPRETATION OF CHRISTIAN ETHICS

MORAL MAN AND IMMORAL SOCIETY

The Self

AND THE DRAMAS

OF HISTORY.

Reinhold Niebuhr

CHARLES SCRIBNER'S SONS

New York, 1955

Library of Congress Catalogue No. 55-7197

to U. M. N.

Contents

vii

Part III

Preface

This volume, written in two years of enforced leisure, elaborates a theme which was subordinate in some of my other books, but which I never developed fully. I acknowledge my indebtedness to the great Jewish philosopher, Martin Buber, whose book *I and Thou* first instructed me and many others on the uniqueness of human selfhood and on the religious dimension of the problem. I make this acknowledgement explicitly because I have not recently studied the remarkable book which prompted my original interest and I have therefore not done justice to it in the text of this volume.

I wish also to acknowledge with gratitude the rigorous criticism which every chapter received from my wife, frequently resulting in changes in both form and content; and to my secretary, Mrs. Nola Meade, whose faithfulness, care and accuracy in transcribing my rough copy into a presentable form, tremendously eased my labors.

Reinhold Niebuhr

Part I

THE DIALOGUES OF THE SELF WITH ITSELF, WITH OTHERS AND WITH GOD.

THE FREEDOM OF THE SELF WHICH MAKES THESE DIALOGUES POSSIBLE. DRAMA AS THE HISTORICAL DEPOSIT OF THE DIALOGUES. IS THE DIALOGUE BETWEEN THE SELF AND GOD REAL OR IMAGINARY?

Chapter 1

THE UNIQUENESS OF THE HUMAN SELF

M an is obviously distinguished from the other creatures by some marked capabilities and qualities. In the Western tradition, composed of Hebraic and Hellenic components, Hebraism supplied the poetic metaphor to designate human uniqueness. In the Bible it is affirmed that God made man "after his image and in his likeness." This assertion of the divine element in human nature was however not elaborated, except by implication. It was left to the Greek philosophers to define the uniquely human more precisely. They did so by equating the divine element in man with his "reason." Aristotle further defined the rational capacity as the ability to conceive universals, in short, the capacity for making conceptual images. But reason also meant for Aristotle, and for all of Western thought since his day, the logical and analytical faculties of the mind. With these man distinguishes things from each other, traces the causal sequences in which they are chained and, having separated distinctive things, tries to bring them into some kind of coherence. Obviously the rational faculty is a very significant part of the unique capacity which is indicated by the metaphor "image of God."

The question is whether any of these classical definitions adequately describe the unique capacity for freedom of the human person. Conceptual tools are no doubt necessary for the self's freedom over the flux of natural events and for projecting ends beyond those set by natural appetites and desires. The self must even use concepts to make itself, as the world, the object of its attention. It uses memory, a force of "reason" which neither Plato nor Aristotle completely understood, to transcend its movement through time and be aware of its self-identity in this temporal flux. Plato and Aristotle did not quite understand memory because they equated "recollection" with the conceptual and mathematical forms which the mind used in mastering the rough stuff of its perception. But the significant power of memory lies in its capacity to retain unique events whether they fit into a conceptual mold or not.

Let us define the uniqueness of the human self by emphasizing the three dialogues in which it is involved according to the Hebraic rather than the Hellenic description of its reality. The implications of these three dialogues may give more accurate content to the original metaphor "image of God" than the Greek emphasis on reason. The self is a creature which is in constant dialogue with itself, with its neighbors, and with God, according to the Biblical viewpoint.

(A) The dialogue of the self with itself is an empiric fact in the sense that every astute person must admit that such a dialogue goes on in the internal life of the self, though there are no external evidences of this dialogue. This internal dialogue is a more significant testimony of the self's freedom over nature than its endowment with conceptual capacities, though these are frequent instruments of the self in the dialogue.

(B) The self is in constant dialogue with various neighbors. This may be a quality which Aristotle was partly describing by defining the self as a *zoon politicon*. But that definition would not necessarily do justice to the endless nuances and levels of the dialogue of the self with others. It is not merely dependent upon others for its sustenance and security. It is dependent upon them for the image which it has of itself and for the spiritual security which is as necessary to the self as its social security.

(C) The self is in dialogue with God. Perhaps this assertion will immediately prejudice our analysis in the eyes of those who have drawn heavily upon either naturalistic or idealistic versions of the Greek tradition. The assertion that the self is in dialogue with God takes the inquiry immediately beyond the limits of empirical verification. It would seem so much safer to follow Aristotle and define the uniqueness of the self as its reason, a definition which is capable of empirical verification. Let us therefore make some at least preliminary concessions to the spirit of contemporary empiricism and say merely that the self imagines itself in an encounter with the divine. For surely the persistence of this imagination is an empirical datum about the self. Perhaps we can be even more moderate and declare that the self distinguishes itself by a yearning for the ultimate. For if we omit this characteristic we have failed to define the total anatomy of human selfhood. We must leave the more exact definition of what this may mean to a later consideration. It is sufficient now merely to call attention to the fact that any datum which illumines the indeterminate character of the self's capacity for transcending itself, its history and its world is necessary for an adequate conception of the anatomy of human selfhood.

Chapter 2

THE INTERNAL DIALOGUE OF THE SELF

W e may safely say that the human animal is the only creature which talks to itself. It maintains a rather constant internal dialogue in which it approves or disapproves its actions, or even itself. Its accusations and defences of itself are quite different from those in which it engages in its external dialogues. The self pities and glorifies itself as well as accuses and excuses itself. It could not carry on this dialogue without using its "reason"; for the dialogue means that the self in one of its aspects is making the self, in another of its aspects, its object of thought. It uses conceptual images for this procedure.

But it is important to note that the self which is doing the judging and excusing, the pitying and glorifying, is not necessarily the "rational" or the "intelligible" self in contrast to the "sensible" self. It was the primary mistake of the philosophers from classical days to this day to equate the self as subject with mind; and the self as object with either the body, or the body-soul unity, or with some other aspect of the self as creature. The fact is that there are not two distinct selves in this internal dialogue. There are merely two foci of the same self. We do, of course, know of a pathological condition in which the self becomes separated into two warring and comparatively discrete entities. This is known as "schizophrenia." There are pathological states which border on this internal division. But the healthy self is always one self, no matter how much it engages in a perpetual internal dialogue.

The dialogue within the self proceeds on many levels. Sometimes it is a dialogue between the self as engaged in its various responsibilities and affections and the self which observes these engagements. Sometimes the dialogue is between the self in the grip of its immediate necessities and biological urges, and the self as an organization of long-range purposes and ends. Sometimes the dialogue is between the self in the context of one set of loyalties and the self in the grip of contrasting claims and responsibilities.

When artists try to depict a character in a novel or drama, they frequently resort to the record of this internal dialogue because it may be more revealing than the self's external dialogue or dramatic action. With artistic license they claim to be privy to the secrets of this dialogue, though it is by its very nature secret; and the self which entertains ambitions and desires is subject to temptations and considers alternative modes of action about which even the most intimate friend may know nothing. Only the victorious, and not the vanquished, forces are known to the outside world. The self remains such a mystery even to its friends because so little is known about the stratagems which produced the victory of the one over the other force.

An interesting witness to the reality of the self's inner dialogue, and more particularly of the phenomenon of the self as spectator of its actions and attitudes, is furnished by Lucy Sprague Mitchell in her biography of her husband and her own autobiography, entitled *Two Lives*.[1] Speaking of her adolescence, she writes: "It was at this time that I became aware of the complexity of one's make-up. When I acted in our

[1] Simon and Schuster, Inc.

stable-theatre I seemed to be two people: one making up dramatic lines and rendering them in fine action, and the other
listening, approving or disapproving. I was actor and critic
at the same time. I found that this was disturbingly true,
whatever I did. When I talked with father or helped mother
with household arrangements, I always heard and saw myself
doing these things. I must be hopelessly insincere, I always
thought. But the sense of guilt did not change me one bit. So
vivid this inlooker self became, that I called it 'the thing in
the corner.' Among my old papers I find a curious document,
written in my fourteenth year and beginning: 'Tis seldom
that one personality speaks to another. Even more rare is it
that one's other personality speaks to another personality.
Too seldom alas, for more often than not they speak another
language." Obviously this is a very significant memory of a
vivid experience of childhood, and throws a bright light on
the anatomy of selfhood which is superior to the analyses of
many learned men.

The analyses of Freud and of subsequent "depth psychology"
into the inner tensions of the human psyche have both illumined and obscured this inner dialogue. They have illumined
it insofar as the analyses proved conclusively that the old
"body-mind" separation was mistaken; and that the inner
organization of the self is much more intricate than was supposed.

The Freudian division of the self into "id," "ego" and
"super-ego" indicates at least two levels of the dialogue, that
between the self in the grip of its immediate necessities and
the self in its more inclusive and coherent organization; and
that between the self as concerned with itself and the self in
its relations to the community. It also proves that the dialogue
may leave many scars. The therapeutic efficacy of depth psychology rests largely upon the discovery that a part of the
"unconscious element in the ego" is but the repressed portions of a preconscious desire. Freud, in fact, denied the freedom of the will, partly because he was so preoccupied with
the limiting forces upon the will by neurotic anxieties, which

he attributed to the baneful effect of repression. Sometimes Freud pictured the task of analysis to be that of freeing the "ego" from the limits placed upon it by the "id" and the "super-ego." The task of psychoanalysts is, he declares, "to strengthen the ego, to make it more independent of the super-ego, to widen its vision and extend its field of organization so that it can take over portions of the id. Where the id is, there shall the ego be." [2]

For all of the therapeutic skill of Freudian psychology, and its wisdom in exploring the labyrinths of the self, it has confused the realities of the internal dialogue in some degree by obscuring the fact that the self is really in both the "id" and the "super-ego." The "id" is defined as a cauldron of "seething excitement." But it obviously has the guile of a real self in trying to evade the guard of the "ego's" "censor." Sometimes Freud pictures the tension between the "ego" and the "repressed" portions of the self. Inasmuch as neuroses are due to these repressions, it is important to bring this repressed material into the open consciousness. The tool of emancipation is the recollection of the experiences in which the repressions took place. Freud notes that the resistance to this process of recollection is offered by the conscious self. "There is no doubt," he declares, "that the conscious and preconscious ego subserves the pleasure principle. It is trying to avoid the pain which would be aroused by a release of the repressed material." [3] Thus the self is in this dialogue between the "coherent ego" and the "id" more than it would at first appear.

The presence of the self in the dialogue between the "ego" and the "super-ego" is even more mistakenly obscured. This is obviously a debate between the self as engaged and obligated to its various communities and the self concerned with its own ends. But the Freudian psychology moves within the limits of a rigid naturalism; and this second level of transcendence is not conceivable within those limits. The "super-

---

[2] *New Introductory Essays on Psychoanalysis,* p. 112.
[3] *Beyond the Pleasure Principle,* p. 20.

ego" is therefore no more than the pressure of society upon the "ego"; and it does not occur to Freud that the self has both the power to defy the community for the sake of its interests and for the sake of interests more inclusive than those of a given community.

The inclination to ascribe the sense of social responsibilities to the external pressure upon the self and to imagine the self resisting these pressures, makes Freudianism pessimistic about the possibility of extending any kind of social discipline to the extent required by modern society. This pessimism is expressed in Freud's *Civilization and Its Discontents*. The conviction prompts the conclusion that there is a tremendous amount of "aggression" stored up by the weight of the "super-ego" and also by the "cultural super-ego." Since there is no possibility of channeling all this aggression, Freud is sceptical about the problem of eliminating conflict in life. This curious conclusion has persuaded our social, as well as psychological, sciences to such a degree that some of them have become practically irrelevant to the serious task of dealing with conflicts of interest on every level of politics and economics. It is certainly not relevant to deal with the monumental collective egoism of nations, compounded of many genuinely historical cumulations; of illusion, and power lusts, as if they were merely the aggregate of individual "aggressiveness." Thus a discipline, which has proved itself therapeutically efficient in dealing with pathological states of individuals, has been betrayed into the inanity of speculating whether the Germans, Russians and Japanese could be cured of their "aggressiveness" by a sufficiently wide application of psycho-therapy.

Freud himself has had some curious evidence of the reality of the self, which he initially obscured in his analysis. He thought, for instance, that many forms of anxiety neuroses were due to traumatic experiences in youth, chiefly of a sexual nature. He was finally made suspicious by the indicated excessively high rate of incest which was confessed in these recollections; and it dawned upon him that the confessions were bogus and merely betrayed the incestuous desires of the patients in their youth.[4] In the same fashion a modern psychologist [5] reports, on the one hand, that the analysis of specific causes has banished the idea of a transcendent self from the consideration of causes as successfully as an earlier natural science had banished God; but, on the other hand, he cautions against the possibility of the banished and guileful self, manipulating the tools of analysis for its own self-justification.

Incidentally, the emphasis put by modern psychiatry upon the voluntary cooperation of the patient and the futility of forcing submission to therapy is another indication of the importance of the banished self and of the reality of the freedom which has been denied.

The inability of Freudianism to comprehend the reality of a free self prompts it to reduce the problem of guilt to the manifestation of neurotic guilt. Neurotic guilt may be defined as the sense of guilt due to fancied violations of arbitrary norms. It has little to do with the sense of guilt, arising from the self's violations of norms accepted by it as valid and validated by the experience of other men. It also tempts psychiatry to reduce all forms of egotism to vestiges of childish egocentricity which greater experience will correct. Thus an approach to the self which is therapeutically adequate for pathological aberrations of selfhood is incapable of comprehending the real problems of the self on either the political or the religious level.

The dialogue which the self carries on within itself is certainly more complex than understood in classical philosophy. Depth psychology has uncovered many of these complexities. But it has no doubt obscured many others because it failed to grasp that the same self is in the various *personae* of the dialogue.

[4] Ernst Jones: *Life and Work of Sigmund Freud.*
[5] L. F. Shaffer: *Psychology of Adjustment.*

Chapter 3

THE DIALOGUE BETWEEN THE WILL
AND CONSCIENCE OF THE SELF

The relation of the conscience to the will of the self is certainly one aspect of the self's internal dialogue. Will and conscience are two levels of the transcendence of the self over itself. More accurately, the will is the result of the self's transcendence over the complex of its impulses and desires. The will is in fact the self organized for the attainment of either a short-range or long-range purpose. This organization requires a rational analysis of the ends in view, a comparison of the relative merits of those ends either from the standpoint of the self's total ends or from the standpoint of some more inclusive system of value. The will is operative on all levels. A young man may, for instance, will to be a lawyer; will to take a college education in pursuit of this ultimate end; and will to join the football squad. He may will the latter course either in pursuit of the ultimate end, or because it is an ancillary end which is deemed by him not to be in conflict with his ultimate end. On all these levels of willing reason is the self's instrument in judging the goals of action. Yet the consistency with which a self pursues its immediate ends and subordinates them to an ultimate end is not an intellectual achievement. Consistency is the achievement of the self rather than of its reason, because there is no power in reason as such to compel consistency though it may have the power to detect inconsistency in the pursuit of goals.

The self's capacity to view itself, and to judge either its short-range or its long-range purposes, gives rise to a reality in its life which is usually termed "conscience." Conscience, like will, avails itself of rational tools but is not subject to these instruments.

It would seem that any judgement by the self of its own actions and attitudes is an expression of conscience. But this is not so. The self may, when viewing its actions, either accuse or excuse itself; and if it accuses itself, it may do so from its own standpoint. That is, it may view its actions as being too "unselfish" and not sufficiently concerned with its own interests.

In short, the self in the position of viewing its own actions is not inevitably expressing its "conscience." The prevalent view that there is some identity between conscience and reason is due to the error of assuming that the self in the position of transcending itself inevitably has a wider concern than the self in its engagements. It has a wider view, but not necessarily a wider interest. The fact is that the self which views its own actions and attitudes is more inclined to be concerned for itself than to judge itself for this concern. We must postpone for the moment a consideration of this aspect of self-transcendence to consider the manifestations of "conscience," particularly in its relation to the will. We will define conscience, provisionally at least, as any aspect of the self's judging its actions and attitudes in which a sense of obligation in contrast to inclination is expressed. Many efforts have been made to deny the reality of such a sense of "ought." Most of these efforts are clearly derived from one-dimensional views of selfhood, usually elaborated within a naturalistic ontology. They try to eliminate the distinction between the desired and the desirable in the view of the self. But they fail to explain why the self is under the necessity of seeking what it desires by proving that the desired is really desirable; or that what the self wants is in accord with some wider system of values than the self's own interests. These hypocrisies are the most telling refutations of one-dimensional views of selfhood. They prove that there is a real distinction between inclination and obligation, between the desires of the self and its conception of a system of value which does not depend upon its inclination or desires. This sense of obligation is powerful enough to allow the self freedom to achieve what it desires only when it is able to persuade itself that what it desires is consonant with this more general system of values.

The "content" of conscience is obviously very relative to time and place. Yet the minimal terms of our obligations to our neighbors, incorporated, for instance, in the prohibition of murder, theft and adultery, are fairly universal. Hume rightly observed that the "preference for benevolence over self regard" was universal, certainly more universal than actual benevolence.

Perhaps it would be correct to surmise that the universalities of the "moral law" are derived from intuitions of the self about the essential nature of its selfhood. To this essential nature belong, on the one hand, its biological structure, and, on the other hand, its social nature. The self would therefore feel obligated to conform to the "law" written into its nature, including the law of love or the law which is derived from the mutual dependence of persons.

Yet the content of conscience is much more relative than the proponents of the idea of "moral intuitions" realize. These relativities point to the social derivation of the moral law. Man is both an historical and social creature. He does not make his moral judgements in a vacuum. The community in which he lives sets the standards by which he judges himself. There is at least that modicum of truth in the moral relativism propounded by modern anthropologists. That this is not the whole truth of the matter is proved by the frequency with which "conscience" expresses itself in defiance of the community. The modern martyrs who have given their life to defy communities which sought to make total claims upon the individual have vividly refuted all theories, whether psychological, sociological or anthropological, which sought to reduce the sense of moral obligation to a purely sociological phenomenon. More particularly they refuted the Freudian theory of the "super-ego" which was no more than the pressure of the community upon the "ego."

It is worth noting however that consistently "liberal" or "bourgeois" notions of conscience as purely individual do not do justice to the fact that the individual is best able to defy a community when his conscience is informed and reinforced by another community, whether religious or political. Perhaps the final paradox of the social and individual dimension of the moral sense is revealed by the fact that the individual may defy a community which directly impinges upon his life and threatens his liberty by its coercions; but his defiance is usually undertaken in the name of another, more inclusive or more worthy, community even though that community makes no overt claims upon him and may exist only in his imagination.

John Wheeler Bennett's study of the history of the German military caste in his *Nemesis of Power* is an interesting survey of the relation of "conscience," both to the pressure of self-concern and to the historical traditions which may inform a conscience. According to this study, the military caste which had strict conceptions of "honor" and a personal ethic which made Nazi practices abhorrent to it, was nevertheless the chief instrument for letting Hitler come to power, and came to an ignominious end, first as partner and then as captive, of the Nazi regime. This result was partly due to the fact that the traditional moral code of its members assumed the predatory character of the nation's morality. There was thus a partial concurrence between their and the Nazi morality. They were secondly motivated by a strong pride of caste which Hitler finally outraged, but initially satisfied, by giving them a seemingly exalted position in the "Third Reich." They were, in addition, so politically inept, that they were unconscious of having given the noose into Hitler's hands, which he used to hang them. This noose was their own exaggerated conception of "loyalty," and their abhorrence of breaking an oath of allegiance. Thus the inadequacy of the moral traditions which informed their conscience was equally responsible with their political ineptness, their lack of personal political integrity, and their personal and collective pride in making them the chief agents of their nation's undoing. Yet there were significant variations in the general pattern of the tradition which informed their moral life. There was a great difference between the integrity of a von Seekt and the capacity for intrigue of a von Schleicher. And the heroic courage which finally made a revolt against Hitler possible was only slightly different in composition from the character traits which made the caste such an ignominious instrument of Hitler's regime. No better symbol could be had in history of the infinitely varied relation of conscience to communal moral tradition, on the one hand, and of conscience to self-concern, on the other.

Since it is the self which wills and the self, on another level of transcendence, which judges what it has willed, there is naturally some confusion about the relation of will to conscience, illustrated in Shakespeare's *Merchant of Venice* in the account of the dialogue between Launcelot Gobbo and his conscience. In St. Paul's confession of the division in his soul (Romans 7), conscience is, on the one hand, a force above the self ("The law is spiritual: but I am carnal, sold under sin") but, on the other hand, the self identifies itself with conscience and feels that there is a force of inclination which operates against both will and conscience ("I, yet not I, but sin that dwelleth in me").

This confusion is heightened by the fact that conscience may become "divided" because it is at different times informed by contrasting sets of loyalties and operates in different contexts of moral claims. Mark Twain is very much interested in this confusion. In his *Huckleberry Finn,* he pictures "Huck" anxious in one moment because telling the truth would deliver his friend the runaway slave, Jim, to his pursuers, and in the next moment uneasy because he has told a lie. Huck thereupon cries out against this confusion: "It don't make no difference whether you do right or wrong, a person's conscience ain't got no sense and goes for him anyway. If I had a yaller dog and he had no more sense than my conscience I would poison him. It takes up more room than all a person's insides and ain't no good nohow. Tom Sawyer says so too."

The relation of conscience to reason is an even greater source of confusion. We have seen that the self, both in its willing and in its judging, avails itself of its logical and analytic faculties. In willing, it uses logic to avoid confusion in the organization of its aims. It also avails itself of reason to detect the contradiction between its aims and desires and a larger system of values of which it has become conscious because it can survey itself in its relation to some larger communal or moral system in which its desires are not as central as they seem to be in its unreflective state.

But it is important to note that the self is always the master, and not the servant, of its reason. That is why reflection is not identical with the operation of conscience. Reflection may prompt a greater self-concern than an unreflective engagement of the self in its responsibilities and affections. The self is, in fact, more, rather than less, inclined to be concerned with itself when it detaches itself from a situation and views it from a transcendent position. This fact gives at least a provisional justification for the lower estimates of the moral quality of "reason" which romanticism advances.[1] It also explains why Hobbes, with some plausibility, could regard the same reason, which philosophers from Plato and Aristotle to Kant regarded as the root of virtue, as the cause of the inordinancy of human ambitions. It was, according to Hobbes, man's "reason" which disturbed the simple harmony of nature. Men by their reason "saw or thought they saw" a better way of organizing their common life. This usually meant organizing to their greater advantage. The self, in short, could use reason to justify its ends as well as to judge them, and there was evidently no

[1] Bergson: "When the self first begins to think of itself it thinks of itself first."

power in reason to limit the desires and ambitions of men. There was no rationally compelling analysis of a complex social situation which could compel the self to moderate its claims in the interests of the whole. The inclination of the self to use its freedom over self and the communal situation to press its claims rather than to moderate them, proves the inadequacy of all theories which equate self-concern with some inertia of nature or some vestige of infant ego-centricity. The chief difficulty in the Freudian analysis of the self is that it is blind to the resources for both love and self-love at the very heights of human personality, rather than in a pleasure seeking "id."

The universal inclination of the self to be more concerned with itself than to be embarrassed by its undue claims may be defined as "original sin." The universality of the inclination is something of a mystery. The orthodox idea of an inherited sinful taint certainly can not explain this tendency. Nor is it meaningful to follow theologians, who, since Origen, have reduced this tendency to an ontological fate and have thus equated the fall with creation. The simple survival impulse may be grounded in our created nature. But we are considering, not the survival impulse, but the tendency to consider ourselves whenever we rise to survey the whole human situation. We will understand the nature of this universal inclination if we note that it expresses itself on many levels, so that its universality does not indicate a uniformity in human behavior. It expresses itself in the action of the deserter, whose self-concern tempts him to evade the risks of war. But it is also revealed in the attitude of the brave soldier who may, upon enlistment in the Army, anxiously speculate on the possibility of attaining officer rank. A person may be thoroughly "devoted" to a cause, a community, or a creative relationship, and yet he may, within terms of that devotion, express his final concern for his own prestige or power or security. This bondage of the will to the interests of the self is what is meant by the "bondage of the will" in Christian theory. There is a significant confusion in regard to this conception, well illustrated in the debate between Luther and Erasmus on the freedom and the bondage of the will. Erasmus, in common with Renaissance thought, conceived of the freedom of the will as the freedom of the self over its impulses. The Reformation, on the other hand, defined the bondage of the will as the bondage of the self to its self, from which bondage there could be emancipation only by "grace" and not by the strength of one's willing.

Chapter 4

THE LADDER OF THE SELF'S AMBI-
TIONS, DESIRES AND QUALMS OF
CONSCIENCE

The self's capacity to view every situation in which it is involved, and to view itself from a standpoint beyond the situation makes for the indeterminate character of all human desires and the corresponding indeterminateness of the qualms of conscience about the legitimacy of those desires and lusts. The self is usually assumed to be "rational" in the exercise of its freedom over natural necessities. But since the self has a freedom beyond its rational capacities it can subordinate its reason to its desires. It can do what Hobbes evidently equated with the idea of "rational." It can use its reason to prove its ends legitimate. In short, both desires and qualms of conscience about the desires are indeterminate; and both are the fruit of the self's capacity to transcend every situation, historical or natural, which offers either preliminary restraints upon its ambitions, limits for its desires or justifications for its undue selfishness.

Thus a civilization, which is technically efficient as ours is, sets no limits to the standards which technics may achieve in establishing the security and comfort of the self against the hazards of nature or of history. Some of the eighteenth- and nineteenth-century dreamers were under the illusion that the triumphs of science, particularly of the medical sciences, would finally change the whole human situation by extending the limits of life set in the traditional "three score years and ten." Time has proved these hopes to be illusory. The brevity of man is an inexorable fate which science can not eliminate. But men will continue to exploit the possibilities of comfort and security above this limit. In this enterprise both the creative desire to master nature and the more egoistic impulse to achieve comfort and power are variously compounded.

There are, in the same fashion, no limits to the possibilities of refining a culture or expanding the treasures of art and science. The purely formal disciplines of culture will expand without limit until a romantic revolt against formalism reveals the perils to spontaneity in the formal disciplines. Everything in human life—its interests, ambitions, lusts, and fears—tends to expand without limit because man has the capacity to survey any cultural or historical situation from a vantage point which does not take its standards wholly for granted; and he has therefore the ability to imagine a more perfect goal or more consistent application of a technique or a more satisfying fulfillment of desire.

These limitless possibilities apply as much to the individual as to a culture or community. There are no limits to human ambitions or securities. Whether people have one house or three or five, and whether the house boasts of two or twenty rooms, is not determined by some logical principle or some primary need because human desires always transcend elementary needs. The scope beyond the primary need invariably includes cultural as well as purely physical values.

This ladder of ambition and achievement is inevitably accompanied by a ladder of anxiety. The poor man is anxious lest he lack sufficient income to satisfy the basic needs of his family. The rich man is anxious that he may not be able to conform to the living standards of his neighbors. He is also anxious lest envy of his wealth destroy, rather than enhance, respect for his person. Human anxieties grow with achievement and the anxieties contain both concern for the adequacy of the social or artistic achievement and for the social prestige, which may follow upon the achievement either contemporaneously or ultimately.

The two-fold nature of anxiety reveals that conscience is subject to the same indeterminateness as ambition. In school or college the young people with moderate gifts are anxious lest they fail in their tests. The more gifted are anxious about the position which they may hold in their class. And, in their anxiety there is a mixture of concern about the adequacy of their mastery of a particular subject and about the social prestige which may be the fruit of their scholastic attainments.

The very creative personalities, who may have succeeded in surpassing every social or historic standard, are not satisfied by this attainment because they have both the ability and the inclination to set themselves more severe standards, whether on aesthetic or moral issues, than those which society sets. This mood of anxiety could be partly defined as "conscience." The qualms of conscience are just as indeterminate as the lust and ambitions of men, ranging from the man of easy conscience because he has desisted from a previous crime, to the man who has an uneasy conscience because his privileges are inconsistent with a standard of justice which he has set for himself, or because he is involved in a social evil from which he sees no escape, or from which a little more courageous action on his part might offer the way of escape.

There are, of course, all sorts of pragmatic ways of limiting the limitless desires of men both for justice and for self-expression, both for self-realization and self-giving. But the limits are provided on the whole by the counter forces of history and of life. A purely "rational" solution is impossible because the contingent factors in every situation are too numerous.

Chapter 5

THE SELF IN SPACE AND TIME

There can be no question, of course, that the self is an object among other objects in space and time. It has its dated existence at some particular time and in some particular location. The conditions of time and space, of age and environment determine its character to a large degree.

But the self also rises indubitably out of the situation of time and place. As Hocking observes, it is in time but it also has time within it. By its memory and foresight it transcends the given moment and is therefore transtemporal in one dimension of its being. It is also spaceless in one dimension. The self-consciousness of the self proceeds in a particular organism. But the self is, in one dimension, non-spatial. Its imagination is free to rove over the boundaries of time and space to which it is bound. But it is more important to note that self-consciousness is ultimately non-spatial. This is a great embarrassment to any rational conception which must insist on the coherence of the various entities with which it deals. The non-naturalistic philosophers of Greece sought to eliminate this scandal by interpreting the self as "reason" and assuming reason to be the "form" of the spatial world. There was a plausible reason for this procedure. The self undoubtedly possesses a rational faculty; and the rational faculty measures the structures of the spatial world. The power of mathematics to unlock nature's secrets filled the mind with wonder from Aristotle to Leonardo da Vinci. This coherence between a non-spatial mind with the forms of space therefore seemed to offer a clue for the solution of the seeming absurdity of a non-spatial entity. The mind is non-spatial, but it is congruent to the dimensions of space. It furnished the forms for spatial objects. That was why mathematical calculations could solve so many problems of spatial relations.

Actually this answer is no real solution for the problem of the self which is more complex than mind and has a more integral and discrete existence. The principles of reason are universal; and idealists of all the ages have sought to swallow up the self in these rational universalities. But the integral self is a highly particular entity which resists these efforts. Yet they have been accepted from Greek rationalism through the whole modern idealistic tradition. Hegel involved himself in all kinds of absurdities in his effort to prove that the real self was not the particular self but a self of universal mind. Kant's "Ego of Transcendental Apperception" is obviously no ego at all but merely the universal principles of rational procedure. Fichte combined romantic with rationalistic influence to project something that obviously had some of the inner vitality of a true self rather than pure mind, but he produced an even more absurd idea when he supposed that this finite self was capable by its own will to create itself in absolute validity.

The fact is that there is no escape from the "rational absurdity" of the real self because it is at once in time and beyond time. It is spatial and yet non-spatial. And there is no sharp distinction between its spatial and non-spatial dimensions. Yet this double fact, which outrages the sense of rational coherence, is a fact of daily experience. The philosophers since Plato and Aristotle have eliminated the absurdity of the self which is in time and yet beyond time and space by reducing self to mind and identifying mind with form and thus establishing it as congruent to space and time. Modern psychology has no such simple way out of the dilemma. It is committed to the study of the empirical self as the object of its study. If any part of that object seems to elude it, the inquiry becomes embarrassing, for only an object in space and time can be the subject of scientific study according to its own presuppositions.

Chapter 6

THE SELF AND ITS BODY

The self is not a particular self merely because it is in a particular body. It can take a partially objective view of its body just as it can of its mind. But it has an internal relation to its body as to its consciousness which makes the idea of "my body" different from the idea of "my property." There is an organic unity in every animal organism which is usually described as its "soul." The self is "soul" insofar as it has an experience of the unity. But it is more than soul insofar as it can think of its body as an object even while it is an inner experience of the bodily organic unity.

In Charles Lindbergh's account of his memorable flight across the Atlantic two decades ago,[1] he gives an admirable account of the unity and the difference between the self and its body and its mind. The statement occurs in his description of his effort to master physical fatigue after thirty hours of flying across the Atlantic. He writes: "For immeasurable periods I seemed divorced from my body as though I were an awareness, spreading through space, over the earth and into

[1] From *The Spirit of St. Louis,* by Charles A. Lindbergh; copyright 1953 by Charles Scribner's Sons; used by permission.

the heavens, unhampered by time and substance, free from the gravitation that binds men to heavy human problems of the world. My body requires no attention. It's not cold. It's not hungry. It's resigned to being left undisturbed. Why have I troubled to bring it here? I might better have left it back at Long Island or St. Louis, while this weightless element that has lived within it flashes through the skies and views the planets. This essential consciousness needs no body for its travels. It needs no plane, no instruments, no engine. Only the release from flesh, which the circumstances I have gone through, make possible. Then what am I? The body substance which I can feel with my hands and see with my eyes? Or am I this greater understanding and greater realization which dwells within it and extends to the universe outside; a part of all existence, powerless but without need of power; immersed in solitude yet in contact with all creation? There are moments when the two appear inseparable and others when they can be cut apart with the mere flash of light.

"While my hand is on the stick, feet on the rudder and my eyes on the compass, this consciousness, like a winged messenger, goes out to visit the waves below, testing the warmth of the water, the speed of the wind and the thickness of the overhanging clouds. It goes north to the glacial coast of Greenland, over the horizon to the coast of Ireland, England, and the whole of Europe, away through space to the moon and stars, always returning unwillingly to the mortal duty of seeing that the limbs and muscles have done their duty while it was gone." [2]

There could hardly be a more perceptive analysis of the essential aspatial nature of the self, combined with its intimate relation to a body in a given space. Mr. Lindbergh goes on to describe the conflict between the fatigued body and the resolute will: "With the faint trace of day an uncontrollable desire to sleep falls over me in quilted layers. I've been staving it off with difficulty during the hours of moonlight. Now it

2 *Ibid.,* p. 353.

looms all but unsurmountable. This is the hour I've been dreading; the hour against which I've tried to steel myself. I know it is the beginning of my greatest test. . . . I've lost command of my eyelids. When they start to close I can't restrain them. . . . My body has revolted against the rule of the mind. . . . Every cell in my body is in revolt, sulking in protest claiming that nothing, nothing in the world could be worth such effort; that man's tissues were never meant for such abuse. . . . I've got to muster all my reserves, all the tricks I've learned, all the remaining strength of mind, for the conflict. . . . I've got to find some way to keep alert. There's no alternative but death and failure, I keep repeating, using the thought too as a whip for my lagging mind, trying to make my senses realize the importance of what I am saying. . . . I set my mind on the sunrise and try to think about that. It will be better when the full light of day has broken. The desire for sleep will give way to the waking habits of the day . . . shaking my body and stamping my feet no longer has any effect. I'll have to try something else. . . . My eyes close and open and close again. I'm beginning to understand that a new factor has come to my assistance. It seems I'm made of three personalities, three elements, each partly dependent and partly independent of the other. There is my body which knows that what it wants most in the world is sleep. There is my mind constantly making decisions, that my body refuses to comply with. And there is something else, which seems to become stronger rather than weaker with fatigue, an element of spirit, a directive force which has taken control of both mind and body. It seems to guard them as a wise father guards his children . . . when my body cries out that it must sleep the third element replies that it may get what relaxation it can but that sleep is not to be had. When my mind demands that my body stay awake it is informed that alertness is too much to expect under these circumstances. . . . But while it must not expect alertness on the body's part, it can be confident that there will be no sleep."

This is as illuminating an account of the constant inner

dialogue in the self as we have in modern literature. It is to be noticed that "my" body is at one time an object among other objects, and in another mode it is different from all other bodies because of its internal connection with the self. It participates in the inner dialogue, or rather it influences a part of the self in the debate, for the body as body obviously lacks an organ for participation. Most interesting is Mr. Lindbergh's suggestion that there must be a "third factor" which he defines as "spirit." This is a significant admission that the division within the self is more complex than the body-mind division. This is the more important in view of the fact that Lindbergh has attributed the power of decision to the "mind" yet he feels that a third element which he tentatively defines as "spirit" is over both body and mind. This tri-partite division of the self falls into a traditional pattern. It is the more significant because Lindbergh has obviously made no academic study of these mysteries. But in common with the scholars he defines as "spirit" what is really the self itself in its awareness of its freedom over its functions. Usually the will, one of the functions of the self, or rather the self in its organization of its impulses and desires, is thought of as more intimate to the self than either its mind or body. But Lindbergh assigns to the self not merely the will which overrules the immediate impulses but also the capacity to reassure the "anxious mind," that is, the anxious self in its immediate consciousness of danger. He has, in short, given us a very accurate description of the complexity of the internal dialogue within the self and of the transcendent unity and freedom of the self in spite of this dialogue. What he defines as "spirit" might be regarded as the ultimate freedom of the self over its inner divisions. This capacity of freedom in Lindbergh's analysis contains elements of will and resolution but also something which seems superior to the anxieties of "mind." It is, in short, the self standing above its functions and capacities and yet proving its relation to them.

Chapter 7

THE DIALOGUE BETWEEN THE SELF
AND OTHERS

The self is engaged in a perpetual dialogue
with other selves in which its dependence upon others becomes
apparent but which also proves its independence over all
relationships. These dialogues create dramatic actions of various kinds which must be considered presently. The dialogues
may be prompted by casual, or by permanent, relationships
with others. While these dialogues represent a dimension of
selfhood which is usually intended by the definition of the
self as a "social animal," they are not in the category of social
life as usually defined. They move above the level of social
cohesion which may be observed objectively. They are dramatic elaborations of these social cohesions.

The self, in its dialogue with others, confronts certain in-
variable conditions of self-fulfillment and self-giving which
may be enumerated as follows:

(A) The self faces the other self as a mystery which can
never be fully penetrated. It can surmise about the internal
life of the other self by way of analogy with its own internal
dialogue. But these analogies are usually misleading because
the dialogues, while very similar in form, may be very dissimi-
lar in content. The self makes many errors by relying too
much on analogy.

(B) The self sees the other as an instrument for its purposes and as a completion for its incompleteness. The sexual relation is the most vivid form of one self seeking completion in another self. The self is completed in the lives and services of a whole community of persons, but these completions do not concern us for the moment. We are considering only those completions which involve dialogic relation between persons who recognize in each other the mystery of similarity and uniqueness.

The most obvious solution of the self's dependence upon others is a relation of mutual dependence which satisfies each self without making one the mere instrument of the other.

(C) Even an ideal relation of mutual helpfulness can not satisfy one condition in such a dialogue. The self can not be truly fulfilled if it is not drawn out of itself into the life of the other. Mutual love seems to be a satisfactory solution for this problem, but insofar as mutual love may involve only cool calculations of reciprocal advantages of the kind Aristotle describes in his analysis of *Philia,* it is always in danger of degenerating into a relation of mere calculation. If so, it will ultimately be corrupted by resentments about the lack of reciprocity in the relationship. For even if Aristotle's elaborate formulae for apportioning "honor" and "profit" in varying proportions to the "superior" and to the "inferior" partner, there can never be perfect reciprocity in any relationship because of the uniqueness of the gifts of the persons in the relationship.

Even a mutual partnership therefore requires something more than calculated mutuality to initiate it and to preserve it. Nature has provided the madness and heedlessness of what is called "falling in love" for the initiation of the most intimate and reciprocal of all relationships. One of the problems is to supply some force more permanent than this original madness to preserve what has been initiated. This fact gives social relevance to what would otherwise seem to be a socially irrelevant form of love, defined in the New Testament as *agape.* This dimension of the dialogue between selves clearly transcends all canons of prudence; and reveals how the dialogue is enriched and sustained by viewpoints which are not directly derived from the ordinary level of mutuality.

The paradox that "whosoever seeketh to gain his life will lose it but whoso loseth his life will find it" accurately and succinctly states the issue encountered in the dialogue between persons when each person is too intent to complete his life in the other in calculated mutuality. If this dimension is not recognized, the paradox will seem to be a contradiction. Thus Gardner Murphy worries about this seeming contradiction: "Psychology can not very well admit," he declares, "without in some way adjusting the paradox that human nature is really capable of effective functioning only under conditions of individualistic fulfillment and at the same time claim that it is the nature of man, so to lose himself in others as to care little or nothing for the enhancement of the self. . . . Christianity extols both ideals and leaves us in confusion." [1]

The confusion is rather in Mr. Murphy's mind; and in the mind of all who would reduce human relations to simple canons of prudence. It is an obvious fact, which may be "empirically" observed, that the self does not fulfill itself most fully when self-realization is its conscious aim. In the same way happiness and virtue elude conscious striving. In any event, prudent calculation is not powerful enough to draw the self from itself as the center of its existence and to find a center beyond itself. That is why sacrificial love is such a "scandal" in any system of prudential ethics, but is so relevant to a full consideration of the problem of human togetherness.

(D) The self recognizes the other as the limit of its expansiveness. It is the "other"; and the otherness includes a final mystery which even the most imaginative love can not penetrate. It is an independent and unique life which, ultimately considered, can not be fitted into any, even common, purpose or project. There must therefore be an element of reservation and reverence for the other in even the most mutual relations.

----

[1] *Personality*, Harper & Brothers, p. 925.

(E) The uniqueness of the individuals which enter into any dialogic relation makes each one of these relations highly unique, however general may be the natural basis of the relation. Thus each marriage relation takes place upon the common ground of hetero-sexuality. But each such partnership is a unique and distinctive drama of mutual adjustment which exhibits some unrepeatable elements. It becomes a moral and artistic achievement rather than a scientific one, though science must master many of the common and general elements at its foundation, such as common problems of sexual adjustment.

(F) While the self is a unique center of life it is indeterminately "open" to other selves. There are no geographic or temporal limits for the self's dialogue with others. Some of the significant dialogues are carried on with heroes of the past or with a deceased parent or absent lover. The dialogue in such cases may seem to lack the "other," so necessary for the dialogue. But memories will furnish the stuff for the dialogue which are almost as powerful as contemporary exchanges.

(G) The pattern of these dialogues is conditioned by historic factors. They may change the basis of the pattern but not annul the highly individual character of the dialogue. Former ages have, for instance, superimposed the pattern of male dominance upon the essential mutuality of the marriage relationship. The modern age has gradually challenged this pattern with the rising power and freedom of the woman. The modern marriage relationship is therefore under the necessity of developing grace within a more rigorously equalitarian standard between the sexes and providing for two foci, rather than one, for the family group. In the same way the pattern expressed in the ancient commandment that "children should obey their parents" has been altered by imperceptible degrees so that, at its worst, the modern pattern defies some basic facts of nature, which include the superior wisdom and power of the older generation. At best, they prove that an amiable disrespect of parents is more compatible with love than an enforced obedience.

Chapter 8

THE SELF AND ITS COMMUNITIES

The self's physical and spiritual need of others is naturally satisfied not only in casual and transient but in permanent relationship. Man is a "social," or as Aristotle has it, a "political" animal. Human communities rise from nature to every type of historical artifact. The simplest, most primordial and most persistent community is the family, which is rooted in nature, that is, in hetero-sexuality, providing for the basic sexual partnership and necessitating a guardianship by the parents in the human being's long period of infancy. The long infancy, constantly extended as civilization becomes more complex and the skills required for maturity more numerous, is not a fact of pure nature. It is because man is an historical creature that he comes upon the scene only partially equipped for life and requiring long tutelage for the acquisition of his various skills. The family lies naturally at the basis of the larger community, which is no more in primitive life than an enlarged family, with kinship feeling as the force of cohesion. Civilization gradually welds these larger families together into more powerful communities. The guile of priests and skill of warriors are operative in this enterprise

signifying the place of organized physical force and of the ideological factor in the forces of social cohesion.

The relation of the individual to the community is a complex one which could be defined as consisting of vertical and
horizontal dimensions. In the vertical dimension the individual is related to the community on two sharply contradictory
forms. He looks up at the community as the fulfillment of his
life and the sustainer of his existence. By its organization his
physical and moral needs are met. Morally the community is,
in the words of Hegel, the individual's "concrete universality."
But there is another direction in which the individual may
look in the vertical dimension, about which Hegel knew little
because he, in common with most rationalists, could not comprehend the heights of human selfhood above the dimension
of reason. The individual looks down upon the community
because he is, as it were, higher than it. It is bound to
nature more inexorably than he. It knows nothing of a dimension of the eternal beyond its own existence. It therefore clings
to its life desperately and may sacrifice every dignity to preserve its mere existence. The highest moral ideal to which it
can aspire is a wise self-interest, which includes others in its
ambition for security. Looking down at the community from
his individual height the individual is embarrassed by the
difference between the moral standards of the community and
his own.

Much of the world's progress has arisen from this embarrassment, for it has tended to lift the standards of the community.
Whenever communities throttle the individual's uneasiness
and insist that the collective sense of the good is absolute, they
sink, as does modern totalitarianism, into a consistent bru-
tality. On the other hand, the idea that the individual's uneasy
conscience about collective morality can be easily transposed
into collective action leads to sentimentality. This has been
particularly apparent in the bourgeois ethos which erroneously
imagined that communities were only provisional entities, to
be dispensed with, as soon as the individual had become fully
emancipated. Looked at from above, the community is the

frustration of the individual, even as it is his fulfillment when looked at from below. No historical progress can change the twofold relation of the individual to the community in the vertical dimension. The community will always remain both the fulfillment and the frustration of the individual. Historical progress may change, or enlarge, the community of primary loyalty; and make that community more complex with a competition of subordinate loyalties. The individual may achieve a degree of emancipation from the community by reason of these competitions, not characteristic of the more monolithic, usually agrarian, communities. But even the most democratic communities can not alter the tension between the individual and the community because it can not alter the difference between the individual and the collective desires and ambitions of men.

The social and political history of modernity is charged with tension between the individual and the community because a technical civilization has, on the one hand, emancipated the individual from his organic ties to the community; and has, on the other hand, given the community a greater cohesion and intensity than any which prevailed in the agrarian societies. Superficially the struggle has involved the agrarian classes, which championed the old organic forms, the bourgeois or trading and industrial middle class, which sought to exploit all the new and more flexible and mobile forms of power which came into their hands, and the industrial workers, who sought a greater degree of collective planning to protect them against the hazards and insecurities of a technical civilization. But the struggle was more than a contest between the classes, in which each class tried to protect the securities, or expand the liberties, which were ideologically appropriate to its mode of life. It was also a struggle in the soul of each individual who was conscious, on the one hand, of his individual destiny and worth, and for whom the presuppositions of a Christian interpretation of human dignity seemed to gain a new social and economic foundation. But, on the other hand, the same individual became dependent upon a greater and greater number of his fellow men for the maintenance of his life and the preservation of his securities, and was more and more involved in the collective destiny of his nation or even his civilization. The emergence of collectivist economies, whether inspired by romantic or by Marxist ideals, were protests against an individualism in which the self became lost in a nameless crowd after its emancipation from the cohesions of an older organic society. The tension between the equally forceful and equally dubious efforts to interpret life either in purely individual or in purely collectivist terms is derived from the contradictory consequences of technics upon the community. For they undoubtedly enlarge the intensity and extent of social cohesion on the one hand, while on the other they emancipate the individual from the close embrace in which organic communities held him.

These contradictory estimates have resulted in equally contradictory moral theories. According to the more conventional theory, conscience is purely a manifestation of the individual's moral sense and its social character is obscured. But the more favored theory among psychologists and sociologists is absurdly collectivist and makes the moral sense merely an expression of the pressure of the community upon the individual. Actually, all moral judgements are expressed in tension between two viewpoints derived from the fact that the individual regards the community both as fulfillment and as frustration. Sometimes the individual is impressed by the claims of the community in comparison with his own private and parochial values. He may espouse the cause of the community freely in his conscience. At other times the individual is embarrassed by the morally mediocre standards of the community. He may be particularly exercised by this aspect of the community precisely when the community becomes coercive and tries to suppress his qualms of conscience. At such times the individual may rise to an heroic defiance of the community and thus refute all simple "social" interpretations of conscience. It is, of course, significant that the individual infrequently defies a community of primary loyalty without having his conscience informed by another community, religious or political; and that he may construct a community in his own imagination, as, for instance, the "community of mankind," though this community may have no direct contact with him.

The individual experiences his relation to the community horizontally, rather than vertically, whenever his community is in conflict with other communities. In moments of competition or conflict between communities, the individual tends to become identified with his community so that its pride and prestige become his own. Indeed its majesty is frequently a compensation for his own real or seeming insignificance. This fact makes the pride of national and racial communities particularly attractive to individuals who suffer from various forms of individual frustration.

We have spoken of "the community" as if it were an exact entity. Actually there are communities based upon every common interest, desire or destiny. The European Middle Ages had a plural communal life, with the small feudal community furnishing the basic loyalty. It was in turn related to some larger community which ultimately became the nation. Both empire and Church tried to be an overarching community with universal pretensions. Modern Western life has been formed by the gradual dominance of the national community, which frequently tried to bring all other communities into subjection to it. But this growing nationalism is qualified by the endless elaboration of voluntary communities, rooted in economic interest, in artistic endeavors, or in religious commitment. The multiplicity of these communities has served to emancipate the individual, for competition between communities for the loyalty of the individual served to bring out his individual decision into sharp relief. The recent growth of totalitarian regimes rooted in either a fanatic national community or in a pseudo-universal class community are rightly regarded as protests, though perverse ones, against the disintegration of community under the force of an excessive bourgeois individualism and under the disintegrating forces of a technical civilization, particularly in its urban centers. The national community has become the community of most inclusive loyalty because it controls the state's coercive power and because geographic contiguity, combined with ethnic or linguistic homogeneity, are sufficient to overcome the potentially divisive forces of the subordinate communities. The supra-national integrations have the best chance of success in Western Europe where unity above the level of the national community has become the necessity of survival for those nations which bear the treasures of civilization against the perils of totalitarianism. These pressures, rather than abstract constitutional schemes, are the forces of communal cohesion because community is always an organic, historical entity rather than a purely rational artifact.

It might be possible indeed to define community as that association of individuals which has coalesced through forces of history, operating upon the cohesive forces given in nature such as geographic contiguity and racial kinship. Human communities have one thing in common with persons. They are historical entities who have reacted to unique historical events. Their memory of these events is one of the basic forces of community. They express their consciousness of their uniqueness by their devotion to heroes, who represent dramatic and poetic embodiments of the peculiar "genius" of the nation. Thus Washington and Lincoln have a special position in the national "myth" which expresses the self-consciousness of our nation. The memory of critical events such as the granting of the Magna Carta and the Declaration of Independence and Lincoln's Gettysburg Address, are also capable of sustaining and giving consistency to the "spirit" of the community. Many communities below the level of the nation, such as racial minorities are more integral as communities if they have the treasure of common memories, particularly those which are centered in some heroic or tragic events. The human community is thus defined in a dramatic historical pattern, just as is the individual. This pattern may develop such a degree of consistency of action that it will be close to natural necessity or ontological fate. But these historical destinies never produce a pattern which could become the basis of confident future predictions. One may predict that the solidity of the British community (as contrasted, for instance, with the French nation) will make a civil war less likely in the one nation than in the other. But beyond that, one can not go. One can not predict how the British community may react to external or internal stresses in the future.

Much learned debate has been devoted to the question whether it is legitimate to ascribe personality to communities. The debate remains inconclusive because communities lack, on the one hand, the integrity and the organ of self-transcendence which the individual person boasts, while, on the other hand, they have, analogous to that of the person, a consciousness of a continuing identity through the flux of historical events. In the case of the Jewish nation, for instance, the power of common memories of a dim historic past is strong enough to preserve the cohesion of the nation though it lacked until recently a physical and geographic basis for its life. Even now, the new nation of Israel will not contain the whole of the Jewish "nation" which continues to live in the diaspora.

Chapter 9

THE SELF AS CREATOR AND CREATURE IN HISTORICAL DRAMA

I t is obvious that the self's freedom over natural process enables it to be a creator of historical events. Both its memory of past events and its capacity to project goals transcending the necessities of nature enable it to create the new level of reality which we know as human history. But the self is not simply a creator of this new dimension, for it is also a creature of the web of events, in the creation of which it participates.

This double relationship naturally causes great perplexities and gives rise to some rather simple contradictory theories which emphasize either the one, or the other, role of creator or creature. The tendency to equate history with nature and to confuse the "laws of nature" with those of history has given rise, since the French Enlightenment, to a determinism which minimizes the creative role of man. The most consistent application of this determinism is the economics of *laissez faire,* drawn from physiocratic theory, and warning men from interference with the "natural" processes and "natural" balances of history.

But the tendency to equate history with nature can also

prompt a contradictory voluntaristic theory according to which man is called upon to use scientific technics to manage history, as he has managed nature. Many modern social scientists have been influenced by this voluntarism since Comte; and have naively insisted on the possibility of transferring the "scientific method," learned in the natural sciences to the management of human affairs. Aldous Huxley has satirized the dreams of such voluntarists in his *Brave New World*.

This interesting combination of determinism and voluntarism usually presupposes a vaguely defined elite of scientists who have the omniscience to manage the events in which ordinary mortals are merely creatures. Modern communism presents us with a much more dangerous combination of such determinism and voluntarism. It has a self-appointed elite, the Communist Party, who, by reason of being the only ones who are privy to the logic, which supposedly determines historical events, are able to intervene at the crucial moments to further the logic and finally to take the heroic step which will insure not only the victory of the "proletariat," but change the whole human situation by making man the unambiguous master of historical destiny rather than merely both creature and creator.

It remained for some modern cultural anthropologist to correct the absurdities of these combinations of voluntarism and determinism which underestimated the freedom of the man who is to be managed, and the finiteness of the man who is to do the managing, by projecting an even more absurdly consistent determinism, according to which all men are the prisoners of their respective cultures with no opportunity to exhibit characteristically universal human traits.

The freedom of man beyond the limits of the historical situation in which his art and life is formed does not necessarily reveal itself in those elements of his art which rise to the height of universally valid insights. It may manifest itself in highly individual insights, transcending the conventions of his society. As an instance: the culture of France, in the period of the Empire, nurtured three great novelists, Balzac, Flaubert and George Sand. Their novels were characterized by a common unconventional attitude toward sexual relations, characteristic of that period. But one of them, George Sand, also expressed a highly individual attitude within the general standards of the period. Her novels left the reader uncertain whether she intended to glorify wantonness or wished to expound the thesis that sexual relations, whether inside or outside of marriage, were intolerable without love. This attitude expressed neither the convention of her period nor some universally valid standard.

The freedom of men above their status as creatures of the historical drama does not necessarily express itself in conscious efforts to determine historical destiny. That ambition may be reserved for a few great statesmen; and the illusion of such creativity is held only by a few dreamers. Actually the creativity which may, or may not, affect historical destiny is open to every man even in the humblest walks of life when he comes to terms with his unique problems partly in terms which his culture supplies, and partly according to his unique gifts and inclinations. Whether his unique response "makes" history or not is largely out of his hands, for only the future can determine whether his unique response is to be the basis of a new historical pattern or is to be stored in the storehouse of history as merely another proof of the endless variety of human responses.

We might speculate endlessly upon such mysteries as the source of the unique moral courage which a man like General Rommel exhibited in his final defiance of Hitler and how it was related to his previous Nazi creed and could be compared with the courage of other generals who had the advantage of non-Nazi background but were not able to show a like courage. We will also have to wait upon history to find whether Churchill's obvious relish in the heroism of this gallant foe restored some of the dignity of gallantry into modern national combats or was merely the last flicker of light from a more romantic age in an age which has no use for such romantic candles in its neon-lighted modernity.

Chapter 10

THE SELF AND THE DRAMAS OF HISTORY

The dialogues, in which the self is involved, are transmuted into dramas whenever they precipitate action. These actions are formed into dramatic patterns which constitute a web of destiny for the individual, determining subsequent actions and dialogues. These dramatic patterns may extend to various communities, family, local or national. The dramatic patterns are historic realities in which freedom and necessity are variously compounded. The most indubitable constancies are those which are rooted in natural necessities, as, for instance, the facts of geography and climate in man's collective life and those of sex and age in man's individual life. But there are constancies of history which are almost as predictable as those founded in nature. Yet they are clearly historical, as, for instance, the constancies derived from the "character" of a culture.

The dramatic patterns contain causal sequences which may be analyzed with some degree of accuracy. It is possible to determine not only that a certain chain of events actually happened but also, to an extent, why they happened. But every answer to the question, why the events happened, must be speculative, since historical causation is very complex, each event standing in various chains of causation. Therefore one could not make a precise estimate of the "real" cause of an event, or even of its dominant cause. Historical analyses do not lend themselves to precise analogies with similar or contrasting patterns, nor can they become the basis of predictions of future events. Therefore the analyses of historical patterns must lack the scientific precision which characterize the conclusions of the natural sciences. In short, they must fail in the test of predictability which is the hallmark of any exact science.

Historical patterns are in a category of reality which can not be identified with the structures of nature. They are to be sharply distinguished from natural structures because they represent a compound of freedom and necessity.

History is the more complex because one pattern is superimposed upon another: the dramatic pattern of a national history, for instance, upon the dramatic pattern of a whole culture. Who can answer the question definitively, whether America is involved in the history of a culture which may be defined as "Western"; or whether the peculiar conditions of American history, our virgin soil, our continental economy, our heterogeneous population and our youthful energies separate our destiny from that of European culture?

It is because historical causation is endlessly complex, and historical dramas overlap one another in bewildering confusion, that history is not subject to the generalizations of either the scientists or the philosophers, who insist on trying to comprehend its multifarious themes in terms of either natural or ontological necessity. There are, of course, valid social or historical sciences. They are most legitimate when the scientists know themselves to be historians, rather than natural scientists; and therefore recognize that their generalizations are hazardous and speculative. The real historians have an instinct for the peculiar quality of history and know the hazards of predictions of the future. Economics, which began under physiocratic illusions, has, in these latter years, become more and more conscious of the endless historical contingencies which it must take into account in its predictions. Economists have therefore become increasingly modest, in contrast to some other social sciences, burdened with more physiocratic illusions about so-called "laws of nature."

Historical facts can be dealt with most "scientifically" when the field of inquiry is reduced to some manageable set of uniformities or recurrences in the behavior of individuals, subject to the same set of natural or historical circumstances— to the attitudes of adolescents or convalescents, for instance, or the behavior of industrial or agricultural labor, or to the conditions of urban life or to the effect of boarding-house existence upon family life. In such, and similar cases, statistical evidence may support generalizations; and uniformities of behavior may be distinguished from the historically variable factors. Sometimes predictions are inaccurate, even in these modest undertakings; in some cases because the unpredictable freedom of man is not taken into account, but more frequently because not enough attention has been given to variable conditioning circumstances. Efforts to predict elections in previous decades failed miserably because sample opinions were taken from people listed in telephone directories; and their ideological bias did not accurately typify the whole political spectrum. Now the samplings are undertaken more scientifically, that is, with due regard for the various groups of a community and their characteristic biases, based on economic and other interests. But no science can determine whether a Polish worker of Hamtramck, Michigan, will vote according to the prevailing opinion in the CIO, or according to his convictions about the adequacy of an administration policy in clearing up the wartime mystery of the murders in the Katyn forests in Poland. If wider generalizations are attempted, as, for instance, covering groups in the same economic class but under differing historical environment, they become more hazardous. What nonsense history made of the Marxist slogan: "Workers of the World Unite." It mistakenly assumed the equal disinheritance of industrial laborers in every nation, and incidentally the primacy of their economic interest. There are, no doubt, legitimate generalizations about the character of bourgeois communities as contrasted with agrarian ones. But will any such generalizations do justice to the variables in the middle-class life of France and Britain, of Australia and America?

In any event, no scientific investigations of past behavior can become the basis of predictions of future behavior. Even if an historian is able to establish causal sequences after the event, he can not make any generalizations about the past the basis of predictions of future actions and events. He can not do so, not only because he has insufficient knowledge of the complex causes of the past; but because he can not predict which one of the many tendencies and forces which determine actions, may have a dominant place in the life of individuals and nations. Only one historian, Jacob Burckhardt, was able to foretell the rise of twentieth-century tyrannies in the nineteenth century. And no one, as late as the beginning of this century, predicted the nightmare which eventuated from the Marxist dreams of heaven on earth. Marx would certainly have been surprised by contemporary realities. These surprising historical events are a refutation of all purely scientific or metaphysical efforts to interpret the drama of history and to reduce its seeming confusion to some kind of simple meaning.

If the analysis of uniformities and recurrences of behavior under like conditions may be defined as the scientific component of historiography, the biographic pinnacles of history are the most vivid reminders of its dramatic character which defies scientific analysis. The career of an eminent contemporary statesman, Sir Winston Churchill, will illustrate how human character rises by gradual stages from the necessities of nature, through historic destinies until it reaches the height of a highly individual and unique response to the unique events of its history. Sir Winston Churchill owes some of his "character" to the fact that he was born an Englishman in the Victorian period, and others to the fact that he was born in the aristocracy of that era. His characteristic differences from Mr. Chamberlain are partly due to his aristocratic background, for instance. Some of the influences upon his life are due to his descent from the Duke of Marlborough and some to the fact that he did not stand in the direct line of descent. The Dukes of Marlborough were inconspicuous country gentlemen. Mr. Churchill's ambition was undoubtedly fired by his lack of an assured place in the scheme of things as a son of a second son. Was the example of his father the determining factor? Or perhaps the neglect by his engrossed father and mother? It would have ruined a less robust lad, but it did not prompt resentment in him toward either his father or mother. It merely encouraged him to seek fame in order to be worthy of a father who ignored him, but whom he adored. One could go on to multiply the multifarious chain of causes which played upon his life. Any conclusions about the relative importance of any set of factors would be highly speculative. Nor would any analysis of his antecedents help to explain how a man, so obviously ambitious, did not involve himself in the self-defeat in which ambition usually becomes involved. "How vain are the calculations of self-interest," said Mr. Churchill, in surveying the pathetic life of the French Admiral Darlan. Why was this observation not true of Mr. Churchill? And what forces in his history caused the extraordinary degree of magnanimity in so resourceful a fighter? None of these questions about Mr. Churchill or any other character can be answered "scientifically," in the sense that one can establish a rationally compelling correlation of causes which lead to a given result. Biography is significantly an art. It is related to the art of portraiture. This latter art has not been superseded by the more exact science of photography. The reason is that portraiture spurns the science of reproducing the exact facial lineaments of a given moment for the art of seeing the quite essential character above and behind momentary expressions of mood. History is more of a science than biography because it can correlate and compare more facts and establish trends under seemingly unique events. But historiography can never be an exact science. The real historians know this and leave it to some modern social scientists to cherish this illusion.

It is interesting to note that Aristotle, who did not have

modern science's knowledge of the evolution of historic as well as natural forms, and lived under the illusion that the structures of both nature and history were fixed, made a sharp distinction between science which would analyze the "constants," and *"phronesis"* (practical wisdom) which must deal with contingent elements in life and history. The fact is that the sharpest distinction must be made between processes in which things "come to be" and "pass away" within a fixed structure of reality and the whole realm of human history, culminating in biography. In this realm there is a subordinate dimension in which events follow in a "necessary manner" as, for instance, the growth of a child through adolescence to maturity.

The radical freedom of the self and the consequent dramatic realities of history are naturally embarrassing to any scientific effort, either to understand or to master history. There is a consequent tendency in the psychological and social sciences to suppress these inconvenient facts about man, and to emphasize the various facts which "determine" his actions and destinies. History is indeed full of these determining conditions of geography and climate, of social and economic conditions, of environment and heredity. They lend plausability to the various determinisms, sociological and psychological, which negate some of the obvious "facts" about man and his history in order to comprehend them "scientifically," which sometimes ironically connotes "empirically."

The impulse to falsify the facts in order to bring them into a comprehensible pattern assails the scientists who try to manage detailed facts and small patterns. Another analogous temptation assails the philosophers and ontologists who try to make sense out of the larger patterns of history and to comprehend the whole drama of history as meaningful. Naturally the mind is baffled by the seeming confusion of the historical drama, devoid of the neat endings, whether tragic or happy, which art gives to the various dramas of history in order to endow them with comprehensible conclusions.

It is significant that working historians have an instinctive

reaction to the ambitions of the philosophers and to their pretension that they have discovered a larger ontological pattern
behind, within and above the phantasmagoria of history. "Men
wiser and more learned than I," writes the great historian
H. A. L. Fisher in the preface to his *History of Europe,* "have
discerned in history a plot, a rhythm, a predetermined pattern. These harmonies are concealed from me. I see only one
emergency following upon another, as wave follows on wave;
only one great fact, with respect to which, since it is unique,
there can be no generalizations, only one safe rule for the historian: that he should recognize in the development of human
destinies the play of the contingent and unforeseen."

Every philosophical effort to understand history is based on
the assumption that in some depth of reality a pattern may
be found in which that which seems "contingent and unforeseen" takes its place as a "necessary" development, as a servant
of the hidden logic which underlies and informs all things.

In the history of Western civilization the efforts to comprehend history ontologically have been many; but they all fall
into two primary categories: (A) the classical idea of the historical cycle and (B) the modern idea of historical development. This modern idea which has been elaborated since the
Renaissance takes such various forms as the Hegelian dialectical view of historical development and the supposedly un-
metaphysical and purely scientific idea of development in the
thought of the social Darwinists. All these ideas of "progress"
express the historical optimism of modern man. In various
metaphysical and scientific garbs they present themselves as
the effective religion of modern man. He endows his own life
with meaning because he can set it into the frame of a simply
meaningful history.

The two ideas of the cycle and of development actually
define two basic facts of historical occurrences. The cycle defines the birth, life and death of the organisms which participate in the historical stream. Since nations, cultures and civilizations are not organisms, in the exact sense of the word, and
have no definitely allotted time span of biological organisms,

the classical analogy between biological and historical cycles
was therefore partly erroneous. The error did not become apparent until the Aristotelian concept of a fixed historical structure was challenged by the idea of historical development.
Nevertheless, it contains a modicum of truth. For historical
cultures, civilizations and communities are mortal, though
their decay and death is never a fate ordained by their nature,
but is always partly the result of historic mistakes and miscalculations.

The modern progressive view is just as true and just as false
as the cyclical view. It is just as true because it corresponds to
one indubitable fact about history. That fact is that there has
been a steady growth of man's control of the natural forces
which furnish the basis of history. This development has
proceeded throughout the rise and fall of particular civilizations. It has culminated in the development of technics, which
have altered the possibilities of cohesion in the community as
well as changing the physical basis of historical existence.
Growing technics include means of communication which
have made larger units of cohesion possible; and the development in weapons of warfare which have culminated in the fearfully lethal atomic weapons of our day. This growth in technics has been so phenomenal that it has prompted the modern
illusion of "progress." But it becomes daily more apparent that
man's technical mastery over nature has not seriously altered
either his spiritual or intellectual endowments nor changed his
essential stature as both creator and creature in history. Technical development has therefore not changed history from its
essence as a drama to a course of predictable development.

The two patterns of the cycle and the forward movement
are therefore not so much dramatic patterns as they are the
two dimensions of the stage upon which the drama is played.
They have only negative significance for the meaning of history. Confusion results when positive meaning is ascribed to
these two dimensions of the stage of the drama. Spengler's and
Toynbee's efforts to restore the cycle as a bearer of positive
meaning prove both the possibilities and the limits of fitting

the drama of history into the cyclical mold. The endless variety of dramatic themes which are superimposed upon the historical cycles and the fact that their life, growth and death do not follow the necessities of the natural cycle but are due to human ingenuity and human failure, make the cycle impossible as a bearer of positive meaning. It may be inevitable that every culture or civilization should die. But it is possible that this death should prove to be the transmutation into another kind of life. This is at least one reason why historical cycles are not analogous to natural cycles, and why they can be bearers of a positive interpretation of the historical drama.

In the same manner historical development is not really analogous to natural growth. The basic fact of historical development is probably caused by man's increasing mastery of nature, and not upon any law of the "survival of the fittest" nor upon some obscure historical dialectic such as Hegel discerns. Certainly the ideas of progress, whether pretending to be "scientific" or "philosophical," tend to obscure the interplay between freedom and necessity which gives the human drama such a bewildering complexity. Yet there is historical development. Problems do recur in ever widening dimensions, as, for instance, the problem of community, which has reached global proportions in our day. But no "progress" can assure the solution of these ever wider and more complex problems. The forward movement can give history no more positive meaning than the cycle. Both describe, not patterns, but conditions for the historical drama.

Chapter 11

THE PROBLEM OF HISTORICAL KNOWLEDGE

W henever we consider the historical drama, we confront not only the fact that it is a realm of such contingency that it is difficult to find the structures and patterns which might be regarded as "really real," but also the fact that the observers of this drama are invariably themselves involved in the historical flux which they are trying to survey. Distance from controversial issues and efforts at "scientific objectivity" may give some historical observers a relative detachment from the issues which they try to interpret. But nothing can give any observer such detachment from the historical scene as would endow his views with the same kind of unchallenged and unchallengeable validity, which the conclusions of the natural scientists well may claim.

Thus the problem of the reliability of any knowledge about history is so serious that one may well be surprised that the logical positivists, who are sceptical about any propositions which do not contain either logical or mathematical axioms or "scientifically verifiable" conclusions, have not given more attention to the problem of the dubious character of all propositions about historical sequences of events. It is in fact an insoluble problem. Yet in the absence of omniscience we do fairly well in allowing various historians, reporting from their various temporal and ideological loci, to report and interpret the events of history. Extravagant biases are, of course, refuted; and it is possible to distinguish a true historian from an obvious propagandist, though it is not possible to draw a simple line between genuine history or propaganda. But it is not possible to get a definitive interpretation of such events as the French Revolution or the American Civil War, for instance, which would refute all conflicting interpretations.

We recently had a vivid reminder of the relativity of historical knowledge, when two former ambassadors to Spain, both historians, Claude Bowers and Carleton Hayes, reported on the civil war in Spain;—Mr. Bowers' *Mission to Spain* and Mr. Hayes' *Wartime Mission in Spain*. The one was favorable and the other unfavorable to the Spanish Republican cause. Mr. Bowers regarded the civil war in Spain as a prelude to the World War, and Mr. Hayes thought of it as a prelude to our present cold war with Russia. Both are honest historians and neither falsified the facts; but they chose very different facts and subjected all relevant facts to contrasting interpretations. Mr. Hayes is a liberal Catholic while Mr. Bowers stands in the Jeffersonian tradition.

Many histories of the French Revolution have been written from the diverse viewpoints of Jacobin and communist dogmas, from Bonapartist and Bourbon perspectives. But historical distance has not resolved the difference between them or given any one viewpoint a clear victory over the others. Sometimes the historical victory of a cause serves to give the viewpoint of the victorious cause a clear priority over the viewpoint of the vanquished. Accounts of our Civil War now remain comparatively unchallenged even though they can not satisfy the South. Even Lincoln is reluctantly accepted by the defeated South as a national symbol, provided Robert E. Lee can be bracketed with him as an equal hero. The Cavalier victory over the Roundheads in the restoration has made the historical interpretation of Cromwell's protectorate a fairly indisputable matter. Significantly, however, Americans have shown a rather more lively interest in the democratic sects of Cromwell's army than the British historians have evinced. Though defeated, their ideas furnished seminal influences for Anglo-Saxon democracy which are cherished on both sides of the Atlantic. Perhaps one reason why the historical interpretation of the French Revolution remains so inconclusive is that the Revolution itself has not been resolved in French political life. Thus history and the interpretation of history are mutually dependent.

An analysis of some larger patterns of history, such as the disintegration of the "Medieval synthesis" in the sixteenth century, will prove the inevitable "ideological" framework of any historical inquiry and the impossibility of refuting any of the conflicting interpretations conclusively.

The disintegration of the medieval culture resulted in the emergence of two religio-cultural forces, generally described as the "Reformation" and the "Renaissance." Both Renaissance and Reformation were rebellious against a culture and civilization, informed by the Catholic faith, which reached its flower in the thirteenth century and is still regarded as the "golden age" by Catholic historians. From the viewpoint of the children of either the Reformation or the Renaissance, the disintegration of this monolithic culture was inevitable. Its decay was apparent from the fourteenth century, that is, before overt rebellion shook its authority. The disintegration is regarded as inevitable because its static social and economic disciplines were not able to contain the new vitalities of a growing commercial civilization. Furthermore its Papal universalism was not able to come to terms with the power of emerging nationalism; and its clerical authoritarianism was not able to do justice to the cultural vitalities of the movement defined as the Renaissance. The children of both Renaissance and Reformation would probably agree in these estimates; but the children of the Reformation would add further indictments. They would place primary emphasis in the indictment of the medieval Church, that it had sought to derive political power from its prestige of sanctity; that it had substituted for the Biblical faith an amalgam of Biblical and classical ideas which guaranteed the individual salvation if he diligently climbed the ladder of merit and rigorously disciplined the "passions of the body," particularly sexual passions; that it presumed to mediate between man and God and to control the keys to Heaven; that it therefore obscured the real Biblical message of salvation, which set the individual under the judgement of God, and promised him forgiveness and renewal of life if he accepted this judgement with contrition and was made aware of his self-worship.

The primary concern of the Reformation was a religious one. Therefore Luther's defiance of ecclesiastical and political authority; and his words "Here I stand; I can do no other, so help me God," is regarded by the Reformation as incidental to the primary religious issue, while it is appreciated by the Renaissance as the one fact which makes the Reformation relevant to the struggle for liberty. The Reformation and the Renaissance also have different motives for objecting to Papal authority. The Reformation regards the clerical authoritarianism as an affront to the majesty of God, while the Renaissance regards it as a threat to the liberty of the mind.

The interpretations of the disintegration of the synthesis are thus partly contrasting and partly similar. There can be no definitive interpretation of what happened which could refute either one or both of these interpretations because the interpretations are informed by specific frames of meaning which must be shared before the conclusions emerging from the frame of meaning, prove acceptable. No amount of "empirical observation" or "scientific objectivity" can resolve such conflicts in the interpretation of historical events because there are few facts which refute interpretations which deal with the motives of the actors, the importance of specific causes of the events and the dominant tendencies of history in which these events are believed to be correlated. In short, the frames of meaning determine the interpretation of facts.

Insofar as Catholicism, though dethroned as the arbiter of

culture and civilization, remains nevertheless a vital religious
force, it is not possible to prove to its adherents that the
Reformation and Renaissance were both inevitable and justified rebellions against both the content and the authority of
the Catholic faith. Some intelligent Catholic historians will
persist in the convictions that these rebellions must be held
responsible for modern nationalism and for every other an-
archic force in life. In short, there can be no definitive refutations of any interpretation of historical events, though the
forces of history may conspire to refute some extravagantly
"biased" interpretations, or those which are too contradictory
to facts so obvious that they do not depend upon interpretations for validation.

This persistence of "ideological" elements in historical interpretation has exercised the epistemologists among the philosophers as much as the peculiar character of historical patterns has baffled the metaphysicians. One philosopher, obviously under the influence of the natural sciences, has offered
a simple solution for the problem of the relativity of historical
knowledge. He would eliminate "evaluations" in order to get
rid of "evaluational distortions." Since all the structures of
meaning which furnish the principle of coherence for historiography are contained in these "evaluations," this solution
is a rather rigorous one which would leave us with little else
but the bare dates of critical events.[1] Historical events are
established in terms of coherence by precisely the "evaluations"
which are so embarrassing philosophically. They point to the
impossibility of reducing historical drama to natural coherences.

At the opposite pole of historical epistemology is the "idealistic" interpretation, initiated by Dilthey and expressed most
consistently in the thought of the late R. G. Collingwood, one
of the most eminent philosophers of our time. He proves that
a philosopher has almost as great difficulty as a pure scientist
in interpreting the dramatic essence of history. He is clear that

---

[1] Maurice Mandelbaum: *The Problem of Historical Knowledge.*

history must be sharply distinguished from nature, for "the processes of nature can be described as a sequence of mere events but the processes of history can not. They are . . . processes of actions which have an inner side, consisting of processes of thought. What the historian is looking for is these processes of thought. All history is the history of thought." [2] The rethinking of the "thought" which inspired historical action, is according to Collingwood, "not a passive surrender to the spell of another's mind. It is the labor of active, and therefore critical thinking. The historian not only reenacts past thought but he reenacts it in the context of his own knowledge, and therefore in reenacting it criticizes it." [3]

Among the many difficulties of this rather implausible rationalizing of history, two deserve special consideration. (1) The unconscious, or only partly conscious, motives of the great actors of history, their resentments, ambitions and jealousies, can hardly be dignified as "thoughts"; and they are in any event more inscrutable than Collingwood supposes. Even if they were entirely overt, the question would still arise whether they could give us the real clue to the meaning of the sequences of events. Collingwood does not consider or refute the thesis of Tolstoi's great novel *War and Peace,* which was that historical patterns develop in ironic disregard of the purposes and ambitions of the actors of the drama.

We can not understand the pathetic period in which Hitler dominated Germany by reconstructing his thoughts or those of all of his lieutenants. Only a philosopher could have attributed such a motive to the historian. The historian would know that Hitler was probably not too conscious of the strange mixture of ambition and resentment which animated him. Collingwood made the mistake of defining as "thought" what is really the dramatic freedom which distinguishes history.

(2) Historical events are the product of a concatenation of social and historical forces, and therefore the thoughts even

[2] R. G. Collingwood: *The Idea of History,* p. 215, Oxford University Press.
[3] *Ibid.*

of the most eminent actors in the historical drama are unimportant in comparison with the interplay of these forces. If we revert once more to the tragedy of Hitler's Germany, we would understand it more completely, not merely by reading Hitler's *Mein Kampf,* but by tracing the strange confluence of historic forces and tendencies which permitted Hitler to dominate a nation momentarily and to involve it in disaster. The historian would have to explain why in Germany the private virtues of diligence and obedience could be so easily harnessed to collective evil; why the German people have preserved such extraordinary docility toward the pretensions of political power; why the German aristocracy was chiefly preoccupied with military tasks, why it became the unwilling tool of the mad Corporal and was unable or unwilling to extricate itself from his power; why the German middle classes, which in other countries became the bearers of democracy, developed an industrial efficiency surpassing that of any other nation while remaining politically incompetent and impotent. The historian would also find it necessary to inquire into the witting and unwitting connivance of other "democratic" nations in the rise of Hitler: why France, which is almost as incompetent on the political scene as Germany, should develop static forms of corruption which provided the foil for Germany's dynamic corruption; and why Britain, politically so much wiser than either France or Germany, should have thought it necessary to remain "uncommitted" in their quarrels and should thus have unwittingly encouraged Germany in her two world wars. These questions are but a few of those which historians have and will ask. In answering them and unraveling the tangled skein of the historical drama, they will make generalizations which will strike the reader as either competent or incompetent, as either hopelessly "prejudiced" or as comparatively "objective." But not one of their generalizations will be able to pass any of the tests which Descartes elaborated in his *Discourse on Method.* The field of causation in historical events is so multiple, and the motives of men so complex and obscure, and the dramatic patterns so multifarious that the artist-historian must certainly rely more on *phronesis* than upon *nous* to venture any generalization. This fact is so obvious that one would have thought that all the genuine historians would have, while admitting scientific and philosophical elements in their labors, long since organized a common defense against the philosophers and scientists who endanger the procedures of historiography by their scientific and "ontological" pretensions.

Both the historians and the average reader have an understanding for the dramatic essence of historical "facts," and discount as far as possible the ideological bias of the historian or correct the bias by other viewpoints, while the scientists and philosophers look in vain for some criterion of absolute truth in history. No such criterion can be found, because all observers are directly or remotely "interested" and the stuff of history is too complex to make it possible to convict any particular correlation of events or interpretation of historical sequences of "bias." Even when events are so far removed from contemporary issues that an "objective" view of them seems possible, some, even remote, analogical possibility may suddenly make a former historical dispute relevant to an immediate issue. The question why the Roman Empire declined ceases to be a remote historical issue as soon as someone tries to prove an analogy between the policies of Rome and those of the "New Deal," for instance.

Chapter 12

THE SELF AND ITS SEARCH FOR
ULTIMATE MEANING

In analyzing the various dimensions of human selfhood, we have thus far concerned ourselves with the presuppositions of the inquiry only insofar as we have called attention to the fact that the tendency to identify the self with its mind is as erroneous as it is persistent. The error obscures the freedom of the self over its rational faculties.

If we now proceed to inquire more rigorously into the dimension and character of that freedom, it will become apparent that the religious inclination of men is derived from that freedom. The freedom makes it impossible for them to consider systems of rational intelligibility, whether conceived in idealistic or naturalistic terms, as a solution for the problem of the meaning of their life. They discern a mystery and meaning above and beyond their rational faculties in themselves; and they also surmise that the chain of causes, whether conceived in terms of efficient or final cause, that is, whether in terms of idealistic or naturalistic metaphysics, points beyond itself to a mystery of creativity. This is true because any previous event is an intelligible, but not a sufficient, cause for the succeeding event. It was Hume's scepticism about causes which first breached the confidence in the intelligibility of the world and prompted Kant to elaborate his critical idealism, in which for the first time the confidence in reason was separated from confidence in a rational ontological order. The result was his conception of a mysterious *Ding an sich,* of a noumenal reality which indicated the mystery beyond the rationally intelligible phenomenal world of finite entities and relationships.

These scruples in modern philosophy have tended to create mystic overtones in any rational system, well-defined in Bertrand Russell's *Mysticism and Logic.* They are indications of the inevitable emergence of explicit religion even in cultures which have ostensibly banished mystery from a world believed to be completely subject to a rational order including both the knower and the known.

It must be noted however that the world views which assume the rational intelligibility of the world, without mystery, are not less "religious" because they disavow explicit religious faith. Confidence in a rational order is, as the great rationalist Bradley admits, also a faith. The self, even of a philosopher, is religious to the degree that the self must commit itself to a system of meaning, even if it has the view that the system is so self-explanatory and that it takes the self as mind so completely into its system of self-consistent truth that nothing more than the elimination of ignorance seems required to prompt the self to its acceptance.

But it is significant that these implicit religions never suffice in the long run, even when, as in the French Enlightenment or in modern communism, they rise to emotional heights of devotion which inadvertently betray a committed self rather than a dispassionate mind. The more explicit religions are, however, the more overt reactions to the fact that the self senses a mystery in itself and a mystery in the world beyond the flux of observable causes. It therefore tries to overcome the threat to the meaning of its life by finding that the one mystery, the ultimate or divine mystery, is a key to the understanding of the mystery of the self's transcendent freedom.

The task of penetrating the ultimate mystery prompts many

responses, but they could all be placed into three general categories: (A) The first category embraces all religious responses in which the self seeks to break through a universal rational system in order to assert its significance ultimately. It may seek to do this individually, as in modern romantic and existentialist thought; or it may be so conscious of its finiteness as an individual that it finds no opportunity to assert the ultimate significance of itself in history except by asserting the significance of the collective self. This category, in short, embraces all the idolatrous religions of ancient history, including both primitive polytheism and the imperial religions of Egypt and Babylon, and (in more artificial terms) of Rome. Until a recent day this idolatry, in which the individual self finds the ultimate source of its meaning in the history of the collective self so much more imposing though also so much closer to the flux of nature, was thought to be a phase of history which was overcome by the rise of the rigorously monotheistic religions and monistic philosophies. But the recrudescence of religious nationalism and the pseudo-universalistic Messianism of communism have instructed us that this idolatry, this worship of the collective self as if it were ultimate and not finite, is not merely due to the limits of a primitive imagination. It corresponds to a perennial desire in the human heart to eat one's cake and have it, too; to subordinate the finite self to something greater than it but not so great that the self may not participate in the exaltation of the finite value. Naturally this idolatrous religion must have baneful effects, not only because it complicates the problem of group relations by exaggerating the claims of contingent historical forces in competition with each other, but because the unconditioned commitment of the self to the collective self must rob it of its freedom; for the collective self is, though more imposing and more long-lived than the individual self, also so much more bound to nature and its necessities, so defective in organs of self-transcendence and therefore so much farther removed from the ultimate source of meaning, that the self debases itself by this uncritical devotion.

(B) The second alternative of explicit religious response has been defined by Aldous Huxley as "The Perennial Philosophy." He is right in asserting that it is a fairly universal response, but wrong in concluding that this universality guarantees its validity. This response, generally defined as "mysticism," stands at the opposite pole of idolatry. It is in fact an heroic effort to transcend all finite values and systems of meaning, including the self as particular existence, and to arrive at universality and "unconditioned" being. The persistence of this mystic tendency in the religions of the world is a telling proof of the ability of the self, in the ultimate reaches of its freedom and self-awareness, to discern some affinity between the mystery within itself and the mystery behind the observable phenomena and to find the key to universality in the joining of these two mysteries. This "perennial philosophy" embraces not only the systems, stemming from the thought of Plotinus, in the Western world but practically all religions of the Orient. It is expressed in the Brahman overtones of Hindu polytheism; in the Sufist tradition of Mohammedanism; in the Taoist tradition of Chinese culture and, most classically, in Buddhism. Here the search for undifferentiated being reaches the height of asserting a type of being as the goal of existence about which one can not be certain whether it is the fullness or the absence of being. It is certainly being bereft of all relationships and meanings.

(C) The third alternative, an explicitly religious answer to the self's search for the ultimate, embraces the two Biblical faiths of Judaism and Christianity. These faiths interpret the self's experience with the ultimate in the final reaches of its self-awareness as a dialogue with God. The idea of a dialogue between the self and God assumes the personality of God, an assumption which both rationalists and mystics find untenable, but to which Biblical faith clings stubbornly. Selfhood or personality is supposedly not attributable to God because the idea of personality is loaded with connotations of finiteness and therefore casts a suspicion of "anthropomorphism" upon Biblical faith. But it is significant that both mystics and rationalists have as much difficulty in ascribing personality to man as to God. This fact suggests that it is not the connotations of finiteness which create the difficulty but rather the fact that personality is characterized by both a basic structure and a freedom beyond structure. The rationalists can comprehend the structure within a system of rational cohesion; and the mystics are able to interpret the freedom as part of a system of undifferentiated potentiality. But neither is able to comprehend the total fact of personality within its system.

The dialogue between the self and God results in the conviction of the self, but not for reason of its finiteness. It is convicted rather of its pretension or "sin"; of claiming too much for its finiteness, and for the virtue and wisdom, which it achieves in its finiteness. The idea of such an encounter therefore permits the Biblical faiths both to affirm the life of the self in history and to challenge its achievements in any particular instance. "Enter not into judgement with thy servant, for in thy sight is no man living justified," declares the Psalmist. Kierkegaard sums up this theme of Biblical religions with the affirmation that "Before God all men are in the wrong." The fact that the self is judged for every inclination which affronts God's "majesty" by pride or lust for power is the religious dimension of sin. The prophets are however equally conscious of the social dimension which is the inclination of the self to take advantage of its fellow men. This "injustice" is never speculatively defined, as in Greek philosophy, but rigorously defined by reactions to injustice in particular situations.

The "severity" of God's judgement is matched by the "goodness" of His mercy. In the dialogue between the individual and God, this validates itself as the indeterminate possibilities of self-realization and fulfillment of the self's potentialities once it has ceased to seek fulfillment of life from the standpoint of itself. The problem of how the mercy of God is related to His justice is a perpetual problem in the Old Testament. The new Biblical faith of Christianity enters into history with the affirmation that the drama of Christ's life is in fact a final revelation, in which this problem is clarified by the assurance that God takes the demand of His justice upon Himself through Christ's suffering love and therefore "God was in Christ reconciling the world unto Himself."

The dying and rising again of Christ is the key to the self's possibilities in history. All of life is given this norm for the realization of selfhood. "I am crucified with Christ," declares St. Paul, "nevertheless I live." This theme is in perfect harmony with the words attributed to Jesus in the Johannine Gospel: "Except a corn of wheat fall into the ground and die, it abideth alone: but if it die, it bringeth forth much fruit." (John 12:24)

Thus the encounter of the self with God is defined in Biblical faith in terms of a norm which has been set by an historical "revelation." And this revelation is an historical event or series of events which are not essentially miraculous (miracles such as the "virgin birth" are afterthoughts) but are events in history which are discerned by faith to have revelatory power into the ultimate mystery. Both Biblical religions are covenant faiths, which organize covenant communities upon the basis of a common commitment of faith in the divine significance of these events. We must postpone until later, then, a consideration of the relation of revelation to the drama of history. In this connection it is necessary to observe that the discernment of ultimate significance of an historic event makes the Biblical religions seem primitive and unsophisticated in the eyes of both rationalists and mystics, who look for the ultimate or "unconditioned" in either the permanent structures of existence or in an undifferentiated ground of being. They may fail to note, however, that the Biblical presupposition is the only one of the three alternatives which asserts a discontinuity between the self and God. This discontinuity makes explicit faith indispensable in the ultimate dialogue; but it also prevents the self either from usurping the place of the divine for itself or from imagining itself merged with the divine. If we test these three alternative solutions for the self's search for the ultimate by the two tests of consistency or coherence with other truth, and by conformity with established facts subject to empirical tests, it will soon become apparent that the religions which tend to the exaltation of finite values and centers of meaning are most easily ruled out, as indeed they have been ruled out in principle for centuries. The collective self may be momentarily imposing; but its mortality is obvious and the perils to the individual self by its pretensions of divinity are very great.

It is however very significant that a religious solution which has been ruled out in principle for centuries should have so much practical force in our day, both in the version of a religious nationalism and in a pseudo-universalistic Messianic creed. These contemporary ventures into idolatry are proof of the difficulty of containing the collective self within any more general scheme of validity than its own interests. They prove that an affirmation of historical meaning as we have it in Western civilization is almost inevitably attended by pretentious efforts to close the system of meaning prematurely with some cherished value of the self at the center of the system.

It is equally significant that modern culture has generated less plausible and dangerous forms of individualistic pretention, in which the freedom and the uniqueness of the individual is asserted in defiance of any systems of consistency or universal meaning. The romantic revolt of the nineteenth century culminated in Nietzsche's effort to achieve the affirmation of unique vitality of the individual and his transcendence over the flux of history, thus seeking to combine classical with Hebraic attitudes toward time and eternity.

It must be apparent that modern existentialism is but another version of this romantic revolt. It has obviously learned from Biblical faith about the unique freedom of the individual and the distinction between the self's reason and personality. It is however unable to make the venture of faith of Biblical religion and therefore ends in the quasi-idolatrous attitude of making the individual his own creator and end. "Thus there is no human nature," declares the French existentialist Sartre, "because there is no God to conceive it. Man simply is. Not that he is simply what he conceives himself to be. But he is what he wills. . . . He is what he wills to be after that leap toward existence." [1]

Heidegger's concern for "authentic being," for the affirmation of the uniquely human freedom against the necessities of nature and the inevitability of death, is distantly related to Nietzsche's defiance of death. It is in the same category of quasi-idolatry. It may not make the self into its own God but it asserts the uniqueness of the self without reference to its relations to the community or to any general value.

If we rule out the idolatrous and quasi-idolatrous, the individualistic and collectivistic forms of these idolatries, as valid answers to the self's quest for ultimate meaning even though we recognize that the popularity of such answers is not confined to past history but is an ever recurring phenomenon, we are left with the two alternatives of the Biblical faith and Mr. Huxley's "perennial philosophy" or the mystic answer to the problem.

The answer of Biblical faith embodies, as we have seen, several presuppositions and affirmations which the modern mind finds particularly difficult, not to say impossible: the personality of God; the definition of the relation between the self and God as a dialogue; and the determination of the form of that dialogue in terms of a previous historic "revelation," which is an event in past history, discerned by faith to give a key to the character and purpose of God and of His relationship to man. It is therefore understandable that when confronted with these two alternatives, sophisticated moderns who have become aware of a depth of selfhood which can not be comprehended within the limits of the self as a biological organism or the self as mind, are inclined to turn to the mystic alternative in preference to the Biblical one. It is even understandable that they should do this at the price of defying the very ethos of their own life-affirming and history-affirming culture and choose an alternative which annuls every partial and

<hr>

[1] *Existentialism and Humanism,* p. 28.

particular meaning including the particular self. This is understandable in the sense that it proves how powerful are the compulsions to comprehend reality in a self-consistent scheme and to leave the mystery beyond the system of rational intelligibility unsolved.

Thus Professor Stace uttered a cry of despair some years ago because he became aware that the world which modern science explicated had no place for the human self or for any of the values which the self holds dear. Subsequently he published his considered answer to this problem in his *Time and Eternity*. He had accomplished his escape from the naturalistic prison by embracing the "perennial philosophy" of Mr. Huxley and the oriental mystics. He defined religion as the search for "the impossible, the unattainable and the inconceivable." Professor Stace thus bears testimony to the capacity of the self to reach for the ultimate; but he is sceptical of any venture of faith in an ultimate which would purify and complete the particular meanings of history. He finds it more acceptable to assert the pure mystery of the divine. He is impressed by the fact that the mystic approach arrives at the conclusion that God is both the fullness and the absence of being. Reporting on the account of divinity in the mystic tradition, he records that "God is non-Being, nothingness, emptiness, the void, the abyss . . . God is the great silence, the great darkness . . . yet God is also in the language of the medieval mystics, the supreme reality, the *'ens realissimum.'* " "This supreme God," he declares, "is contrasted by the mystics with the worthlessness of the world . . . the world then is worthless trash. This is seen by all men more dimly or more clearly, but it is seen by the mystics with absolute clarity." [2]

Professor Stace refers frequently to the Hindu desire to achieve unity of the self and God, to realize the assurance that "Brahman and Atman are one." This seems to him to be pure religion in comparison with the religions of the Bible with their appreciation of particular selfhood.

[2] *Time and Eternity*, p. 126.

The impulse to annul the meaning of particular selfhood and the significance of the whole drama of existence is expressed even more significantly in the view of the eminent philosopher George Santayana. Despite his essential Platonism, and his consequent faith in a "realm of essences," Santayana makes it clear, in his *Platonism and the Spiritual Life,* that the final goal of religion must be to transcend even these ghostly structures of particular meaning. "At the risk of parting company with Dean Inge, or even with Plato," he declares, "the spiritual life is not a worship of values, whether found in things or hypostasized into supernatural powers. It is the exact opposite. It is the disintoxication from their influence. . . . The great masters of the spiritual life are evidently not the Greeks, not even the Alexandrian Greeks, but the Indians and their disciples elsewhere in the East; and those Moslems, Jews and Christians who have surrendered precisely that early unregenerate claim to be enveloped in a protecting world." Santayana makes it quite clear that such a faith annuls all historic possibilities and responsibilities. "Obligations are moral," he writes, "they presuppose physical and social organisms and immanent spontaneous interests. . . . All values fall within the preview of ethics, which is a part of politics. Spirituality is the supreme good for those who are called to it, the few intellectuals who can be satisfied only by the impartial truth and by the self-annihilating contemplation of all being." [3]

It is rather revealing that Santayana reserves the mystic *summum bonum* for a few intellectuals. It reveals how aristocratic is the conception; and how closely mysticism is related to rationalism. From Aristotle to Santayana, mysticism is in fact the perennial overtone of rationalism. The drama of history is not comprehended in the categories of meaning supplied by either the rationalists or the mystics. In the one case the categories fail to comprehend the dramatic variety and the complex causal relations of history. In the other case the mystic conception of the fulfillment of meaning obviously

[3] Pp. 34-40.

results in the annulment of any particular meaning in history.

It will be regarded as futile by all pure "empiricists" to compare the Biblical and the mystic conceptions of the ultimate dimension of selfhood and to judge between the thesis that the self is in "dialogue with God" and the thesis that the self on that level is in the process of merging with a universal divine consciousness. But if the evidence of introspection is accepted (though it is admittedly inexact) it can not be too difficult to prove that the abstraction of the universal subject from the self as particular object is a futile procedure because the particular self always remains obtrusively in these exercises of introversion. There is furthermore the social evidence that the mystics never succeed in eliminating particular selfhood or in transcending the self as a particular organism. The erotic overtones in the mystic visions of an absolute consciousness is a rather pathetic symbol of the futility of the self's attempt to escape from the "body" and time into an undifferentiated eternity.

In short, we are confronted with evidence that the thesis of Biblical faith, that the self is in dialogue with a God who must be defined as a "person" because He embodies both the structure of being and a transcendent freedom, is more valid than the alternative theses which find much greater favor among the sophisticated. The Biblical thesis requires a more explicit act of faith because it leaps a gap of discontinuity between man and God and because it dares to give a specific meaning to the divine, which is relevant to the partial and fragmentary meanings of history. It both fulfills and corrects these meanings, loyalties and values, and therefore has a more valid attitude to the self's historic existence which the various rationalistic systems affirm too simply and the mystic thesis annuls too absolutely. This character of Biblical faith is therefore the crux of the question, why a faith which is more explicit than alternative ones should be more justified by actual experience than these. It gives a key to the seeming mystery of our whole cultural history. That mystery is why an allegedly "dogmatic" faith should be justified by the experiences of the human self more than the allegedly "empirical" approaches to selfhood, which obscure their potent, though implicit, dogmas within their prescriptions for empirical observation.

We must examine this strange paradox by an historical analysis of the long debate between the Biblical-dramatic and the rational approaches to the problems of the self in the history of Western civilization.

Part II

THE TWO COMPONENTS OF WESTERN CULTURE AND THEIR ATTITUDES TOWARD THE SELF.

THE HEBRAIC COMPONENT IN ITS APPRECIATION OF DIALOGUE, FREEDOM AND HISTORY. ITS INDIFFERENCE TOWARD NATURE. ITS TRUST IN AN HISTORICAL "REVELATION" FOR A DISCLOSURE OF THE MEANING OF THE HISTORICAL DRAMA. THE HELLENIC COMPONENT, ITS SEARCH FOR THE STRUCTURES AND PATTERNS WHICH UNDERLIE THE FLOW OF DRAMA AND HISTORY. ITS INTERPRETATION OF THE SELF AS MIND. THE HEBRAIC AND HELLENIC COMPONENTS IN REFORMATION AND RENAISSANCE. THE CHANGE IN MODERN CULTURE FROM INTEREST IN STRUCTURE TO PROCESS; FROM MIND TO NATURE. THE EFFORT TO UNDERSTAND MAN AS PART OF NATURE.

Chapter 13

THE HEBRAIC AND THE HELLENIC
APPROACHES TO THE PROBLEM OF
SELFHOOD AND HISTORY

W e have sought to interpret the unique character of human selfhood without particular references to the
presuppositions which governed the inquiry except the frequent references to the misunderstanding of the self which was
occasioned by the identification of the self with mind. This
had an obvious origin in Greek philosophy and has persisted
through the whole course of our Western civilization. Our
analysis of presuppositions became more explicit as we finally
turned to the examination of the religious dimension of self-
awareness and found that a rationalistic approach to the problems of the self easily leads to a mystic one. There is a path
not only from Plato to Aristotle, but from Plato to Plotinus in
the history of Greek culture. And both Aristotle and Plotinus
fail to understand the self in its wholeness, its uniqueness, its
particularity, and in its involvement in the dramatic realities
of history.

The simple fact is that the same Greek component in our
culture which is responsible for laying the foundations of all
our philosophy and sciences and is celebrated by every intelligent person as the fountain and source of what is "enlight-

ened" in our history is also responsible for all our most serious
misunderstandings about man and his history. These misunderstandings have two sources in Greek rationalism. The one
is the failure to distinguish between the self and its mind, resulting in the illusion that the true self is mind, subordinating
the passions to rational control. The other is that the history,
which the self elaborates and in which it is involved, proceeds
on a "rational," that is to say an ontological, pattern. The
drama in history is obscured by the alleged ontological framework of history. For "ontology" means the "science of being."
A science of being, to be distinguished from the particular
sciences which analyze the structure of particular beings, seems
confronted with the alternatives which Aristotle and Plotinus
adumbrated. Either being is defined as an essential structure
which is represented as the final cause, determining all processes of actualization; or being is described as an undifferentiated "ground" of all particular realities from which they
emanate. In either case, the ontological analysis of selfhood
and of history is productive of error. Historical drama is
equated with natural occurrence by Aristotle because the forms
and structures determine actualization as much in the historical, as in the natural, scene. History, on the other hand,
is made meaningless by Plotinus. It is merely an emanation
from an eternal ground, and its actions have no significance.
Aristotle can not find the particular self. The self's mind is
identical with a universal mind. Plotinus also seeks emancipation from particular selfhood, not however by rational but
by mystic means, that is, by extricating universal consciousness
rather than universal mind from particular selfhood.

Modern ideas of a temporal process have altered these alternatives somewhat. But they have not succeeded in giving
the self or its dramas any real significance.

There is no doubt, on the other hand, about the wholeness
of the self in its finiteness and freedom, about the height of
that freedom above the limits of formal reason, about the
dramatic reality of history, and about the distance and the
relation of God to that drama, in the culture of the Hebrews,

which furnishes the other component of our Western civilization, and which is embodied in the Bible. It is commonly asserted that we have our religion, and possibly our ethics, from the Hebraic side, and our philosophy from the Hellenic side, of our heritage. This generalization is, broadly speaking, correct, but it does not point accurately to the peculiar virtues and defects of each part of our heritage. It does not do justice to the fact that there is a yearning after the ultimate in the Hellenic, as in the Hebraic culture; and that there are ethical and religious concepts in both. But the Hellenic is defective in understanding the self and its dramas because it tries to understand both rationally and ontologically. The Hebraic, on the other hand, is defective in analyzing any permanent structure in the flow of temporal events. For the one history is made into another dimension of nature; and for the other nature is subsumed under history. Both nature and history are understood as standing under a divine sovereignty, rather than as subject to self-explanatory laws. Thus the one culture misunderstands human selves and their history, where freedom is more apparent than laws. The other misunderstands nature because it is primarily to be understood in terms of analyzable laws.

The Hellenic heritage has been so serviceable in our understanding and "conquest" of nature and has won such increasing prestige by these accomplishments that it has threatened to discredit the Hebraic component more and more, relegating its characteristic insights to outmoded "superstitions" at the precise moment in history in which its insights would be most serviceable in understanding man's history; and the more consistently a proud Hellenic culture tended to misinterpret that tragic drama, the more its philosophies and sciences became "empirical" and more intent upon the "facts."

Christianity is commonly believed to be a joint product of Hebraic and Hellenic cultures. This is true only in the sense that, beginning with the Johannine literature in the Bible, it sought to come to terms with the Greek concept of the permanent structure in things, and has embodied in its own life the

permanent tension between the Greek and the Hebraic ways
of apprehending reality. But this does not change the fact that
when it is true to itself, it is Hebraic rather than Hellenic. It
believes in a personal God despite the embarrassment of its
philosophers. It has, as Judaism, the other religion of the
Bible, the sense of a covenant community based on commitments and memories of past revelations; and it relies on these
historic revelations to penetrate the divine mystery rather than
upon an analysis of the permanent or "eternal" structures
through which the temporal events flow. It is therefore Hebraic
rather than Hellenic in its essence, even though in popular
piety the Greek idea of the immortality of the soul has usurped
the Hebraic idea of the "resurrection of the body." This usurpation is significant because the idea of the resurrection clearly
implies the finiteness of historical man and the wholeness of
the person in his finiteness and freedom. That there should be
a transmutation of that person "in the resurrection" can clearly
only be held "by faith." On the other hand, it is supposedly
more rational to believe that an immortal soul flees from a
mortal body upon death. It may seem a more rational belief,
but it rests upon a very dubious distinction between an immortal "mind" and a mortal body. This distinction is the key
to the Greek understanding of the self.

The sharpness of the contrast between Hellenic and Hebraic
ways of knowing must not obscure the similarity of their
origins. Both cultures began with a poetic-dramatic apprehension of historic reality, which was probably not so different
from the poetic ways of knowing in all early cultures and
analyzed so perceptively in Henri Frankfort's *Intellectual Adventure of Ancient Man*. The similarity was preserved beyond
the primitive beginning of the cultures and was apparent in
the period when a developing reason and imagination refined
the early myths. For this refinement in the Hebrew prophets
and the Greek dramatists was remarkably similar in ethos.
The *dramatis personae* of Greek drama were real persons, engaged in actual history, subject to conflicting claims upon their
consciences which were not easily resolved. They were actuated

by compulsions which were derived from their *thymos* rather than from the lusts of the body to which the philosophers attributed all non-rational compulsions.

The persons in Greek drama were not under the illusion that they could bring all the vitalities of life and history into a neat order if only the subrational impulses were subordinated to the order of "mind." These persons were men of spirit, who were betrayed into evil by the same capacity which made their creativity possible: their freedom over natural impulses. The Dionysian impulses may have been at war with the Apollonian sense of order in Greek tragedy. But there is no suggestion of a war between the mind and the body. That division was introduced by the philosophers.

The idea of an inner conflict in man does, however, introduce the first real difference between the Greek and the Hebraic analysis of the human situation. The Promethean theme in Greek tragedy and the myth of the Fall in the Bible both deal with the inclination of man to defy the limits set for him as a creature. But they arrive at different answers of the problem.

Both in the "Fall" myth in the Bible and in the Promethean theme in Greek drama this tendency, defined as *hybris* or pride, is regarded as the root of evil rather than the subrational impulses of nature. But in the Promethean theme, Zeus is regarded as motivated by an unjustified jealousy against the creativity of man or against Prometheus, the quasi-divine protagonist of man. Prometheus is responsible for giving man all the arts of civilization. It is, in short, not possible to exploit all the capacities of man and establish civilization without violating Zeus' rather unjustified restraints upon those capacities. It is unnecessary to say that Zeus is the forerunner of the principle of order which Greek ontology exalts as the rational basis of existence. In the "Fall" myth it is not regarded as inevitable that man offend God in his creativity. God sets limits for finite man; but those limits do not exclude his dominion over nature and all that this dominion implies. God is, in short, much higher than either the order of nature or some principle of rational coherence. He is "transcendent" to any conceivable order; but He reminds man that there are limits which he must not exceed. Man's sin consists in a pride which pretends to defy those limits. Human creativity has much wider scope than in Greek tragedy. Therefore the Old Testament does not reveal the ambivalence between Zeus and Prometheus of Greek tragedy. God is not unjustifiedly jealous; and the defiance of God is not the tragic prerequisite of man's creativity. The myth of the "Fall" obviously derives from an interpretation of the human situation, first elaborated by the great prophets of Israel. Both this and the Greek dramatists' interpretation are poetic and dramatic; not ontological. But the Hebraic frame of meaning is superior because the principle of meaning is placed in a position of transcendence over the actual structures of existence. Therefore the whole scope of human striving does not inevitably violate the principle of order in human existence. This is the first clearly stated difference between the Greek and Hebraic modes of "knowing" God. It is the beginning of what finally becomes a clear distinction between an "immanent" and "transcendent" God. This distinction also involves the derivative distinction between the immanent and the transcendent human self. Throughout the course of Western history men found the facts of selfhood to correspond to the symbol of transcendence. But they never ceased to be apologetic for the "irrational" symbol of the transcendence of both God and man. In their embarrassment, partly occasioned by the spatial implications in the symbol of transcendence, and partly by the fact that transcendence could not be fitted into a system of rational coherence, they violated all the "facts" of experience in order to achieve the "rationality" of divine or human immanence. One side of our culture, and significantly that side which was proudest of its "culture," took the superiority of Greek monism for granted and regarded even the most rigorous prophetic monotheism as a slightly cruder form of the monotheism which the Greek philosophers achieved.

From the sixth century, when Xenophanes first seriously

challenged the anthropomorphic Gods of Homeric legend and constructed a rigorous rationalistic monism or monotheism, to the flowering of Greek philosophy in the thought of Plato and Aristotle, the Greeks were agreed in the proposition stated by Plato that *nous,* or mind, was "king of heaven and earth"; that the rational principle of order, immanent in the variegated structures and "natures" of existence, was really God. And since that time almost every philosopher, even Christian ones, have celebrated this Greek emancipation from both parochialism and anthropomorphism. In comparison with this achievement the faith of the prophets of Israel seemed less impressive. Did not their God exhibit anthropomorphic traits? Did He not manifest love and hate and all the passions of a finite self? Histories of culture had to do some justice to the Hebraic side of our culture. But the average historian could not bring himself to any judgement fairer than that of Hegel, who regarded the Biblical faith as a crude and picturesque form of poetic thinking which, in every case and every age, philosophy had to refine. The prophets arrived at their truth "by revelation and authority" in the words of Gilbert Highet,[1] and their God was, though one and not many, still irrationally "transcendent." The prophetic achievement could not compare with that of the philosophers who had achieved a conception of God thoroughly "immanent" in the world's processes and established as a certainty by the most rigorous rational disciplines.

There is, in fact, a rather rapid descent from the appreciation of the "existing individual" in Greek drama to the loss of the individual in the ontological systems of Greek philosophy. The individual is partly known and partly obscured in Socrates' thought. His dialogic procedure, his emphasis upon the maxim "know thyself," his belief that his conscience was "a little God" with which he conversed—all revealed an awareness of the realities of the inner and outer dialogue in which the self is engaged. In Plato this residual understanding

---

[1] *Man's Unconquerable Mind.*

is partly obscured by his elaboration of the dictum of Socrates
that "men would do the good if they only know it." The
supremacy of the mind and its identification with the self is
established. The Eros doctrine of Plato however is a qualifica-
tion on the later mind-body dualism. For it assumes that the
mind has the task not only of suppressing and ordering the
physical impulses of the self, but of transmuting the "spirited"
element of the self beyond its immediate goals to the ultimate
ones. Thus the idea of "intellectual Eros" is elaborated. It
does not, of course, change the essential contempt of the body
in Greek dualism. Those who "take themselves to women and
beget children" are regarded as engaged in a lower enterprise
than those who harness *thymos* to the search for "truth, beauty
and goodness." These insights into the complexities of the
self's creativities are more consistently obscured in the rationalism of Aristotle. He excludes self-knowledge specifically from
the competence of the mind, acknowledges that the mind is
involved in the body, but insists that pure mind is impersonal
and universal. It is, as it were, provisionally imprisoned in
the body. It is the "form of forms" and therefore the principle
of meaning for all sensible things in their structures and forms.
Thus the inconvenient self is dissipated into mind; and mind
into the structures of existence.

The identification of mind or *nous* with God and the belief
that the rational order is really the creative principle of life
is succinctly and religiously expressed in the words of Anaxagoras: "Everything else has a share of everything. *Nous,* however, is infinite and self-ruling and is mixed with nothing, but
is alone itself by itself. For if it were not by itself but mixed
with something else, it would not share in all things, it would
not have a share in all things if it were mixed with any. . . .
Mind arranged all such things as were to be and were (that is
things which now are not) and such as are present; and it
arranged this whirling, too, which the stars and the sun and
the moon and the air and the ether—as they separate off—
perform." [2] Thus did the Greek mind identify meaning with

[2] Werner W. Jaeger: *Theology of the Early Greek Philosophers,* p. 160,
Oxford University Press.

rational intelligibility and state its confidence in the power of reason, which remains a strong motif in our culture and expresses itself in even such strong anti-Aristotelian philosophers as John Dewey.

Rationalists of all ages of Western history have regarded the rigorous monotheism of the Hebraic prophets as inferior to this philosophical monism. But they did not observe that the God of the prophets convicted all particular forces in history, including the "elect" nation and its "rulers" and "princes," of violating the divine command of justice while the Greek philosophers were complacent about the social realities of the Greek city-state and lived under the illusion that the rulers were the instruments of justice because they possessed a higher measure of mind. In short, the contingent character of all social achievements was discerned by prophetism and obscured by even the most sophisticated Greek philosophy. The God of the prophets made judgements which left even the elect nation uneasy. The God of Aristotle was a universal mind with which the mind of the philosopher claimed a complacent identity. So the tension between the finite self and the divine self was obscured.

The contrast between the two forms of monotheism was revealed even more clearly in their attitudes toward the "rulers" of their respective civilizations. The prophets were severely critical of the rulers or "elders" of Israel. Their criticism was directed at their pride and injustice. ("They turn aside the needy at the gate," declared Amos; and Isaiah charged that "the spoil of the poor is in their houses.") This happened to be an accurate description of the actual behavior of ruling groups throughout the ages.

In contrast we have both Plato's and Aristotle's complacent acceptance of the aristocratic structure of Hellenic society, and Aristotle's conviction that some men were "by nature" slaves. The basis of this conviction was clearly their confidence in the "reason" of the "guardians" as a source of justice and as the agent of order in the *polis*. Ignorant men would strive for immediate ends, but the "philosophers" would, with superior intelligence, strive for more inclusive ends and thus create a political order which would imitate the cosmic order created by the divine mind. The provisional truth in this assessment of the human situation lies in the fact that some men excel others in the rational comprehension of the forces and factors which are involved in any political situation. These are the potential rulers in a community. But their superior rational endowment guarantees nothing in regard to the justice with which they will wield their power or exercise their eminence. The basic fallacy of the Greek philosophers was to regard the rational faculty as the source of virtue. This error was partly due to their failure to recognize the ability of the self to use its reason for its own ends. It was partly due to the inclination to find in the sub-rational impulses the cause of confusion and egoism in human behavior. This error was to be repeated again and again in the history of Western thought. It has made the whole Greek tradition inferior in the understanding of human nature to the Hebraic one. Nevertheless the Greek tradition is still preferred to the Hebraic because it displays a neater coherence of the world, of the self and the world, and of the self and God. For the world, the self and God are all contained within the continuities of "reason."

The Hebraic tradition, which is allegedly more crude and less rational, is still relegated to the sphere of "pre-scientific" or "pre-philosophical" thought. It is, despite these prejudices, more "empirical" than the Greek tradition. Its superior empirical accuracy consists in its understanding of the wholeness of the human self in body, mind and soul, in the appreciation of the dramatic variety of the self's encounters with other selves in history, and in the discontinuity between the self and God. The self feels itself in dialogue with God. In this dialogue, God is not the "wholly other"; but he is certainly the divine other.

The self is not related to God by sharing its reason with God and finding a point of identity with the divine through the rational faculty. The self is related to God in repentance, faith and commitment. All these forms of relation imply a certain degree of existential discontinuity with God. The self is always a creature, conscious of its finiteness, and equally conscious of its pretension in not admitting its finiteness. Insofar as it becomes conscious of its pretensions it is capable of repentance and a new life. The encounter with God is in short a dramatic one. The personal encounter takes place in the context of a framework of meaning defined by a collective encounter between God and His people. The prophets speak to Israel, and finally to individuals in Israel (particularly in the case of Jeremiah and Ezekiel) on the basis of the assumption that God has a covenant with Israel. This covenant is at once the presupposition and the fruit of prophetic inspiration. The Covenant of God with Israel is an article of faith. It is not altogether clear whether it was Moses or Abraham who was the human agent of the covenant. This indicates either a confusion in the tradition or perhaps the collation of two traditions, perhaps stemming respectively from Palestinian and Egyptian sources. But the confusion does not prevent the gradual consolidation of the idea of the covenant and its service as the ground upon which prophetic thought proceeds. The circular movement between the presupposition of prophetic thought and its consequence will disturb the rationalists. There is a perfect analogy in the thought of the early Church about the "second Covenant" in Christ. For the "Christ event" is at once the presupposition of the faith of the early Church and the consequence of the increasing confidence of this community of faith that the drama of the Christ event which was the basis of its life disclosed both the kernel of meaning in the mystery of the divine and provided a norm for the life of man. Both were comprehended in the *agape* of Christ.

Prophetic consciousness assumed a covenant between a God, "who laid the foundations of the earth,"—a God who did not depend for His prestige upon the victory of a nation, who was sovereign of both nature and history;—and a particular people. The Covenant is involved in the same scandal of *Einmaligkeit* as is the later Christian revelation. A particular event in history is believed to be the clue to the mystery of the divine maj-

esty, which is sovereign over all of history. In the modern mind
(and for that matter the classical mind) such revelations are
identified with theophanies which the credulous believe and
the intelligent reject while they look for the ultimate in either
a principle of rational order in the world or in a mystery which
annuls all historic purposes and meanings.

But meanwhile the prophets gave ample testimony of the
fact that they were in encounter with the "true" God rather
than the idols of human imagination. From that encounter
they returned to preach judgement upon the "elect" but rebellious nation. They warned against the prophets "that
make you vain. They speak a vision of their own heart and
not out of the mouth of the Lord." They proved the falsity of
their imaginings, these false prophets, by increasing the complacency of the human heart, intent upon its own ends: "They
say still unto them that despise me, 'the Lord hath said you
shall have peace'; and they say unto every one who walketh
after the imagination of his own heart, no evil shall come unto
you." (Jeremiah 23:17) The prophets did not engage in the
fruitless debate whether "religion," or "reason," was most
serviceable in eliminating human vanity. They knew very
well that the religion of false prophets accentuated human
vanity and pretension. "Can any hide himself in secret places
that I shall not see him? saith the Lord," Jeremiah continues,
"Do not I fill heaven and earth? saith the Lord. I have heard
what the prophets said, that prophesy lies in my name, saying,
I have dreamed, I have dreamed . . . The prophet that hath
a dream, let him tell a dream; and he that hath my word, let
him speak my word faithfully." (Jeremiah 23:24-28) It might
be observed that rational discrimination is undoubtedly a
resource in distinguishing religious visions which are in the
service of human pretension and the "word of the Lord" which
punctures all human vanities. But it must also be apparent
that the prophets had no difficulty in distinguishing between
a genuine word of the Lord, which was "sharper than a two-
edged sword," and the "dreams" and "imaginations" of the
false prophets. The latter always accentuated human complacency and pretension.

It was left to a later Alexandrian Jew, Philo, anxious to make the prophetic tradition acceptable to the Greek world, to interpret the prophetic encounter with God as "ecstatic," which is to say, as consisting of precisely those "imaginations" which the prophets defined as the marks of the "false prophets." For the Greek culture could understand "ecstasy" as the visions of men who were "beyond themselves"; and it might even make religious ecstasy more tolerable by purging it of caprice and identifying it with mystic efforts of the self to escape from itself. Thus the effort to make the scandal of prophetic consciousness acceptable to the Greek mind robbed it of its genius.[3]

The community of the covenant was maintained, on the one hand, by prophetic interpretations of the Covenant, which had the effect of increasing the sense of the significance of the Covenant and of purging the Covenant people of any false pride and security because of their "elect" status. It was preserved, on the other hand, by memories of critical historic events by which the people were separated out and became a "peculiar" people, part nation and part church. The force of these historic memories, refreshed by liturgical observances year by year (most of which were festival of nature religions transmuted into historical anniversaries) —the force of these memories has been powerful enough to preserve the self-identity of a nation through the centuries, though it has lacked a "homeland" and lived in the "diaspora" for many centuries until very recently. The other means of survival has been the observance of the *Torah*, the law, about which a Christian can not speak sympathetically because one of the reasons for the emergence of a "new Covenant" was precisely the problem of the adequacy of the law as a mediator between man and God in the final encounter. It is possible only to say as one who stands by religious commitment outside this Covenant, that the religious consciousness of the Jews is determined from the beginning by two strains, legalistic and prophetic, which were expressed in the very idea of the covenant. For it was the

[3] *Cf.* Abraham Heschel: *Die Prophetie* (shortly to be had in English translation).

Sovereign of history ("I am the Lord thy God, who brought thee out of the land of Egypt") who also enjoined the precepts of the Decalogue which follows that introduction. For the Christian it would seem that the "new covenant" is the fulfillment of the prophetic consciousness about God, man and history and the negation of the legalistic interpretation. But he must certainly guard against the misinterpretations which have contrasted the New Testament as containing a "religion of the Spirit" with the Old Testament, as a "religion of the 'law.'" Certainly, despite the ages of post-exilic legalism in Judaism, the prophetic-dramatic-historical genius of prophetism was sufficiently vital in Judaism to produce two thinkers, Franz Rosenzweig and Martin Buber, in our own generation, who perceived the realities of both human and divine "selfhood" and of the dramatic character of history more acutely than any Christian theologian.

Furthermore, if Jewish legalism proved as inadequate as Christian obscurantism in dealing with "modern" situations and the modern man's quest for rational understanding of his world, both survived in an unfavorable environment because their approach to the mystery and meaning of the self and of God, and of the reality of human history, made their "foolishness" a source of wisdom. It might be necessary to cherish this wisdom in a corner but it was cherished nevertheless by men who knew themselves to be selves and to be in encounter with God, in ages in which this dimension of human existence was denied. The fact that such men as Spinoza and Freud, not to speak of Philo, were Jews, and that Maimonides was as anxious in the medieval period to conform Judaism to Aristotle's wisdom as Aquinas was to conform Christianity, merely proves how difficult it was to appreciate the peculiar genius of one's own culture and faith in ages in which everything tended to make that faith seem to be primitive and picturesque but not rationally respectable.

Chapter 14

FAITH AND DOGMA IN THE NEW COVENANT COMMUNITY

The structures of meaning in religions of history and revelation are undoubtedly sustained by specific and explicit acts of faith in contrast to those world views which also have some ultimate principle of meaning but which seek to obscure the act of faith which sustains them by making the system appear to be sustained by a rationally analyzable coherence.

Thus, for instance, the obscurity of meaning in the Prophetic interpretation gave rise to the Messianic faith that God would "act" to eliminate the obscurities. These obscurities and ambiguities can be briefly enumerated. Reward and punishment were not justly apportioned to virtue and vice. The innocent suffered and the "wicked flourished like a green bay tree." Israel itself, which rightly stood under divine condemnation according to the prophets, was nevertheless an innocent sufferer compared to the mighty nations which were the executors of divine judgement. When would the "righteous" be vindicated? When would Israel be vindicated? When would the tension between the law and the inclination of the human heart be overcome by a "new covenant" providing for a law written into the human heart? (Jeremiah) These obscurities persuaded the more rationalistic Greeks either to dismiss history as having no moral meaning or to hope that "reason" would gradually eliminate its obscurities and cross purposes. The prophets hoped instead that the drama of history would be clarified not by the gradual emergence of a logic immanent within it or by the imposition of logic upon it. It would be clarified dramatically by a divine action in which the "mercy" of God first revealed in the covenant would be displayed in a new way. This dramatic action was "expected" in the sense that it seemed to follow inevitably from the "constancy" of the divine mercy. But it was also unpredictable in the sense that mercy was not subject to any law inherent in history. It must be observed that many human ends, which can not be regarded as ultimate, were supposed to be vindicated in that final vindication. Israel was to be restored as a nation. (Is the establishment of the present State of Israel a fulfillment of that Messianic promise?) The "righteous" were to be vindicated despite the fact that in the final reaches of prophetic insight there were no significant distinctions between the righteous and the unrighteous. The "innocent" were to be avenged despite the fact that it seems to be a permanent character of history to establish norms which are equally painful for both the criminals and for the truly innocent.

In short, there were many false expectations in the hope of this dramatic Messianic denouement.

The Christian community came into historic being by a common venture of faith that this expected act of God took place in the whole drama of Christ's life. Christ had to be accepted by an act of faith, for the event took place in history and nothing takes place so inevitably that it can be proved to be the natural consequence of the previous "conditions of history." The early Church accepted Christ as the "expected" one, as the "desire of the ages." It interpreted the "new covenant" as a logical extension of the first covenant. But this faith could not compel the original nation-church to accept him. He was rejected by the original covenant community, and there were thus two, rather than one, faiths. At best, the two can regard themselves as two versions of one faith, each thinking of the other as an heretical version of the common faith. Since such faith is by commitment, the interpretation of the faith can not follow as a rational deduction from the given facts. Yet faith can not be irrational or capricious. It must validate itself as an interpretation of the facts of existence.

Looking at these facts from the standpoint of the commitments of the Christian faith, they would appear as follows: The Christ event which Christian faith regards, retrospectively, as the culmination of history could not be regarded prospectively as such a fulfillment. It is however the more impressive retrospectively because it could not be fully anticipated. It is the more impressive because some of the expectations hoped for the fulfillment and vindication of forces and factors in history (the nation and the "righteous") which do not deserve to be singled out as the bearers of historic fulfillment. The Christ was expected to be a triumphant Messiah, and he is in fact a "suffering servant" who does not bring the struggle between good and evil to a triumphant conclusion. Instead, the drama of his life reveals that the nominally "righteous" are involved in the crucifixion and that the only resolution of the variance between God and man was for God to take the sins of men upon Himself. Thus the suffering Messiah became, in the eyes of faith, a clue to the mystery of the mercy and the justice of God, and the atonement became the real content of the revelation. On these grounds the Christ event was recognized to be the "end" of history, not in the sense of its "finis" but as its *telos*. History would go on, and human pride and arrogance would create unimaginable evils. But nothing would surprise or dismay the person who had once penetrated to the mystery by the help of this key.

It is important to note that the analysis of the whole human situation anticipates the unlimited possibilities for good and evil in every human life and of developing human freedom in history, and of the continued variance between men and God whenever human actions are ultimately considered.

In short, the truth of the interpretation of life and history, derived from the revelation in Christ is most apparent at those points at which the revelation outraged and disappointed the Messianic expectations and defied the canons of "rationality" which were subsequently used to justify or to refute the truth of the revelation. We shall have occasion later to analyze the corruptions which have obscured this truth whenever men have sought to accommodate it to their perspective. It is true precisely because it comes as a refutation of partial and parochial viewpoints, and of the desire of men and nations, of priests and philosophers, of cultures and civilizations to vindicate themselves. It can be empirically verified as the truth, but it can not be anticipated or established by an empirical analysis of any human situation because every such empirical analysis will lack the challenge to the egoistic corruption in the viewpoints of nations, cultures and classes, which insinuate themselves into every definition of the ultimate truth, and will reduce the height and significance of human freedom in order to fit the human drama into some scheme of natural or rational coherence.

The Christian Church soon faced the problems of preventing a truth apprehended by faith, and not subject to the tests of coherence which govern the test of truth in philosophy and science, from degenerating into private caprice. What was to prevent anyone from appropriating this revelation and corrupting it according to his own fancy?

The answer to this problem was the establishment of the authority of the covenant community, the Christian Church, which would try to reach a consensus on the interpretation of the revelation and prevent the caprice of private visions and fancies. In a series of Church Councils dealing primarily with the Christological issue, that is, with the question of the significance of the Christ revelation, the agreements which were arrived at were promulgated as "dogmas." The word "dogma" was adapted from Roman imperial usage in which it meant imperial decree. It has achieved a hated connotation in the lexicon of modernity, for it connotes the arbitrary assertion of what can not be proved scientifically. As a matter of fact, it was intended to avoid the arbitrariness of private interpretation and to assure the "public" character of the truth in a realm of truth in which poetic and dramatic symbols of the truth did not allow for establishment of the kind of universal validity which modern science boasts and which the philosophers seek in vain.

In short, dogma, in the best sense, is the inevitable guard of truth in the realm of history and drama in which a religion of history and revelation moves, in contrast to the realm of structures which may be analyzed exactly and meticulously until unanimity of interpretation is reached. Dogma, at its best, represents the consensus of a covenant community which lives upon the basis of common convictions and commitments to a revelation of the truth which can not be accepted as true in the manner of philosophical and scientific truths, because the truth does not follow inevitably from the analysis of the processes of nature and history. We must consider presently the baneful effects of trying to enforce any such consensus upon a political community by political power.

Chapter 15

DOGMA AND ONTOLOGY IN THE CHRISTIAN CONSENSUS

The essence of the Christian faith is drawn from the Hebraic, particularly the prophetic, interpretation of life and history, and is erroneously interpreted as the consequence of a confluence of Hebraic and Hellenic streams of thought. However, it must be admitted that the elaboration of the meaning of the Christian revelation demanded from the very beginning, that the truth about life and God apprehended in an historical revelation be brought into conformity with the truth which may be known by analyzing the structures and essences of reality on all levels. Historically this meant co-ordinating these truths with the findings of Greek philosophy and science. The beginning of this enterprise was made in the Scriptures, more specifically in the Johannine literature with its conscious effort to interpret the Messianic faith to the Hellenic world. The Johannine prologue significantly initiates the story of Christ's life not with the history of his birth, as in the Synoptics, but by the bold assertion that this Jesus of history was in fact the *"logos* made flesh." It appropriated the Philonic *logos* concept and insisted that the *logos,* the pattern of creation, the structure of existence, was in fact identical with this character in history. "The world was made by Him and without Him was not anything made, that hath been made." This encounter between "natural" and "revealed" theology was to provide the pattern for the creative tension between structural and dramatic ways of apprehending historic reality which have persisted throughout the history of Western civilization. This is true even if one assumes that the *logos* concept of Philo was not purely Hellenic but added some connotations taken from the Hebraic idea of God's "almighty and creative word."

The Johannine literature is most instructive when it interprets the love of Christ. His *agape* corresponds to the created structure of human existence but it is also a "new Law" revealed in Him: "Brethren," we read in the first Epistle of John, "I write no new commandment unto you, but an old commandment which ye had from the beginning. The old commandment is the word which ye have heard from the beginning. Again, a new commandment I write unto you; . . . because the darkness is past, and the true light now shineth." (1 John 2:7-8) In other words, the *agape* of Christ is not arbitrarily imposed upon life. It is "from the beginning"; that is, it is given in the essential and created nature of man, which involves a freedom for which love is the only law. But the historic revelation clarifies that commandment: "for the darkness is past and the true light now shineth." There are nuances in the *agape* idea, there is a depth of "grace" of self-giving and suffering love in *agape* which does not follow inevitably upon an analysis of the character of human freedom, but which is an historic extension of what has been given in the created nature of man. One might add that neither Plato nor Aristotle was able to conceive of the idea of *agape* though their analyses touched the edges of the mystery as they explored the limits of *eros* and of *philia*.

The Christian Church elaborated its faith that Christ was more than a character in history and that the drama of his life was more than an event in history, by the Trinitarian dogma, which asserted that the revelation of the divine mystery in Christ was related, on the one hand, to the divine power of creativity, which was the mystery presupposed in all rational analyses of causes. It was, on the other hand, related to the mystery of the God whom the individual encountered in the final reaches of his self-awareness, where he met God as the "other" who judged and forgave him. This Trinitarian formula was, though a "stumbling block" to the Jews, not derived primarily from Greek ontology. It was a stumbling block because it violated, or seemed to violate, the rigorous monotheism of Hebraism and also the first commandment of the Decalogue, which forbade the construction of an "image" of the divine mystery. It was nevertheless more Hebraic than Hellenic, for it appealed to two aspects of the divine mystery, which prophetism acknowledged: the creation and the personal encounter between God and man. It merely inserted the Christ event for the first covenant at the center, and as the point of revelation of meaning in this mystery. Even the idea of Christ's pre-existence in the Johannine Prologue had antecedents in apocalyptic thought, in the concept of a pre-existent Messiah who was "from the foundations of the world."

The corollary dogma of the "two natures of Christ" was intended to emphasize the two perspectives in which Christ was viewed as "truly man," that is, as a character in history and not a theophany, and "truly God," that is, as a revelation of the divine mystery, particularly the mystery of God's judgement and mercy. This dogma did indeed avail itself of Greek speculative categories, but not with great success. For how could this man be declared to be at once God and man when it was the nature of God to be "impassible," and nothing in history can be "impassible"? Obviously the difficulty was in transposing symbolic, dramatic statements into ontological ones. But this difficulty has not invalidated the central truth of the Christian faith, which stands or falls with the assertion of Christ's uniqueness, however much this affirmation may be a "stumbling block to the Jews and to the Gentiles, foolishness." We must consider subsequently how every effort to reduce this scandal by "liberal" Protestant Christianity, whether they availed themselves of Kantian, Hegelian or Whiteheadian ontologies, has led to a blunting of the truth embodied in the *kerygma* and to a consequent misreading of the human situation, usually with the result of conforming to the sentimentalities of our age. For our age did not take seriously enough the intimate relation between the creative and the evil possibilities of human freedom. This would apply, too, to the recent efforts of Rudolf Bultmann, engaged in the laudable enterprise of saving the *kerygma* while cleansing the message of the Bible of "pre-scientific" myths. But he ends by equating the *kerygma* with the message of existentialist philosophy. The *kerygma* was obviously not left untouched because the existentialist philosophy, while understanding the unique freedom of man, is more intent to assert it in defiance of death than to acknowledge that it is subject to corruption; that therefore man must be saved from sin, rather than from death.[1]

Bultmann's desire to cleanse the Scripture of "pre-scientific" myths is in accord with a responsible attitude toward the dangers inherent in the dramatic and poetic attitudes toward reality. They may obscure the "laws" and structures on every level of reality which science analyses and metaphysics seeks to bring into a total system of coherence. For this task the Hellenic tools of rational discrimination are more adequate than the dramatic symbols of the Bible. But Bultmann's failure to guard the truth in the *kerygma,* despite his professed concern to leave it untouched, proves that he has not made a sufficiently sharp distinction between pre-scientific and permanent myths. Pre-scientific myths disregard what may have always been known, or have now become known, about the ordered course of events in the world. Permanent myths (it would be better to use the word "symbol" to avoid the sceptical connotation of the word "myth") are those which describe some meaning or reality, which is not subject to exact analysis but can nevertheless be verified in experience. The experience which verifies it and saves the myth from caprice is usually in the realm of history and of freedom beyond the structures and laws of existence. Thus the question of myths and symbols contains the whole problem of the tension between the Hel-

[1] Rudolf Bultmann, *Kerygma and Myth.*

lenic and the Hebraic components of our culture. Modern physics certainly avails itself of symbols as much as does poetry and religion, but its symbols are verifiable by strict measurement and observation.

There is certainly a great difference between the symbols by which modern physics describes the realities which have taken the place of the older concepts of "substance" or "matter," and the symbols, for instance, of a dynasty or an historic figure in its history by which a nation comes to the consciousness of its unity and continuity. And there is even a greater difference between the scientific and the religious symbols by which a community of faith, using events in history, sees in them clues to the eternal mystery which hovers over and in history. But these symbols are verifiable on their own level. That "God was in Christ reconciling the world unto Himself" is verifiable in the experience of everyone who experiences the mercy and new life which flows from true repentance in the encounter with God. It is also verifiable by the proofs that alternative methods of explaining or dissolving the mystery and the meaning which governs and surrounds us lead to observable miscalculations in regard to the nature of man and of history. Thus there is a significant distinction between the "myths" with which a pre-scientific world describes natural phenomena and the symbol which is central to the structure of Christian faith, namely, the assertion that a Jesus of Nazareth was the "Son of the living God."

The Christian Church is certainly guilty of "fideism" when it affirms that an historically apprehended motif, the *agape* of Christ is the chief characteristic of the ultimate "being" which the Greek philosophers described in purely static terms, eliminating all temporal character, and which Hebraic thought described as the Creator. In either case an ontological concept is involved in the definition of God. But the Christian faith does not derive its idea of love from the idea of "being." When Hellenic concepts of "being" are substituted for the idea of a "creator," and of the mystery of creation as the ontological anchor for the historic revelation, the emphasis is invariably shifted from the content of the revelation, which is, according to the Bible, the reconciliation between God and man on the divine initiative. The "Incarnation" becomes instead the revelation of the eternal in the temporal [2] and the dramatic account of the reconciliation between God and man is obscured. The consequent estimate of the human situation is altered so that the achievement of the "eternal" under conditions of time becomes the *summum bonum,* whereas the Biblical message is of forgiveness by God toward man and the corresponding forgiveness which men must practice toward one another and will practice the more successfully if they realize the fragmentary character of their own virtues and achievements.

An even more striking difference is achieved when the myth of the "Fall" in the Bible is transmuted into strictly ontological, rather than historical, terms. The Biblical myth seeks to do justice to both the universality of sin and self-regard and to the element of personal responsibility in each sinful act. The fateful universality is accounted for in Christian orthodoxy by assuming that Adam's first sin is transmitted as a taint from generation to generation. Beginning with Origen, theologians under the influence of Platonic philosophy, have changed the idea of a universal guilt as historical fate to an ontological one, that is, to a necessary consequence of man's finiteness.

It is probably significant that finite men should have imagined so persistently that the guilt which they feel is the consequence of their finiteness and particularity. It is significant because it effectively cancels out their guilt and because it points to a dimension of their existence from which it is possible to survey the whole temporal drama and estimate it as "appearance" or "illusion." This Platonic transformation of the Christian concept of the drama of history is nevertheless a grievous error. It can not be made plausible at all without imagining a purely hypothetical "transcendent Fall" which must account for the actual "Fall," that is, the creation of a temporal world. Augustine's Biblical concepts of selfhood, and of the corruption of freedom in the self, corrected the Platonic aberrations of Origen and many of the pre-Augustinian

---

[2] *Cf.* Lionel Thornton's *Incarnate Lord* for an Anglo-Catholic interpretation of the Incarnation on the basis of Whitehead's metaphysics.

fathers of the Church. But nothing could correct the ancillary consequence of the error, which was to define sin as sensuality rather than as self-love and to construct a system of salvation in which ascetic spirituality became the path to redemption. The seat of sin was placed in the "belly" rather than in the self. (Origen) Thus the self was withdrawn from judgement. There is a corruption of every Biblical concept involved in this Platonism. The "goodness of creation" and the significance of the whole temporal and historical process is placed in question. The wholeness of man in body and soul is made dubious, and the evil he does is attributed to his finiteness rather than his freedom and is regarded as an inevitable consequence of that finiteness.

Augustine arrested for a time this baneful absorption of a Biblical dramatic faith into an ontology. In him, the Biblical account of the self in its freedom and wholeness of body and soul triumphed over Neo-Platonic presuppositions. Perhaps it was significant that the classical thought-world in which he was nurtured was Neo-Platonic rather than Platonic or Aristotelian. It therefore emphasized mystery beyond meaning rather than rational structure as the basis of meaning. There was more room for the elaboration of the significance of the meanings of the drama of Biblical revelation. Thus Augustine restored the Biblical accounts of creation, of selfhood, and of the sin and the grace in the dimension of human freedom. Augustine was not capable of refuting one other error which had crept into the interpretation of Biblical truth. That error was to eliminate the studied paradox of Biblical faith in its interpretation of redemption. For redemption was, on the one hand, the emancipation of the self from itself by its devotion to God. It was, on the other hand, the constant forgiveness and mercy of God toward all men, for even the most devoted among them would be involved in the sin of setting their will and interest against the divine, usually by assuming a too neat identity between the human and the divine will. Augustine elaborated a fairly complacent idea of grace and perfection according to which "we may be denominated perfect if we walk perfectly on the road to perfection." This doctrine persuaded Augustine to draw a sharp line between the *civitas dei* and the *civitas terrena,* between the saved and the lost; and to lay the foundations or to offer the first example of the perennial inclination of the religious community to make itself odious by its pretensions of righteousness.

The long history of medieval Christianity was the story of the gradual consolidation of the synthesis between Biblical-dramatic and Greek ontological modes of apprehending reality. The synthesis culminated in the thought of Thomas Aquinas, which became definitive for Catholic thought. In this synthesis the sense of structure derived from Aristotelian thought gradually took the place of the more Platonic and Neo-Platonic sense of a divine mystery above the observable structures. Since it is necessary to do justice both to the structural aspect of reality and to elements which appear in man and his history by reason of human freedom above the structures, it would seem that the Thomistic synthesis was the most adequate method of dealing with both aspects of reality. But the synthesis was inadequate because it did not fully recognize the degree to which historical freedom reached down into the structural aspects of life. The Aristotelianism of the Middle Ages was challenged progressively as the discoveries of historical development in both nature and history made the Aristotelian ontology otiose.

The most serious consequence of the incorporation of classical ontology was in the field of ethics where the Biblical idea of love as the final norm of life was added as an extra "theological virtue" together with faith and hope upon an ethical system defined by the classical conception of "natural law." The content of "natural law" was much too specific and the "intuitions" of reason which were drawn from it were much too inflexible to do justice to the ever new historical occasions which appear in history. The moral intuitions also failed to define the good adequately for man in the wholeness of body and soul. The most absurd consequence of this classical scheme was in the field of sex, in which a very negative attitude toward sex, partly drawn from Hellenic dualism and partly from Pauline attitudes, was combined with an effort to define the function of sex from an analysis of "nature." The consequence was the prohibition of sexual relations even in marriage except for the end "intended" by nature, namely procreation. The fact that a sexual partnership is also a comradeship between two persons who would express their love for each other in sexual terms, even beyond the obvious "intention" of "nature," is thus negated. The whole system of classical ethics, as incorporated into the Biblical mode of thought about the providence of God in and over history, is highly dubious. Thomas' assertion that God's providence is expressed in an "eternal law" and that the "natural law" is the rational creature's participation in "the eternal law" clearly substitutes rational ontology for the Biblical dramatic apprehension of the meaning of history. The rational "intuitions" of natural law are much too rigid and neat to give adequate moral guidance to men in the unique occasions of history and under the shifting circumstances of historical development.

If the medieval synthesis is too rational on the one hand, it does not provide sufficient "rational" checks upon the religious imagination on the other hand. Thus the religious life of the Middle Ages had no protection against the growth of "superstition," against the tendency of reducing concepts of grace to magic, and of using the ecclesiastical control of magic as a source of political power.

Whatever errors were incorporated into the medieval synthesis were aggravated by the political supremacy which the Church established over the whole of the medieval culture. It is important to analyze the consequences of this supremacy fully because it had the most fateful consequences in the whole political and spiritual history of the Western world. It is always dangerous to establish any unchallenged human authority because human pretensions tend to grow when they are not subject to challenge. It is particularly dangerous to establish a priesthood in such an unchallenged position because religion lends itself particularly to the pretension of possessing absolute truth and virtue by finite and sinful men.

The establishment of the Church as the undisputed sovereign power over a whole culture and civilization is due to unrepeatable historical contingencies. The disintegration of the Roman Empire left the Church as residuary legatee of this dying world and as tutor to the yet unformed European culture, making its way from barbarism to civilization partly by appropriating the cultural treasures of the civilization which it had vanquished. These events and facts gave the Church an initial advantage which it exploited, particularly by using its possession of the "keys of Heaven" in a religious age, to unlock the doors of power on earth.

The establishment of papal supremacy was not possible without violating one of the cardinal tenets of Biblical faith which asserted that "in God's sight is no man living justified," and thus implied the ambiguity of all human virtues and achievements. The violation of this Biblical affirmation was made explicit in the claim of the Pope to be "Vicar of Christ" on earth and to govern the world in the name of Christ. Beginning with this claim, Christianity has been inferior to Hebraic prophetism in failing to observe a proper distance between the divine and the human, and not heeding the prophetic warning, "For as the heavens are higher than the earth, so are my ways higher than your ways, and my thoughts than your thoughts" (Is. 55:9).

The effect of this pretension was manifold. Three facets of it deserve special consideration: (A) It made a religious experience of the ultimate, which must remain a matter of personal commitment and repentance, into an article of faith which could be enjoined by political authority. It thereby robbed the religious experience of its essential character and emptied it of both religious meaning and moral prestige. It was this facet against which the Reformation protested so vehemently. The corruption of religion was aggravated by the general tendency to reduce "grace" in the religious life to a power which could be magically transmitted.

(B) The derivation of political power from the pretensions of sanctity was very effective in a religious age; but it was bound to generate increasing resentments, which came to a head in the Renaissance as well as the Reformation, but which even pious Catholics anticipated long before the sixteenth century, notably Marsilius of Padua and Dante. Dante, in *De Monarchia,* sought desperately to rescue Catholic universalism, the one virtue of papal absolutism, from the odium in which it was enveloped by religious pretension of the papal Church.

(C) The papal authority over the whole of culture had the special effect of giving the concept of "dogma" in religion a very unfortunate connotation. For "dogma" was the expression of a religious authority against the growing desires of a culture to explore all human possibilities, including the possibilities of investigating every coherence and sequence in the natural world and history. The compound of Biblical religion with Aristotelianism was particularly unfortunate because it accentuated the idea of a world of fixed and eternal essences in which deductive rational processes could explore the unknown upon the basis of the known. Modern empirical science, beginning with Francis Bacon, was forced to insist on the right and the necessity of empirically examining "causes" and tracing the actual course of events in nature and in history.

Ironically the empiricism on which Bacon insisted and which became the basis for all the triumphs of modern science had to be asserted against the authority of a Christian Aristotelianism, though the idea that reality is not totally rational and that it is necessary to account for "the irrationality of the givenness of things" is derived from the Biblical doctrine of creation as contrasted with the classical idea of creation through the rational forming of the formless matter or the unformed stuff. But this idea of creation was corrupted so that a divine act becomes in each particular instance an explanation of an event, which obviates the necessity of finding a particular cause for it. Therefore Bacon protested against the effort to understand nature *ex analogia hominis* instead of looking for the laws and structures which actually determined actualization. He could hardly anticipate that the empirical method which he initiated would end by trying to understand man *ex analogia naturae* and that the empirical method which unlocked the mysteries of nature so well would become the basis of an implicit dogma which obscured the salient facts about the human situation.

Chapter 16

THE SELF AND ITS DRAMAS: REASON AND NATURE IN THE DISINTEGRATION OF THE MEDIEVAL SYNTHESIS

We have sought to clarify the effect of the synthesis between the Biblical-dramatic forms of thought and the classical confidence in reason and its emphasis upon a rational ontology which entered into that synthesis.

With the disintegration of that synthesis under the impact of the Renaissance and Reformation, one of the effects of the disintegration was that the Reformation re-emphasized the Biblical and dramatic approaches to the self and to God, while the Renaissance separated out the classical identification of the self and mind, of reason and reality and sharpened the tools of rational discrimination. This division had some very marked effects upon our culture. For the Renaissance initiated movements of culture which led to an even more extravagant confidence in reason as the source of human virtue than characterized either the classical or the medieval period. But, on the other hand, it initiated all the rational disciplines which have enriched our culture and which finally led to the modern triumphs of science in the knowledge of nature.

The Reformation, on the other hand, in returning to a purer Biblical interpretation of the human situation, disclosed some "facts" about man which are only disclosed on the presupposition of the dramatic encounter between a divine and

human self. These facts are validated continually by experience; and their discovery places the Reformation in the unique
position of contributing to the sum of human knowledge
despite its lack of interest in the pursuit of knowledge and
despite, or perhaps because of, its "fideism" that is its appeal
to faith rather than reason, and its cavalier attitude toward
the disciplines of culture, particularly toward philosophy.
Among its contributions to the understanding of human selfhood are: the emphasis on the wholeness of the person in body
and soul, derived from the Bible (Luther's *totus homo*) ; the
conception of the height of human freedom and of the encounter of the person with a personal God in this dimension
of its existence; the idea of the critical and total nature of
this encounter, involving the whole of the person and shattering his pride and self-esteem. This idea, derived from Paul
("I am crucified with Christ; nevertheless I live") purges
Christian piety of all the complexities introduced by ascetic
ideals and mystic efforts at flight to the eternal. It places the
religious emphasis upon the final encounter between man and
God, upon the promise of a renewal of life, if human pretension is destroyed in that encounter; and upon the paradox of
a divine mercy and judgement of God which is met in that
encounter. Thus the "Atonement" was seen to be the real
content of the "Incarnation" and the relation between judgement and forgiveness is the real mystery in the divine which
must be clarified. Finally, the Reformation insists that even
the most radical shattering of the old self and the reconstruc-
tion in terms of a commitment beyond itself can not eliminate
sin, that is self-love, in the life of the redeemed.

The Reformation maxim *justus et peccator simul,* and its
insistence that the redeemed are just as needy of forgiveness
at the end as at the beginning of their striving because the
righteous as well as the sinners are at variance with God,
ultimately considered, clarified a truth of Biblical religion
which remained obscure throughout previous Christian history. It was in fact partially obscure in both prophetic and
Pauline thought. It was obscure because the prophets insisted,
on the one hand, that the judgement of God would fall with

equal severity upon the "circumcized and uncircumcized" (Jeremiah) but, on the other hand, they had a lively sense of the difference between the righteous and the unrighteous. St. Paul was certain that "if any man be in Christ, he is a new creature" (2 Cor. 5:17) while he also insisted that all human righteousness was unavailing in God's sight and that men would be in need of God's mercy, no matter what their moral attainments might be. The Protestant Reformation may be said to have clarified the prophetic and the evangelical tradition by profiting from the ages of testimony on this perplexing ambiguity in Scripture and in life. The testimony proved that pretensions of perfection were new causes of sin and conflict in the world. This discovered or rediscovered truth about man has a unique relation to the whole enterprise of truth. For it is an obvious truth to which every kind of experience bears witness. Yet it is a truth which can not be comprehended except on the basis of the particular presupposition of the Biblical faith; and it is constantly obscured by the universal inclination of men to find some ground of either reason or faith, of piety or intellectual attainment, which will assure them of an unambiguous "righteousness" and of the opportunity to hold their fellow men, who do not share this ground, in moral contempt. The Reformation did not always exploit this knowledge about human nature to its full extent; but that merely proves that even the final truth about man can not overcome the inclination of the human heart to misuse any truth for its pride or prestige.

Nor was the Reformation conception about the wholeness of man in body and soul fully exploited. It did prompt the Reformation's fierce anti-asceticism, its opposition to the effort to establish goodness by the suppression of physical desires, particularly sexual ones. But this anti-asceticism did not suffice to persuade either Luther or Calvin to rethink the whole Christian attitude toward man's sexual problem. Luther could, when he thought unsystematically and expressed himself occasionally, rejoice in marriage as a source of grace and joy. But when he thought of the sexual problem theologically, his strong Paulinism prompted him to define marriage as "a hospital for sick souls," emphasizing with Paul the purely negative advantages of a stable sexual partnership between man and woman. It fails to recognize the fact that a community in which mutual fidelity between husband and wife, and between parents and children, disciplines life has a more positive contribution to the achievement of grace than the mere channeling of sexual passion. The errors of the Reformation thus frequently derive from a lack of rigor in exploiting its own Biblical presuppositions.

The truth which emerged in the Reformation was not dependent upon a literalistic interpretation of Scripture. It was, in fact, obscured by such interpretations. For they reduced to a miraculous historical fact, the fact of history which had to be discerned by faith to be a disclosure of the divine judgement and mercy, which would shatter the self in its self-esteem and renew to a more creative life. Luther, in contrast to Calvin, was not given to Bibliolatry but described the Bible as the "cradle of Christ," thus emphasizing the central revelation which must be definitive for the Christian life. But it is fair to say that the whole Reformation in both its Lutheran and Calvinistic varieties, was Biblicist in comparison with Catholicism. This was an inevitable consequence, on the one hand, of its polemic against the authority of the Church, which could not be carried on without the undue exaltation of the authority of a Book; and, on the other hand, it was due to the indifference of the Reformation to the disciplines of culture, to the scornful attitude of Luther toward "philosophy" and to problems of ontology, which re-enacted the old Hebraic indifference toward all speculations about the coherences and essences of life, and particularly of nature. The resulting obscurantism seemed to relegate Protestant faith to those portions of the population which were not abreast of the phenomenal developments in the various fields of culture and to give it the appearance of a remnant left over from a pre-scientific age. But it was not merely due to cultural backwardness. That is proved by the quality of Neo-Reformation thought, as in Karl Barth, for instance, which was able to combine a sophisticated knowledge of all the disciplines of modern culture with a frantic effort to isolate the Christian faith from the allegedly debilitating effects of philosophical and scientific speculations.

We must postpone for the moment the various honest and heroic efforts made by what is usually defined as "liberal Christianity" to establish contact with modern culture, and need only record now that these efforts did usually result in dissipating a part of the Biblical heritage and giving a version of the Christian faith which incorporated one or more of the modern illusions about the self or the dramas of history. These abortive efforts, together with the cultural obscurantism of orthodox Protestantism, fully reveal that the problem of doing justice to both the dramatic and the structural or ontological aspects of human existence are as difficult now as when the debate between Hebraism and Hellenism first began. How difficult it is may be gathered by a consideration of the rather pathetic debate between modern science and Protestant orthodoxy on questions of human nature and destiny, initiated by the Darwinian discoveries in biology. In that debate, Darwinianism seemed to crown the whole structure of modern interpretations of a progressive history by proving natural forms to be as subject to development as historical structures. It also proved an historical relation between the human "animal" and its "mammalian" forebears. These were all "scientific" discoveries, consequent upon an empirical observation of historical and natural sequences. Modern culture drew some illicit, though seemingly plausible, conclusions about these discoveries. It concluded that man's opinion of himself was too optimistic and that he was no doubt a part of "nature." It also concluded that history was but an extension of the natural process so that evolution in biological forms was supposed to give the final proof for modern man's confidence in historical progress. Thus in the words of Clutton-Brock, "Science told a lot of little truths in the interest of a great lie." The great lie was the belief that human freedom was not real and that man had no unique characteristics which would distinguish him markedly from the other animals. Orthodox Protestantism countered this great lie by "telling a lot of little lies in the interest of a great truth." The truth was the unique character of man; and the little lies were the pathetic efforts to refute undoubted scientific discoveries about biological evolution by illicit appeals to the Biblical doctrine of creation, as if it were an alternative to scientific analysis of causes rather than a reference to the mystery which lies beyond all causal sequences and prompts reverence for the emergence of any novelty in the temporal flux, particularly the emergence of such a novelty as the human being. This controversy was in a sense the pathetic climax of the long warfare between science and religion and seemed to prove that the warfare had finally ended in the complete victory of science over religion. All that had been accomplished, however, was to give a modern naturalistic version of ontological structure a spurious triumph over the "empirical" reality which can be attested by any honest "experience." That reality is the significant freedom of man expressing itself not only above the level of nature but above any conceivable ontological level whatsoever, and able by that freedom to elaborate various dramatic patterns of history.

There can be no question about the futility of the effort to guard the idea of the uniqueness of the human person by resisting and defying the evidence of the biological scientists in regard to the evolution of natural forms. This is the more true since it is an accepted fact and truth that man is related to the natural order and is therefore in a sense an animal. But it is also true that Darwinian conclusions did materially influence the modern estimate of man's nature so that it seemed impossible to conceive of man as a unique creature. This fact has persuaded a modern philosopher, Karl Jaspers, that it is necessary provisionally to question the validity of the evolutionary idea of the emergence of man at a particular point in the evolutionary development in order to get a hearing from modern men about the thesis of the radical difference between man and the other creatures. In other words, a justified empiricism in regard to the natural order may become so dominated by ontological (in this case, naturalistic) presuppositions that it becomes impossible to be genuinely empirical about facts of a different order which do not fit into the onto-logical presuppositions.[1]

The fact that Christian obscurantism actually sought to guard an important "fact" about man, though with an abortive strategy, does not excuse the cultural obscurantism, the indifference to the task of tracing the causal relations in nature or in history. But it does prove that the *History of the Warfare between Science and Religion* (Andrew White) was not so simply the story of the triumph of science over religion as was generally supposed. It was certainly not a simple triumph of truth over error and superstition. A system of thought which was based upon a justified "fideism" and which became corrupted by an unjustified obscurantism did possess some true insights into the nature of man and his history. On the other hand, a scientific and rationalistic culture was blind to some obvious, not to say obtrusive, facts about the dimensions of selfhood and of history. Its prescriptions of inquiry contained some hidden ontological dogmas which blinded the culture to those facts which were incompatible with its dogmas.

We must postpone for a moment a consideration of the long and tortuous process through which the culture of a free society winnowed the truth about the self and its dramas, contained in a Biblical faith, from the errors caused by its cultural obscurantism and at the same time extricated itself from the errors due to an uncritical reliance upon reason and the scientific method. For these dogmas betrayed it into the effort to comprehend history within the dimension of nature and to derive virtue from man's reason. The political history of the Western world achieved triumphs of freedom and justice by winnowing truth from falsehood in both forms of faith.

---

[1] Karl Jaspers, *The Perennial Scope of Philosophy:* "Man can not be derived from something else . . . to be aware of this signifies man's freedom, which is lost in every other total determination of his being. . . . All empirical causalities and biological processes of development would seem to apply to man's material substratum and not to himself," p. 59.

Chapter 17

UNDERSTANDING NATURE AND MIS-
UNDERSTANDING HUMAN NATURE

The Reformation restored the Biblical-dramatic modes of thought and reclaimed knowledge of those aspects of human nature which were obscured by either the classical-medieval ontology or the classical identification of the self with its mind.

The Renaissance separated out the classical elements from the medieval synthesis. It therefore initiated all those forces and tendencies in modern thought which either equated mind with self and derived virtue from reason, or which tried to understand the self in the context of some ontological framework. Naturally the Renaissance also restored the capacities for rational discrimination which characterized a classical culture and which, expanded by modern scientific technics, have contributed so much to the modern man's understanding of his world and of himself within the limits of the culture's dogmas. However, the modern movement developed two characteristics which were not anticipated in the classical world view. The first is the idea of a temporal development of both nature and history. This progressive view had its rise in the optimism of the Renaissance which expected human reason to march to new triumphs, once reason escaped from the prison house of ecclesiastical authority. This optimism was fed by a multitude of real and spurious causes until it became the dominant principle of interpretation for the understanding of both nature and human nature. The discovery of the growth of historical forms, implied in the thought of the Roman Lucretius but not able to break through the cyclical dogma of the classical age, gave a great impetus to the idea of progress. It turned the cycles into spirals in early Renaissance historiography, thus transmuting the classical into the modern view of historical reality. The discovery of the development of historical forms was supplemented by the later discovery of development in biological structures. Darwin's biology seemed to provide the final key for the understanding of the world.

It also accentuated a second characteristic of modern culture, not evident in the classical world-view which it ostensibly restored. That was the interest in nature and the consequent or at least ancillary conviction that nature as a system is the ultimate reality to which man must orient himself. A naturalistic ontology was a subordinate element in classical culture. But Plato and Aristotle triumphed over the early naturalists or "atomists," and naturalism never became a serious option for men throughout the history of Western culture until the phenomenal triumphs of modern science and its conquest of nature seemed to make it plausible. Man was understood as a part of nature. Thus modern culture marched inexorably toward the understanding of nature and the misunderstanding of man. For it not only tried to contain human freedom within an ontological framework but it conceived that framework in naturalistic terms, which is to say, in terms which denied the freedom of the self and falsified the drama of history more consistently than any other ontology. A special ironic touch is given to this development by the fact that it was partly due to the "empirical" method of modern science which was intended to ascertain the "facts" by careful observation and to discount the "deductive" method which was based on confidence in the strict rationality of reality and upon the consequent validity of proceeding from the known to the unknown by rational deduction.

In the words of Francis Bacon, the father of modern empiricism: "Our method is continually to dwell on things soberly . . . to establish forever a true and legitimate union between the experimental and the rational faculty. . . . Those therefore who are determined, not to conjecture or guess, but to find out and know; not to invent fables and romances of the world, but to look and dissect the nature of the real world must consult only things themselves." [1] This empirical ambition, which is responsible for all the triumphs of the natural sciences, was directed equally by Bacon and his followers against both the Aristotelian rationalism and the Christian authoritarianism in the medieval synthesis. It gave modern culture a special animus against "dogma." But unfortunately it was not prepared to deal with the hidden dogmas in the prescriptions of science itself. It was therefore not prepared for the illusions which spread in the name of "empiricism." It is important to consult the evidence of "things themselves." But inquiries can not be undertaken without presuppositions or what President Conant defines as "conceptual schemes." These conceptual schemes are the hidden dogmas. They are usually the more potent for being implicit rather than explicit. "Science," declares President Conant, "is an interconnected series of concepts and conceptual schemes, which have developed as a result of observation and experimentation, and are fruitful of further experimentation and observation." [2]

Conant's regard for the necessity of "conceptual schemes" reveals the impossibility of observing the "things themselves" without a frame of meaning for the inquiry. Among natural scientists these conceptual schemes are assumed to be limited and to be subject to constant re-examination in the light of empirical evidence; for empirical observation may prove the tentative conceptual scheme to be at variance with the facts. Thus the first empirical science of the modern period, astronomy, invalidated the conceptual scheme underlying Ptolemaic and Aristotelian astronomy by the evidence of facts which pointed to a different astronomical order than had been as-

[1] Francis Bacon: *Preface to De Augmentis,* pp. 6-16.
[2] James B. Conant: *Science and Common Sense,* p. 25.

sumed in the older pre-Copernican astronomy. From that day to this, it has been assumed that it is a fairly simple procedure to change conceptual schemes when the evidence of the "facts" discredits them. But an "empirical" culture was not prepared to deal with the problem of wide, rather than specific, conceptual schemes, that is, with presuppositions of inquiry which referred not to a specific type of being under scrutiny, but with the very character of being itself. Ideally these conceptual schemes were subject to re-examination; but practically they proved themselves powerful enough to determine the evidence by which they were supposed to be tested. Thus Professor John Dewey, the most typical of modern naturalistic philosophers, never tired of insisting that the "experimental method" must be rigorous enough to re-examine its own hypotheses. But it never occurred to him that his insistence that the "methods of science" could be transferred from the field of nature to that of history, and that only the intrusion of irrelevant religious and political authority prevented this consummation, rested upon an erroneous and, unexamined presupposition. That was the universally held belief of modern culture that the realm of history was essentially identical with the realm of nature. This belief reduced history to the realm of necessity and obscured the freedom of man and the reality of the drama of history.

Two figures dominated the thought of the seventeenth century and contrived between them in their diverse ways to develop Renaissance thought in the direction which finally resulted in modern culture. They were Thomas Hobbes and René Descartes. They had quite different views of human nature but both contrived to sow the seeds which flowered in later confusion about the character of the human self.

Thomas Hobbes did not share the confidence of modernity in "reason" as the source of human virtue. In that respect he was not typically modern. His realism, not to say cynicism, probably established the difference between the realism of our political sciences in contrast to the more prevalent illusions about human nature in social sciences. "Reason" in Hobbes' esteem was the servant of the egoistic self. It was not therefóre, as for all rationalists, the instrument of justice and the guarantor of universal, as contrasted with partial and parochial, values. It was "reason" which made the difference between the harmonies of nature and the competitions within the human community. For reason was responsible for the inordinancy of all human desires. It justified men in following their interests with a consistency which made conflict with their fellow men inevitable and necessitated a tyrannical government in the interest of social harmony. We must postpone for the moment a consideration of the relation of realism with political conservatism in Hobbes, which has persuaded all typical children of the Enlightenment that it is necessary to encourage at least mild illusions about human nature for the purpose of validating democracy. Our present concern is with Hobbes' empiricism, and with the ancillary naturalism, not to say, "materialism" in his thought. Hobbes was more rigorous than any eighteenth-century French materialist in reducing reality to corporeal dimensions and in dismissing every other type of reality as "fantasy." He declares: "That a 'man is a living body,' we mean not that 'man' is one thing and 'living body' another thing and 'is' or 'being' a third; but that 'man' and 'living body' are the same thing . . . the consequence 'if he be a man he is a living body' is a true consequence, signified by the word 'is' . . . Therefore 'to walk,' 'to be speaking,' 'to see'; also 'walking,' 'speaking,' 'sight,' 'life' and the like signify just the same and are the names of nothing." [3]

Hobbes' polemic against "fantasies" includes every kind of abstract concept or generalization which describes any "fact" of nature and history above the level of sense object, or discrete event. It fully reveals the ontological implications of a rigorous empiricism. Naturally every aspect of selfhood beyond the dimension of the "living body" is excluded from his system. So, too, are all historic generalizations which describe some pattern of history.

Descartes, the other and greater figure in the thought of the seventeenth century, was very conscious of that dimension of

[3] Thomas Hobbes: *Leviathan,* Chapter 6.

selfhood which rose above Hobbes' "living body." But he was as concerned as was Hobbes to banish religious fancies and credulities from the realm of knowledge. This he did by rigorously separating the mind from the body, assuming that the depth of selfhood which was not contained in a mechanically conceived body would be described in the definition of "res cogitans." His "Cogito ergo sum" is obviously indebted to Augustine's speculations about the certainty of self-knowledge. But the sum of Descartes' thought comes out at a refurbishing of Aristotelian rationalism, in contrast to Hobbes' rigorous anti-Aristotelianism. In his *Passions of the Soul* [4] in which he distinguishes the passions which have their origin in "animal spirits" and those which are subject to the mind, he reveals the difficulty of destroying the idea of the unity of the self, inherited from Hebraic-Christian culture so that the mind may be fitted into a system of rational coherence and the body take its place in a mechanically conceived "nature."

Naturally there is little more awareness of an integral selfhood than in Hobbes, and the type of knowledge which Descartes insists upon for the sake of certainty, as contrasted with credulous imaginings, could not grasp historical realities any more than Hobbes' empiricism. Descartes however was typical and generative of two characteristics of modern culture. His passion for exact knowledge laid the foundation for the achievements of modern science; and his confidence in the mind's control over "passions" restored the classical idea of reason as a source of virtue. "Even those who have the weakest souls," he declares, "can acquire a very absolute empire over their passions, provided they employ sufficient skill in the management and guidance of them." [5]

The French Enlightenment managed to forget Hobbes' realistic account of human self-interest, to adopt his materialism and to compound it with Cartesian rationalism. The result was a fanaticism in the name of "reason" and of "nature," which was to offer indubitable proof that the worship of "reason" as the source of virtue and of order both within the individual

[4] See Norman Kemp Smith: *Descartes' Philosophical Writings,* p. 285.
[5] *Ibid.,* p. 305.

and in the community was certainly not conducive to that "reasonableness," which Montaigne extolled in skeptical reaction to Catholic rationalism. Nothing in Western history proves more conclusively that there is a great distinction between the use of reason for the sake of making discriminate judgements and the worship of "reason" as the source of virtue. Every error which infects a modern liberal culture in its estimate of the human situation—and most of the errors which reached a tragic culmination in modern totalitarianism in the name of "science"—were hatched in the French Enlightenment. History was simply equated with "nature" and regarded as subject to "nature's laws." These laws were regarded as fixed and inviolable as anything in nature; and therefore subject to "reason's" analysis. All the illusions of the type of social science which would destroy ideological taints in historical judgements by stricter scientific procedures, were anticipated in the Enlightenment. It had no awareness of the self's capacity to influence the mind or of the inability of any mind to give a rationally compelling account of historical reality. Therefore it equated "reason" and "nature" sometimes because it believed nature itself to be "rational" and sometimes because it believed it to be subject to the rational control of man. It was only necessary for reason to discern the laws of nature to accomplish this object. This confusion led *inter alia* to the economy of the physiocrats, who not only believed that the knowledge of the laws of nature would free men of all irrelevant political control, but also that an enlightened despot might be necessary to accomplish this emancipation. All these confusions led to what has been defined as "totalitarian democracy." [6] The irony of the fact that the worship of reason resulted in Jacobin fanaticism and cruelty; and that a nation which imagined itself emancipated from religious fanaticism should fall so quickly into a new fanaticism, informed by a very religious anti-religious rationalism, has not been fully appreciated by all post-revolutionary "liberalism." It still adheres to absurd notions about the perfectability of man, chiefly of

[6] *Cf.* T. L. Talman: *Totalitarian Democracy.*

his reason. It refuses to admit the plain evidence of history, that democracy is necessary because man's reason is corrupt, that is, corrupted by his interests. Therefore it is not possible to trust anyone with unchecked power or to allow any position in the community to remain unchallenged. The Enlightenment spawned every illusion which produced despotism in the name of liberty, civil war in the name of fraternity, and superstitious and uncritical politics in the name of reason. Thus Condorcet criticized the classical age for its "empiricism," and rejected Montesquieu's relativism as being based too much on geographic factors and neglecting the immutable conditions or "necessities" of human nature and the "rights" which were allegedly derived from them. Probably no era in modern history has been at once more insistent upon restoring the credos of a classical rationalism, and more engulfed in confusion about the nature of the human self and its dramas, than the period of the French Revolution. That is, among others, the reason why the promises of the French Revolution remain unfulfilled in France to the present day. The unhappy nation is still unable to find stability in the perpetual conflict between social forces which are informed by contrasting rationalistic illusions. The one force rejects, and the other accepts, the doctrine of man's perfectability. The one regards the Church, and the other holds reason, to be the fountain of truth. But neither is capable of that charity and accommodation to the other which makes community possible. So the French Revolution remains unresolved in France after more than a century of history. Evidently the abstract principles of the "dignity" of man and of his right to "liberty" are not as fruitful in creating a free society as the wisdom which recognizes the modicum of truth in error and the modicum of error in the truth of every political credo, and as the sense of community which overarches the political conflict in a healthy society and robs it of its venom.

The nineteenth century added little to the wisdom of the contrasting types of naturalists who both regarded history as identical with the realm of nature, the one believing that men should not interfere with its laws and the other seeing in sociology the power of a "scientific" mastery of history by man. Herbert Spencer was the proponent of the one theory and Auguste Comte of the other. Darwinian biology gave rise to a "social Darwinism" which seemed to give an added scientific prestige to the physiocratic theory, with the difference however that men were warned against interference, not with the "harmonies" of nature but with the "struggle for survival." In America, William Graham Sumner was the most prominent proponent of the theory of social Darwinism, warning that "the law of the survival of the fittest is not man-made, and can not be abrogated by man." [7] Lester Ward, on the other hand, propounded the philosophy, or rather sociology, of Comte, with equally absurd conclusions. He was convinced that a proper engagement of "disinterested intelligence and scientific investigation" would enable "sociocracy" to replace monarchy, aristocracy and plutocracy. This rule of the "whole of the people," to be distinguished from the "majority of the people," which characterized conventional democracy, would be made possible by the triumph of scientific intelligence over all partial and parochial viewpoints. Both Sumner and Ward abjured metaphysics. Yet it is apparent that the "scientific method" played the same role as the guarantor of the absolute as the Aristotelian *nous*. Modern empiricism, whether it regarded man as merely the creature or as the creator of history, evidently understood little about the endless competitions of interest in the drama of history and the impossibility of resolving these conflicts by the application of "disinterested intelligence." In short, it had learned nothing from the refutations by history of the illusions of the French Enlightenment. Decades were required to deliver our social sciences from the naivetés of this new empiricism, so ignorant of the real character of the human self and of the historical drama.

The idealistic reaction to the naturalism of the Enlightenment in the nineteenth century supposedly cherished the unique spiritual qualities of man in its "idealistic" ontology.

---

[7] William Graham Sumner: *Sociology.*

Hegel, particularly, dominated the thought of the nineteenth century. He managed to create a very imposing system of thought which combined elements of classical rationalism, Christian piety and the modern idea of a progressive history. Hegel's early writings reveal some awareness of what Kierkegaard defined later as the "existing individual"; his hopes, anxieties and frustrations. Furthermore, a deposit of Biblical-Christian awareness of selfhood, particularly of the uniqueness of the self's self-consciousness, made it necessary for Hegel to go through considerable "dialectical" legerdemain before he could arrive at the identification of the self with its mind, a procedure which was accomplished without much ado in classical rationalism. The struggle within the self between its self-centeredness and its desire to commit itself beyond itself was transmuted into the tension between the self as particular object in nature and the self as subject and as potentially universal mind. This was an intellectual task, which, though difficult, offered no real difficulties to the intelligent man who could disavow the Christian ideas of "sin" and of "grace," as it attempted self-redemption by rising above the "unhappy consciousness" of this tension to a serene attainment of its universal validity. Of course the real self in its organic unity of finiteness and freedom disappeared in this procedure. Hegel regarded Biblical religion as merely a crude and picturesque version of his scheme of redemption. He was blind to the fact that its dramatic forms revealed truths about the self and its history which would be obscured by a rationalism which sought to identify the self with its mind and to comprehend the drama of history in ontological terms.

Hegel's interpretation of history was even more imposing and absurd than his interpretation of selfhood. His philosophy of history was a grand theodicy in which he tried to justify the ways of God to man, or in this case to endow the drama with meaning from the standpoint of his faith in an ultimate. His ultimate was a God who required time to achieve divinity or to realize both the freedom and the order which are in the nature of the ultimate. The concept of God, requiring time to become truly God, thus combined Christian and modern religious feelings. But the classical motif was added by the fact that the impulse which created historical movement was furnished by logic itself, so that history became a logical or at least a rational process. Parmenides had been concerned, at the dawn of Greek philosophical speculation, with the logical impulse to posit the antithesis of a concept, so that, for instance, the concept of "being" posited the concept of "non-being." But Parmenides could not regard anything as "being" which was touched by the flux of "becoming" in its passage from "non-being" to "being." This passion for identifying "being" with a fixed structure, so that temporal events are cast into the category of "appearance" remains a permanent characteristic of the metaphysical mind. An eminent English philosopher of the nineteenth century, F. H. Bradley, living in an age intent upon finding "reality" in the temporal flux, could nevertheless insist that every aspect of reality, involved in flux, is only "appearance," while "reality" can be affirmed only of the fixed rational structure of existence. It was Hegel's genius that he placed logic in the service of historical movement. It was his idea that the motive power of the historical flux was provided by the very tension between opposites of which Parmenides spoke. This tension between being and "non-being" was responsible for "becoming." But the force of temporal events was not circular as in classic thought, according to which all "motion" was created by the "coming to be and passing away" of particular entities, as they actualized their essential nature and then decayed. The temporal flux was logical in a different way. It moved from "thesis" through "antithesis," to a synthesis of opposites; which in turn became a new thesis for another "dialectical" advance. Everything, including God, the self and man's history was driven by this dialectic motive power. Thus all of reality including history was thoroughly "rational."

It was an imposing structure of thought which had a few, but only a few, "empirical" facts to support it; among these were the distinction between nature as a realm of necessity and history as a realm in which freedom and necessity were compounded. There was also the tension between freedom and order in the life of cultures which Hegel used to construct a dialectical movement in history, beginning with primitive life, moving through the ancient empires and culminating in the perfect synthesis of the European (more particularly Prussian) synthesis of order and freedom of his day. There were some facts to give plausibility to the picture. But Hegel falsified or obscured every dramatic pattern and reality of history in order to preserve the unity and consistency of his picture of the world, the self and history. The real cause for its seeming plausibility was the modern man's faith in consistency or coherence as a test of truth. He was willing to deny the reality of a "living God," that is, of a God who was more than a dialectical process, and the reality of his own selfhood and the dramatic realities of his history, if only he could believe this vision of an absolute which incorporated time and history within it.

So imposing was the structure that for a century it was possible to make only such portions of the Christian faith acceptable to the "intellectuals" as could be fitted into the Hegelian world picture or could plausibly be reinterpreted in terms of its outline. This was the triumph of the "rational" element in the Greek inheritance over the experimental modern element which Francis Bacon desired to compound with it. There were not however enough "facts" to support this structure. It was a great inflated balloon waiting for someone to puncture it.

Feuerbach proceeded to supply the puncture, whereupon a swarm of "left wing" Hegelians tore up and redesigned the whole conception until Marx came up with a grand redesign. He managed to wed the materialism of the French Enlightenment to the Hegelian "dialectic." Marx gave his philosophy a seeming relevance and social motive power by a dash of religious apocalypse dressed in the new "logic of history." According to Marx, the Hegelian speculations could be dismissed as irrelevant except at one point. What "evidence" could support them? But was there not historical evidence for a "dialectic" in man's social history? Did not history begin with an original communal wholeness of man which represented his true "essence"? Did not his primitive innocency disappear in the antithesis of a "class society" in which man was "alienated" from his "true essence"? Did not this class society then proceed through various chapters of feudalism and bourgeois society until its "contradictions" reached a "climax" in modern capitalism? Did not the injustices of this capitalism produce a disinherited class whose resentment would provide the antithetical thrust against it? All that was necessary was to instruct the class of the disinherited, the "proletariat," what the logic of history was, and that it had been marked out by that logic to accomplish the heroic task of not only emancipating men from injustice, but of changing the whole human situation so that man is no longer creature and creator in history but becomes unambiguously its master, not only "proposing but disposing." Every religious reverence for the mystery of history or of life is thereupon abolished as no more than an outmoded remnant of a previous impotence.

It is not surprising that this version of Hegelian logic should have become plausible enough to become the basis of a new world religion; and one which fills the world with cruelty and with pretensions of world dominion in the name of world redemption. Instead of being involved in ambivalence between visions of an absolute God beyond the conditions of time and the impulse to conform the conditions of time to the vision of the absolute, it gives itself to the unambivalent ambition to bring every historic reality under the dominion of its vision, forgetting, of course, that all such visions are partial and parochial, and that they are therefore the source of evil in the application. The new religion harnessed the resentments to the hopes of the disinherited and gave them the pride of believing themselves prospective world emancipators. Furthermore, it wedded the rationalistic passion with the empirical interest so that it could pose as a "science," the "Marxist-Leninist science" in modern communist parlance. Furthermore, it gave a group of intellectual idealists the chance to compound their idealism with their lust for power. They had to instruct the proletariat, ostensibly the saviors of the world, but unconscious of their destiny until instructed.

Thus it provided the opportunity for secular prophets to become the atheistic theocrats or priest-kings of a utopian state. They could fulfill every unfulfilled dream and ambition of the eighteenth-century philosophers. The vision was so attractive that it held many intellectuals bound long after history had proved that this dream had turned into a nightmare of cruelty.

A footnote must be added about the discredit to the cult of "reason" involved in this tragic history. The communist tyranny had been preceded by the fascist one. The fascists were corrupt romantics, trusting in their intuitions and in the glorification of the sub-rational vitalities of life, of "Blut und Boden." Hence the devotees of the cult of reason warned the world about the danger of lack of confidence in reason. They conceded that reason might be, on occasion, weak or corrupt. But was it not better to cherish reason, they argued, than to succumb to the flood of unreason? They were right, of course, in emphasizing the creative function of rational discrimination. But they have not yet made their arguments relevant to the historic fact that communism has proved the cult of unreason not to be the sole source of tyranny. The other is an uncritical cult of reason, which manages to derive cruelty and tyranny from its scientific pretensions, thus proving how unreasonable a pretentious reason can be. We have two lessons in the limits and the corruptions of man's reason, one in the French Revolution and one in modern communism. The latter is not "irrational" in the same sense as the Nazis were. It surveys the world with cool calculation. But it may bring a final disaster upon the world because its cool calculations are founded upon, or informed by, wholly illusory ideas of a "logic of history." How can we prove that this "reason" is irrational? We could of course prove that the presuppositions of inquiry are very important; that they may obscure the facts which the inquiry is supposed to ascertain; that they are, in fact, rather like all the implicit dogmas of modern men, who may pride themselves upon their freedom from explicit dogma. The communist dogmas are rather more restrictive than some other dogmas; and have proved to be so even when they are

not supported by a police power which suppresses inconvenient evidence in conflict with them.

Fortunately, the drama of history was more unpredictable
and its facts less "logical" than either Hegel or Marx had
believed. Therein lay the salvation of Western civilization, at
least its avoidance of the prison which Marx's logic (as
amended by Lenin) had prepared for it. The class structure
of a technical civilization became ever more complex rather
than more simple. The government proved not to be simply
the "executive committee" of the "ruling classes" as the theory
averred. In fact, economic power was not as superior to
political power as both classical liberalism and Marxism
thought. The free societies possessed more resources for react-
ing to injustice and for adjusting the disbalances of power
which created them. The most advanced "capitalistic" national community, far from subjecting its industrial workers
to the logic of "increasing misery," actually allowed them to
share a fabulous prosperity, which was indeed subject to serious fluctuations, but which increased rather than gave promise
of moving toward a catastrophic climax. Most of these "facts,"
which refuted the Marxist logic, were so obvious that they
could not be denied. They changed the social and political
history of the Western world into a destiny such as no Marxist
had anticipated. Perhaps this proves that empirically ascer-
tained facts have the power to refute even the most plausible
dogma. On the other hand, a modicum of facts is able to
sustain the prestige of even an implausible dogma. Consider,
for instance, the prestige of the Marxist faith in that part of
the world in which a decaying feudalism and the remnants
of "imperialism" produce enough facts to sustain the dogma
which has been refuted by obvious facts in the technical civilization for which it was designed and where its logical promises
were hoped to be fulfilled. In addition, the two countries of
the Western world in which it still has prestige either have not
completely overcome a traditional feudalism (Italy) ; or have
a tired and corrupt capitalism (France) which produces some
of the facts which seem to validate the Marxist dogma.

Chapter 18

THE CLIMAX OF AN EMPIRICAL CULTURE: ITS BLINDNESS TO SOME OBVIOUS "FACTS"

Fortunately, the larger part of Western civilization was able to refute the logic and pseudo-empiricism of Marxism by developing a common life in which both freedom and justice were preserved, and in which the resentments of the poor did not prompt rebellion against its institutions. It is the fond illusion of a modern liberal culture that it vanquished this pseudo-empiricism by a more genuine empiricism which was thoroughly "scientific" and not quasi-philosophical and quasi-religious. Actually the wrong theory of Marxism was refuted by social and political facts, which were not intended by any of the various contestants in the cultural and political contests. To this development we must devote our concluding chapters. In this context it is important to observe that the "empirical" emphasis in the culture of the West contains almost as many hidden dogmas as the empiricism of Marxism. Furthermore, these dogmas make our historical sciences blind to some obvious facts about human nature and history which simpler cultures apprehended by the wisdom of common sense. But the empirical method has been so successful in the understanding of nature that the prestige of the triumphs of the natural sciences could always be used to obscure or deny the obvious deficiencies in the understanding of man. Thus modern culture has moved toward an ironic climax of misunderstanding man by the same alleged methods which helped it to understand nature, and to cover up the significant failure in one field by a phenomenal success in another.

If we make the charge that an empirical culture is blind to some very obvious "facts," it is necessary to define what is meant by "facts." We have seen that Hobbes could recognize only corporeal realities as "facts." Traditional scientific empiricism recognizes only sense data as facts. But who would deny the validity of the concept of "fact" to such "realities" as the self's freedom, the self-corruption of that freedom in self-concern, or the self's "historical" character? These are the kind of facts with which the average man must deal daily.

(A) Common sense attests the reality of each one of these facts. When we say "the self's freedom," this "fact" is interpreted in common-sense terms as the self's ability to determine its actions, despite the determining influences upon those actions in the environment, and despite the possible inhibiting forces in its own "sub-rational" nature upon the power of its will. Its freedom is never absolute; but the common sense of all the ages, free of metaphysical subtleties, has agreed to define this freedom in terms of holding the self responsible for its actions. Despite all modern scientific or metaphysical deterministic theories, the jurisprudence of the world has never varied in assuming a responsible freedom of the self, though "insanity" may be recognized by law as limiting responsibility; and presumably psychopathological derangements, short of insanity, might be recognized as limiting responsibility, if not in law then certainly in popular opinion. Furthermore, a charitable survey of the determining influences upon the life and actions of a delinquent child, for instance, will qualify the severity with which responsibility is apportioned. But these qualifications do not seriously challenge the general assumption that the self is in possession of a responsible freedom.

It is not only common sense and jurisprudence but the art of every culture which attest to this capacity of the self, for self-determination. The novels and dramas of every age have based their depiction of characters upon the assumption that human beings have the capacity of self-determination. Any other assumption would destroy art as surely as it would distort the realities with which the common man feels himself to be in touch.

This free and responsible self is either denied or obscured in the prevailing theories of the psychological and social sciences of our day. Sometimes the strict naturalistic presuppositions obscure the reality to which common experience attests. Sometimes the methods of empirical science, drawn from the natural sciences, serve to obscure the facts about the self which can be known only through introspection and in dramatic encounter. Thus disciplines which have ostensibly disavowed all metaphysics are as unable as the more rigorously metaphysical disciplines to see the responsible self and its involvement in sin or its capacity for grace.

The thought of an eminent psychologist, who is not governed by strictly naturalistic presuppositions, reveals how the methods of the natural sciences, applied to human realities, obscure the real self in its integrity and freedom. After analyzing all the intricacies of human personality, Gardner Murphy asks the question: "Should the student of personality, at the present stage of research, posit a non-empirical entity, distinct from both organism and its perceptual responses to forms and symbols, which are called a "self"? He decides that "a tentatively negative answer to this question seems advisable." [1] Mr. Murphy is too much of a realist to give more than a "tentatively negative" answer. But the standards of his science will not permit any but a negative answer, though he promises that another answer might be given when "the present stage of inquiry" is more advanced. Actually no advance in the inquiry will ever enable his type of empiricism

[1] Gardner Murphy: *Personality,* Harper & Brothers, p. 490.

to find the free and responsible self. It may be known in introspection and in dramatic encounter but not by methods of empiricism which make the self an "object" of empirical inquiry. It is a "non-empirical entity" only in the sense that it can not be seen through the spectacles of an empiricism, derived from the natural sciences. It is of course not distinct from either its "organism" or its "perceptual responses," i.e., its mind; but neither can it be equated with either.

It is rather significant that this self, which Mr. Murphy can not find, is the same self upon which Descartes rests his final certainty in his famous dictum *cogito, ergo sum,* though it must be admitted that the self was obscured as quickly as discovered by Descartes' definition of this self as *res cogitans,* as the thinking thing. The various versions of depth psychology seem involved in the contradiction of implying the responsible self in some facets of their thought while they explicitly deny its reality in other facets.

Freudianism explicitly denies the free self because it is so impressed by the power of the various sub-rational compulsions which destroy its freedom. It regards the emancipation of the self from both subrational and social compulsions as the object of therapy: "Where the id is there let the ego be" is the Freudian slogan. But the reality of a real ego is by no means unambiguously acknowledged. Freud was, of course, aware (as aware as Samuel Johnson) of the introspective testimony to the reality of free will. But he regarded this testimony as a "subjective feeling" which had no legitimacy beside the scientific evidence, which related every action to a previous cause. He was thus able to deny the reality of the real self more simply than Hegel, who had to engage in considerable dialectic subtlety before he transmuted the self into mind or "understanding." Freud is reluctant to use the word "soul," probably because of the connotation of immortality which adheres to that word. But he is forced to reintroduce the banished word in terms of its Greek equivalent *psyche.* Furthermore, the banished freedom and responsibility are inadvertently acknowledged when a Freudian psychiatrist insists on the necessity of voluntary rather than compulsory submission to therapy. (The co-operation of the unacknowledged self is important.) Sometimes a warning is issued against the inclination of the unacknowledged self to use the technics and insights of psychiatry for purposes of self-deception or self-justification.[2]

The self is obscured in modern anthropological theory, even when extreme (mechanistic) forms of naturalism are disavowed. Thus Kluckhohn and Murray attribute the "extreme position of nineteenth century mechanism" to the reaction of modern psychology to their possessive mother, philosophy, and their dogmatic grandfather, theology. But the consistency of their own naturalism and the consequent obscuring of the free self, is evident in their conclusion that, "Personality must be located in nature, within some field where there is togetherness of all these processes or of representations of these processes. . . . Thus we can state that personality is the organization of all the integrative processes in the brain." [3]

It is significantly the "brain" rather than "mind" which is defined as the source of the organization of integrative processes. Either the problem of the correlation between brain and mind, which has exercised the philosophers, has not been considered, or, having been considered, the "mind" was dismissed as not belonging to, or being located in, "nature."

When Neo-Freudians try to correct Freud's lack of understanding for the self's dependence upon others and elaborate a "cultural psychology" which emphasizes the dependence on the self for its security and self-esteem, upon the love and the esteem of others, particularly the "mothering one," they only contrive to obscure the freedom of the self more absolutely,

[2] L. F. Shaffer: *Psychology of Adjustment,* p. 534.

[3] Clyde Kluckhohn and Henry A. Murray: *Personality in Nature, Society and Culture,* pp. 8-9. Quoted by Albert C. Outler in *Psychotherapy and the Christian Message.* His chapter on "The Human Self and Its Freedom" deals with the blindness of psychiatric theory to the realities of the responsible self.

for they regard it as merely the product of its immediate social environment, particularly in its infancy.[4]

The "objective" psychologists are frequently as incapable of discerning a real self as the psychiatrists. They are even more ready to propose schemes for "conditioning" persons for "socially approved" ends and are vague about the criteria which determine the legitimacy of these ends. Thus a psychologist [5] projects a psychologist's vision of utopia in terms which betray both a lack of humor and any social wisdom. He would establish ideal communities, preferably not too large lest the passions and complexities of the larger community corrupt the ideal harmony of the "conditioned" community. In these communities men would be conditioned from childhood to live in frictionless harmony with their fellows. This harmony is made possible because the individuals have been purged of all jealousies and egoistic ambitions which would set them at variance with their fellows. They are significantly without any trace of dignity and nobility as well as of jealousy or competitive impulses. These conditioned persons of the psychological utopia are obviously not real selves, and are bereft of the indeterminate possibilities of good and evil, characteristic of free selves.

Modern anthropology has lately developed a theory of cultural relativism [6] which makes the individual completely the creature of his culture. They have not resolved the problem with which Socrates challenged the Sophists and have not enlightened us why it should be possible to learn anything about man in general, if men are completely relativized by their particular culture. They have hit upon an important truth in recognizing the historical character of man; but the rigor of their cultural determinism has made them blind to the freedom of man over the culture of which he is obviously, in one sense, a creature.

[4] *Cf.* Harry Stack Sullivan: *Conceptions of Modern Psychiatry*, The William Alanson White Psychiatric Foundation, 1947.

[5] *Cf.* B. F. Skinner: *Walden Two*.

[6] *Cf.* Ruth Benedict: *Patterns of Culture*.

"In the man-culture system," the anthropologist, Leslie White, informs us, "man is the dependent, and culture the independent variable." Mr. White is certain that man's dependence upon his culture makes it impossible for men to solve such conflicts as the present one between the free and the collectivist societies. He compares all efforts to guide historical destiny with the efforts of primitive magic workers to control the weather. Every significant difference between the realm of history and the realm of nature is obscured in the rigor of his determinism. "Why is it," he asks with incredible naiveté, "that if one employs the principle of cause and effect in physical phenomena, no one cries 'fatalism'; but the moment one employs the principle in cultural phenomena the accusation springs forth?" [7] Mr. White has evidently never considered the historical complexities which arise from the ambiguity of man as both the creator and the creature of the cultural process; nor asked himself the question why human cultures should ever have arisen and become distinguished from the animal society.

(B) In addition to the contradiction between the wisdom of common sense and that of the academic empiricists on the question of the freedom and responsibility of the self, there is another contradiction between the two in the awareness of the one and the blindness of the other to the curious mixtures of egoism and creativity in human selves, manifesting itself on all levels of behavior. Since the eighteenth century there has been a good deal of speculation on the relation between "egoism" and "altruism," and about the elimination of the one in favor of the other. But the mixture of the self's concern with itself and its creative and responsible interests is infinitely varied. Children in their relation to their parents, soldiers dealing with their officers, workmen and office people seeking tolerable relations with their superiors, develop an almost instinctive method of appealing, on the one hand, to the sympathies of those who have greater power than they

[7] Leslie White: *Science and Culture*, p. 343.

and, on the other hand, trying to satisfy the vanity or pride, the sense of power or the sense of importance of their superiors. The taint of egoism, both individual and collective, is taken for granted by all men of affairs in government and business.

Common-sense wisdom also takes the infinite variety of the compounds of self-concern with creative energy for granted and is not surprised to find it on the highest as well as the lowest levels of character. Even the most perfectionist Christian sects and the most ascetic Christian monastics have practical ways of dealing with the vanities and jealousies of their bishops and abbots, which, according to their theories, are not supposed to be tainted with this corruption. The pervasiveness of egocentricity is observed by a modern poet, E. E. Cummings, who wisely does not seek to distinguish between harmless and harmful versions of it in bearing testimony to its universality. "Who, if I may be so inconsiderate to ask, is not egocentric?" asks Mr. Cummings.[8] "Half a century of time and several continents of space in addition to a healthily developed curiosity, haven't enabled me to locate a single peripherally situated ego. . . . My slight acquaintance with pickpockets and scientists leads me to believe that they are far from being unselfcentered. . . . So, I believe, are all honest educators. And so, I am convinced, are streetcleaners and deaf mutes, mothers, murderers, mountain climbers, cannibals, fairies, strong men, beautiful women, unborn babes, international spies, ghostwriters, bums, executives, out and out nuts, cranks, dopefiends, altruists (above all), obstetricians, ambulance chasers, and lion tamers."

Mr. Cummings' list is interesting primarily because of its calculated lack of discrimination. Only one of his categories could be safely challenged; that of "unborn babes."

The effort to discriminate between "harmless" and "harmful" types of egotism would probably lead to endless and inconclusive debates. It is fairly easy to refute the contention

[8] E. E. Cummings: *Six Nonlectures*, Harvard University Press.

that egoistic ambition is a necessary prerequisite of creativity; but it is obvious that egoism is a fairly universal concomitant of creative efforts of all types. Sometimes it militates against the person's usefulness; but at other times it is a harmless excrescence. Artists are generally assumed to be "temperamental," which is to say, vain. Their vanity usually feeds on their success. But only in extreme cases does it seriously affect their art. Eloquent preachers are under the same temptation as artists, and succumb to the temptation as frequently. Men of power are corrupted by the love of power and by pride in its possession. Powerless idealists, on the other hand, frequently reveal a great concern for their reputation as idealists; and scholars are jealous of each other because of possible inequalities of academic prestige. It is one of the mysteries of commonsense reaction to this universal tendency that no one can define at what point egocentricity ceases to be a harmless foible and becomes a harmful vice. Yet there is a fairly consistent reaction which distinguishes the harmless from the vexatious egotism. Soldiers are wont to discount the human foibles of their commanders with gentle cynicism, but beyond a certain undefined point they react with hatred to this egotism. Politicians are expected to be ambitious; and their ambition for personal advancement is not believed to militate against their capacity to serve the commonweal. Yet there is an undefined point which the politician must not exceed if the public is not to react cynically to his ambitions.

Common sense, in short, takes human egotism for granted in all forms of human relations, and reacts with gentle or harsh cynicism to it according to its degree, its vexatiousness and possibly according to the degree of self-deception in the critic. For the illusion of freedom from a universal taint is very common and is productive of resentful reactions to the egotism of others. The wisdom of the "man in the street" never fails to comprehend the mixture of creativity and self-concern in the behavior of all his fellows. This is the achievement of a genuine non-academic "empiricism."

In contrast, the academic wisdom deals abstractly with this

mixture of motives in human behavior. The wisest understanding of the complexities is characteristic of those disciplines which are most genuinely related to the historical
studies and those which pride themselves least on their
empiricism.

The discipline of economics was cradled in a physiocratic
theory which assumed both the universality and the harmless-
ness of self-love. Classical economic theory also identified self-
concern too uncritically with the economic motive and regarded self-concern in too individualistic terms. But all these
errors have been overcome as the discipline of economics developed and as it surveys economic behavior in the whole context of communal relations and in the mixture of motives in
individual and collective man. It is still inclined to obscure
the primacy of the power motive as distinct from the economic
motive; and it certainly has less understanding for the inordinancy of human ambitions than has political science, for
instance. On the other hand, it was the achievement of
classical economics that it harnessed self-interest in contrast
to its moral and political suppression in the classical and
medieval period, though the force of self-interest proved not
to be as harmless as classical economists assumed. Democratic
society found it necessary to equalize disproportions of economic power in the interest of justice, whereas the original
theory assumed that economic forces alone would make for
balances of power. The contribution of economic theory
toward the growth of a free society was nevertheless considerable.

It may not be possible to generalize about the attitudes
toward self-interest by the diverse schools of political science,
but it is not too hazardous to assert that political science is
nearer to the discipline of historiography than any other
social science and therefore is more likely to appreciate the
power of self-interest as an historical phenomenon. Political
scientists understand, better than the economists, the primacy
of the power impulse in human egotism. And they have no
difficulty in realizing the force of collective self-interest in

history. They do however find it difficult to appreciate the mixture of motives in the behavior of nations as well as of individuals. Hence those who emphasize the power of collective self-interest are inclined to a too cynical interpretation of the facts. There is therefore a constant debate between the "idealists" and "realists" about the interpretation of man's collective behavior, particularly that of the nation. The idealists do not understand the power and persistence of collective self-interest and invent various schemes for suppressing and transmuting it. The "realists," on the other hand, frequently approach Thomas Hobbes' cynicism in their emphasis upon the power of national self-interest and in their belief that no moral consideration can avail against it.

The errors in modern culture in regard to the mixture of self-regard and creativity in human behavior occur particularly in those disciplines of our culture which pride themselves particularly on their methods of empirical observation. Whether they are betrayed by the limitations of these methods (since they are not calculated to measure the complexities of "normal" human behavior) or whether they are too much under the influence of the dogmas of the Enlightenment, they have an almost universal attitude toward the problem of egotism. It consists in regarding self-interest as ordinate and harmless, provided it is not unduly frustrated by what Holbach defined as "bad rulers." In the modern context this means any political, cultural or religious efforts to criticize, suppress or transmute egotism. They also look for specific causes of inordinate forms of egotism, which become in effect the causes of egotism in general, so that the progressive elimination or mitigation of the factor of self-regard is assumed in these analyses.

Professor Dewey summarizes a great deal of modern sociological and psychological theory of human nature in his *Human Nature and Conduct.* He asserts: "Moralists are led, perhaps, to think of human nature as evil because of its reluctance to yield to control, its rebelliousness under the yoke. But this explanation only raises another question. Why did morality set up rules so foreign to human nature? . . . We are forced therefore to consider the nature and origin of the control of human nature with which morals has been occupied. . . . Control has been invested in an oligarchy. Indifference to regulations has grown in the gap which separates the rulers from the ruled. Parents, priests, chiefs, and social censors have supplied aims which were foreign to those upon whom they were imposed, the young, laymen, ordinary folk. A few have administered and given rules; and the mass have with reluctance and in a passable fashion, obeyed." Professor Dewey, following this diagnosis of the contradictions in which human beings are involved by reason of the fact that "there is a law in their members which wars against the law that is in their minds," proceeds to prescribe a cure. It consists of a more "scientific" projection of rules and aims of human conduct, and would be formulated by more competent "rulers" than parents and priests. It would overcome the contradiction between man's self-regard and his social impulses by a more scientific channeling of all the "drives" in human nature. Professor Dewey explicitly disavows the Marxist implications of his theory. "No matter how much men have turned moral rules into an agency of class supremacy," he declares, "the theory which attributes the origin of rules to deliberate design is false. . . . Lack of understanding of human nature is the primary cause of the disregard of it. . . . When men had no scientific understanding of nature they either passively submitted to it or sought to control it magically." [9] Dewey naturally promises that the scientific knowledge of human nature will work all the transformations which the knowledge of nature accomplished. It will particularly provide more competent rules to which men will not be so reluctant to conform because they will be constructed in greater accordance with the potentialities of human nature.

The most impressive modern psychological version of the Enlightenment theory of an essentially harmless self-regard,

[9] John Dewey: *Human Nature and Conduct,* Henry Holt and Co., Inc., pp. 2-3.

which becomes harmful only when frustrated, is given by the Neo-Freudian Erich Fromm, in his *Man for Himself*. He presents the thesis that men must first seek their own happiness, whereupon they may then love others as a "phenomenon of abundance." "Authoritarian religion" interferes with this simple fact of human nature by confronting the selfish self with the "command" to love the neighbor. Naturally a contradiction is established between the natural desires of the self and the moral command. Fromm sees very clearly that love is not a simple command to be obeyed. It is truly a phenomenon of abundance. The self, which is engrossed with its own security or prestige, is not free to love. But Fromm does not see that the security of the self is furnished not by its own efforts at security, but by the love of others. He also does not realize that the desire for security or for prestige is, like all human desires, indeterminate. There is no point at which the self, seeking its own, can feel itself self-satisfied and free to consider others than itself. The concern for others is as indeterminate as the concern for itself. These concerns are not in the "id" on the one hand and the "super-ego" on the other hand. Fromm has merely elaborated Freud's picture of the "ego" as torn between the demands of the "id" and the "super-ego."

"The demand to love our neighbors as ourselves is the strongest defence against human aggressiveness and is a superlative example of the unpsychological attitude of the cultural super-ego," declares Freud. "The command is impossible to fulfill. The enormous inflation of love can only lower its value and not remedy the evil. Civilization pays no heed to all of this. It merely prates that the harder to obey the more laudable the obedience." [10]

Actually there is no such tension between a pleasure-seeking "id" and a demanding "super-ego," not to speak of a "cultural super-ego." The ego is not an embarrassed broker between the two forces. The fact is that there are indeterminate de-

[10] Sigmund Freud: *Civilization and Its Discontents*, p. 140.

sires within the self, both for self-aggrandisement and for self-giving. The failure to recognize this fact makes Freudianism, whether in its early or in its later and refined forms, quite irrelevant to political problems. For political life must deal with the bewildering mixture of self-concern and creativity on all levels of community.

There is no "empirical" evidence for Freud's thesis that "aggressiveness" increases with the wider and wider demands upon the self with an ever-widening social organization. The evidence for this thesis is taken from neurotic individuals but is irrelevant to the behavior of "normal" individuals, who are involved in varied mixtures of ambition (not "aggressiveness") and creative concern for family, community, nation and civilization. This miscalculation probably accounts for the difference between the therapeutic success of Freudianism in dealing with deranged persons or neurotic individuals, and its irrelevance to any political problem faced by modern men. It is significant that the professional jealousies which Freud encountered in his early life as he rose to success and the element of jealousy which entered into the friction between him and Jung in later years are not explained in any Freudian theory. Only one of the younger colleagues who were envious of his success was obviously neurotic.

A Neo-Freudian of great insight and wisdom, Karen Horney, has attempted a further refinement of Freud's protest against the baneful effects of the demands of the "cultural superego." [11] According to Miss Horney, human beings would grow naturally to fulfill their potentialities if the demand for the unconditioned and the perfect did not interfere with their nature. She wisely recognizes that the search for absolute power and for absolute goodness are generically alike; and she proves that they may both lead to neuroses. She attributes the demand for absolute goodness to the influence of the religious demand "Be ye therefore perfect as your Father in Heaven is perfect." But she does not realize that the same teacher who uttered

[11] Karen Horney: *Neuroses and Human Growth.*

this demand rigorously rejected the claim which men make of achieving perfection.

The parable of the Pharisee and the Publican, in which the repentant sinner is "justified before the other," namely, the Pharisee who thanked God that he "is not as other men," is a clear refutation of the pretension which men make of standing upon some absolute ground, and which distinguishes them from other men who are obviously involved in the ambiguities of human history.

The desire for the absolute, whether for power or perfection, is not introduced by any particular doctrine or religion, but grows up spontaneously in human nature and creates many effects in human relations, even when the impulse does not create the neuroses which Miss Horney analyzes so effectively.

An anthropologist, Professor Ashley Montagu, has a version of the rise of human selfishness which resembles the psychiatric theories of Harry Stack Sullivan.[12] He recognizes that the security, which frees men to love their fellow men is provided by the love and esteem of their fellow men, or rather more particularly by the mother who guards the security of the infant (or in Sullivan's phrase the "mothering one," that is, anyone who has chief responsibility for the infant's security). Any undue self-concern is therefore due to a defect in love in the infancy of the child.

"Science points the way to survival and happiness," declares Professor Montagu, "through love and co-operation. Do what we will, our drives toward goodness are as biologically determined as our drives toward breathing." [13] Montagu derives defects in human character from defective securities in the life of the child, "particularly in the first six years." All this is true, of course, upon its own level; but hardly explores the possibilities of both good and evil above the biological level. It must also be observed that the theory places a rather heavy

[12] *Cf.* Harry Stack Sullivan: *The Interpersonal Theory of Psychiatry.*
[13] Ashley Montagu: *On Being Human,* p. 101.

load upon the shoulders of the mothers because it can not conceive of egotism arising in the individual without specific cause. Montagu is not able to explore this dimension because he does not know the self in its depth of selfhood. "Free will the person does not have," he declares. "The will that he has operates strictly within the limits determined by the pattern of the social group. What he has is the *illusion* of free will." [14]

It is this preoccupation with particular causes of particular forms of egotism which grows out of the denial of the self's unique free selfhood. "Man is suffering from an organismic dislocation from the environment, from an 'I' complex or 'I persona,' " writes a modern anthropologist in this vein of seeking for specific causes of a universal malady.[15] "The result is a divisiveness of function, in which disassociation and conflict assume supremacy over the organisms, unity and centralization of function." Mr. Burrow fails to state that this "dislocation" characterizes all human social organisms, as contrasted with the harmony of the ant-hill.

(C) The naturalistic presuppositions of the modern behavioral sciences, particularly the strong influence of Freudian thought upon, not only psychology, but anthropology and sociology, creates a contradiction between their view and that of common-sense wisdom with reference to the dramatic essence of history.

The determinists and voluntarists may quarrel on whether a man is the creature of his culture or whether a scientist is the potential master of it. But in any event, what they are talking about is not the tragic historical drama in which we are all involved, which we feel challenged to deflect from the most dire possibilities sensed by all men and over which we feel nevertheless no power to control and no omniscience to foretell even generally feared probabilities. The drama remains unpredictable. There is nothing in the behavioral

14 *Ibid.*, p. 74.
15 Trigant Burrow: "The Social Neurosis, a Study in Clinical Anthropology," in *Philosophy of Science*, Vol. 16, pp. 25-40.

sciences, for instance, which would prepare a nation like our own for the fate of being more impotent to control its destiny in the days of its seeming omnipotence than in the impotence and innocency of its infancy.

Nor is there, for all the "cultural relativism" of our anthropologists, an appreciation of the genuinely historical difference between the cultures of, say, Britain, France and Germany. The tragedy of Germany must be analyzed in terms of a dozen complex historical factors, involving such geographic factors as its place in the heart of the European Continent; such social factors as the political incompetence of its middle class and the military preoccupation of its aristocracy; and such cultural factors as the political ineptness of a metaphysically gifted people.

It certainly can not be explained as the consequence of defects in the toilet training which German mothers give their children. For that matter the excessive libertarian tendencies of American political thought have obviously more complex causes than the "anthropological" one of the rejection by American immigrants of their European "father." [16]

The tragic phenomenon of world-wide communism, with its Russian center and base, does not yield its secrets to an empiricism which draws comparisons between the present Russia and "Eastern Christendom," nor to one which surveys the historic swaddling of infants in Russia as the alleged cause of the docility of a people. Communism is in fact a monstrous mergence of power impulses with utopian dreams for which the whole history of a Christian culture is required to explain.

It is not too broad a generalization to say that the empiricism of the "free world" is pervaded almost as much by Freudian and quasi-Freudian thought as the culture of the tyrannies is dominated by Marxist thought. This Freudian psychology and anthropology is, however, therapeutically skillful in dealing with maladjusted individuals, irrelevant to all genuinely historic situations. It does not understand how the individual is creatively involved in the historic situations of

[16] *Cf.* Geoffrey Gorer: *The American People.*

which he is also the creature and victim. Freud is ambivalent toward the realities of cultural development. On the one hand, as, for instance, in his *Civilization and Its Discontents,* he is in the romantic tradition of pessimism toward the achievements of civilization and betrays a characteristic romantic preference for primitivism. Each elaboration of culture and civilization merely increases the almost intolerable tension between the pleasure seeking "id" and the ever more rigorous demands of the "cultural super-ego," i.e., the moral requirements of a complex civilization. The poor "ego" is caught in this tension; and its frustrations create ever more dangerous increments of "aggressiveness."

On the other hand, Freud is a modern exponent of Enlightenment doctrine who believes that "our best hope of the future is that the intellect, the scientific spirit, should establish a dictatorship over the human mind." [17] The one theory is as irrelevant to historic situations as the other because the self and its mind create ever new elaborations of culture; and there is no increasing tension between the cultural situation and a primitive "id." On the other hand, the self and its mind are too involved in every historic situation to be simply redeemed from them by the "dictatorship" of the scientific spirit.

In short, a "Freudian" empiricism is as incapable as Hegelian metaphysics to comprehend the self in its dramatic environment. For the self is at once the creator and the creature of every historic situation; and it maintains the wholeness of its person in all these situations, whatever may be the tensions between its "mind and body" or its "id" and "super-ego."

We thus confront the ironic fact that a culture, intent upon understanding nature and boasting of ever more impressive achievements in the "conquest" of nature, has become involved in ever more serious misunderstandings of human nature, of the self in its uniqueness, and in its dramatic-historical environment.

[17] Sigmund Freud: *New Introductory Lectures in Psychoanalysis,* p. 234.

Part **III**

DRAMATIC, ORGANIC AND CON-
TRACTUAL ELEMENTS OF THE SELF'S EFFORTS TO
BUILD COMMUNITIES. THE DIFFERENCE BETWEEN
ORGANISM AND ARTIFACT DUE TO THE DISTINC-
TION BETWEEN THE SELF AS CREATURE AND AS
CREATOR OF HISTORICAL DESTINY. THE INCREAS-
ING PROPORTION OF ARTIFACT IN MODERN COM-
MUNITIES. CAN THE WORLD COMMUNITY BE
FASHIONED PURELY AS ARTIFACT?

Chapter 19

THE RESOURCES OF THE CHRISTIAN
FAITH IN A DYNAMIC CIVILIZATION
AND AN EXPANDING SOCIETY

The Christian faith undoubtedly survives in a so-called "modern" age in which scientific development is supposed to have invalidated it. It survives, in part, because all the testimonies of philosophers and scientists against it can not avail against the inner witness of the human self, that it is a real self, burdened with both responsibility and guilt (burdened with the latter because it has not adequately fulfilled the former).

Religious faith in both Catholic and Protestant versions of Christianity and in the Jewish version of Biblical faith survives most vitally in the backward "regions," that is, in those sections of culture in which the failure of religion to come to terms with the undoubted truths disclosed by the disciplines of philosophy and the sciences is not found too embarrassing, and where the efforts to disabuse the self of its selfhood are not too effective. It is however a serious mistake to relegate Biblical faith merely to the backwaters of our culture. For men need not be too obviously simple to escape the baneful effects of a sophisticated culture, which erroneously regards faith as merely the remnant of man's earlier impotence (Marx) or as the projection of infantile fantasies (Freud).

The persistence of the problem of selfhood and the inability to fit the self into any system of coherence which the wise men of this and other ages devise for it is not, of course, a proof of the validity of a faith which discerns, or thinks it discerns, another dimension of reality beyond the coherences of nature and reason, in which both the freedom and the guilt of the self are understood and in which the former meets judgement, and the salve of forgiveness is applied to the hurt of the latter.

But even if the private relevance of faith be granted and it be understood that it is more than a source of comfort for individuals in the hours of their extremity (that is, when they confront the facts of both death and sin), it is not clear whether or how there is any resource in Biblical faith for the problems of the community, for aiding men in organizing and reorganizing their common life, particularly in a civilization, in which growingly powerful technics continually alter the conditions of human togetherness both by expanding the communities on all levels and by making the requirements of justice increasingly complex. The task of harnessing, deflecting and suppressing self-interest for the sake of the larger interest becomes ever more difficult, and the equilibria of social power upon which justice depends become ever more tentative in the shifting circumstance of a technical age.

These communal problems require above all the application of discriminating intelligence, which knows how to distinguish between constant and variable factors in a social situation and which is informed by the empirical spirit, by a genuine "humility before the fact" in defiance of dogmas, whether of a religious or rationalistic variety. It would seem therefore that the modern prejudice, which looks to all the disciplines informed by the spirit of the Renaissance for guidance, were justified. But unfortunately some of the facts which a modern empiricism obscures because of its own hidden dogmas must be clearly seen if men are to solve the problems of their togetherness. Thus the seemingly irrelevant Biblical faith becomes relevant to the social situation. It was relevant even in the days when it seemed to have been permanently relegated to the status of *ueberwundener Standpunkt*. Insofar as modern men have solved their social problems and achieved communities in which the individual had a tolerable freedom and the community preserved a tolerable stability, and classes were related to each other in a tolerable justice, it will be found that both components of our culture, the Hebraic and the Hellenic, the Biblical and the classical made, if not equal, yet equally necessary contributions to the result.

At its best the Biblical faith guarded the "facts" of freedom and responsibility and acknowledged the self-concern of the self, which a more pretentious empiricism denied. It also introduced a sense of the dramatic quality of history and the uniqueness of its various occasions which underlies the empiricism of an Edmund Burke as contrasted with the alleged empiricism of the French Revolution. At its best, the Renaissance faith introduced the disciplines of rational discrimination which religious dogmas effaced or obscured.

At their worst, the two forces of piety and rationalism introduced similar errors into the social situation in the very debate in which they polemicised against their respective errors. There is an ironic quality in the debate between the pious and the rationalistic exponents of freedom and justice. Each accuses the other of introducing false absolutes into the contingencies of history. For the pious, the absolute is the will of God; and for the rationalists, it is the dictate of reason. Yet each side is guilty in its own way of the error of which it accuses the other.

The pious conceive of the worship of God to be a guarantee against the worship of idols, that is, against undue reverence for, or loyalty to, contingent and finite values. Ideally the worship of the true God emancipates the soul from the worship of self, either individually or collectively. Actually the history of religious fanaticism proves that it is fairly easy to claim identity between the absolute and the contingent value, and thus to claim divine validity for a

"Christian" civilization despite all of its moral ambiguities, and to use the Christian faith as a weapon against the foe in all kinds of historic encounters.

Reason, according to the faith of a rationalistic culture, will dissolve all these irrationalities and force men to claim for themselves only those privileges which will fit into a total scheme of coherence. Reason, argued Condorcet, would force the privileged to yield their privileges, and education would arm the simple with new weapons against the shrewd. Were not most injustices due as much to the shrewd taking advantage of the simple as of the strong taking advantage of the weak? All class distinctions were, according to an anthropologist, Robert Briffault, due to religious prejudices, which would be dissolved by rational analysis.[1] He forgot that it was Aristotle who gave the most plausible justification of slavery in rational terms when he declared the institution to be the natural consequence of the difference in the endowments of men, of whom the intelligent were by nature destined to command while the unintelligent were by nature "tools."

The simple fact is that neither the classical, the medieval nor the modern rationalists recognized that it is as easy to identify the interest of the self with a universally acknowledged right or value as to identify it with the will of God. That is why we have had such an ironic conflict between the pious and the rationalists, each of them aware of the hypocrisy of the other but neither of them aware of the dishonesty in themselves. Ideally a Christian faith makes for humility and charity because it subjects both the claims and the pretensions of the self to an ultimate judgement. Actually religion makes for fanatic claims as frequently or more frequently than it generates charity for reasons already analyzed.

Ideally the cultivation of reason makes for "reasonableness." It moderates claims by weighing each claim against competing claims and by challenging traditionally estab-

[1] Robert Briffault: *Rational Evolution.*

lished privileges with the question whether they are justified by social function or any consideration of the commonweal. Actually the logical process does no more than work out conclusions on the basis of the premises upon which the process is based. The logical man will not assert that all men are mortal because Socrates is mortal. He will assert that Socrates is mortal because all men are. But if we apply logic to human affairs, we readily see how the premises determine the conclusions and how interest determines the adoption of the premises.

Kant tried to place logic in the service of morals by his dictum, "So act as to make thine action on the basis of universal law." But if we begin with the not unjustified premise that special services to the community require special incentives and that special functions justify privileges related to the function, we can rationally claim every kind of special privilege for ourselves by the sanction of "universal law." Therefore, the Enlightenment was not as successful in establishing "liberty and equality" as it had hoped. It failed not only because so many privileges and coercive restraints were more justified than it had thought, but also because power is able to justify even unjustified privileges if it begins the logical process with premises which seem to justify them. Gradually, of course, a rational analysis of all the permanent and the contingent factors in a social situation will reveal liberty and equality to be the regulative principles of justice, and will discover how much these regulative principles must be compromised in practice in order to permit society to organize by the inevitable hierarchy of authority by which all communities are integrated. Ultimately, the two principles of liberty and equality, both of which were regarded as "self-evident" by the Enlightenment, proved to be in conflict with one another, the middle classes insisting on a preference for liberty, and the industrial classes for equality. These preferences were the occasion for the civil war which rent the unity of most Western societies. The preference for each value by the respective class was advanced the more fanatically because it was supposed to be rationally justified. Yet each preference was ideologically motivated. The middle classes preferred liberty because they wanted as little as possible control by the State of their economic activities. The industrial workers, on the other hand, having no significant social power of their own and being prompted by justified and unjustified resentments against the hierarchical structure of society, preferred equality to liberty. If the premises of communist logic are granted, namely, that "all history is the history of class struggles," and that class distinctions are progressively heightened until they lead to the climax of a revolution, then everything in the communist conclusions proceeds in an inevitable manner from these premises. It is of course also "rational" to refute the premises of communist logic empirically, to prove that there are more complex class tensions than are assumed in the communist premises and that they are modified rather than heightened in a technical society, and that the institution of property is not the sole cause of social injustice.

Thus it would seem that empirical reasoning is a safeguard against the fanaticism of abstract reasoning, which begins with premises not warranted by the facts of experience. But we have previously noted that the causal chains of history are so complex that it is impossible to refute even the most fanatic theory with absolutely compelling logic.

It is significant that not only political arguments informed by obviously untrue presuppositions lead to erroneous results. Even non-communist political parties seek their ends by reasoning which is an offense to common sense. Thus, for instance, it has been a favorite argument of Republicans that during the Democratic Administration over a billion people in the world came under the yoke of communism. This argument was supposed to prove that any administration in America could, by a different policy, have prevented the course of events in the revolutionary ferments of Asia. The argument involved the logical fallacy of *post hoc, ergo propter hoc* and it assumed an American omnipotence in world affairs which was contrary to the obvious facts. But since America is very powerful and since our foreign policy is designed to prevent events unfavorable to our interests, the inherent absurdity of the political logic is not universally apparent. Political arguments are in fact both a proof of the inner necessity of men to reason so as to make their interests seem to be in accord with universally valid values and of the inclination to bend reason more or less patently to their ends. Political arguments certainly prove that it is not possible to compel the self to abate its claims because a fault has been proved in the logic by which those claims are advanced.

In short, reason may be as obedient a servant of particular interests as religion. Both are the more plausible servants because the presumption of truth, transcendent to interest, is implied in both faith and reason. This is why rational discrimination is necessary to weigh the claims made for the self in the name of both faith and reason. That would make the virtue of a scientific culture an antidote against the defects of both religious and rationalistic claims. But the insight of an historic faith is required to understand the self which is both able and inclined to use either religion or reason, or both, as the servants of its interests, even while it may honestly long for the absolute truth which one or the other allegedly guarantees.

The irony of the conflict between the pious and the rationalists, each accusing the other of introducing partial interests into their vision of the truth, is exceeded by another irony in the modern debate. In that irony only the typically modern element in our culture is involved. It is created by the modern belief that traditional religion is too "other-worldly," too interested or preoccupied with trans-historical consummations of life to be effective in establishing freedom and justice upon the earth. It believes that it is only necessary to disavow "heaven" and concentrate upon historical goals to achieve whatever *summum bonum* the imagination may suggest. Yet it is precisely this consistent this-worldliness which has introduced the final evils into contemporary history. For the claim of having realized the final consummation in history is certainly even more dangerous than the claim of having reached the final truth.

The irony of modern utopian pretensions and illusions, which have corrupted our culture since the Renaissance and reached their climax in the French Enlightenment, has been heightened by the fact that these illusions of the absolute goal, being either reached or reachable, have been generated in a culture which professed to be interested merely in the process of history, and thought that history was but a variation of the process of nature. Nothing could bear more telling testimony to the fact that man is more capable of betraying himself as a creature, worried about the absolute, than these inadvertent yearnings, even when he explicitly disavows any dimension of his life above the temporal process. Thus we have been involved in renouncing an incredible heaven only to build a more incredible, and much more dangerous, heaven on earth. To add to the depth of the irony, these utopian illusions have developed not only within the limits of a strict naturalism, but in the name of a rigorous empiricism. A culture which has prided itself on tracing the specific causes of specific evils either expected utopia when it had rid the world of all specific evils by improvements in government, education and psychiatric technics, or it came to the surprising conclusion that all evils were due to one specific cause, the institution of property, for instance. Therefore the elimination of this cause would guarantee the creation of a heaven on earth. Unfortunately it occurred to none of these empiricists that each individual self might, in its radical freedom, be the fountain source of ever new evils in history, its destructiveness having the same root as its creativity.

This failure of modern culture to solve the problem of the relation of the self and its history to the absolute or unconditioned is revealed not only in its disavowal of the transcendent goals of life. It is betrayed, too, in the lack of comprehension for the double truth which the Christian faith beholds in the Christ-drama. In classical versions of the Christian faith Christ significantly symbolizes both the indeterminate possibilities of historical achievement and also the divine mercy which understands the tension and contradiction between all forms of human virtue and achievement and the divine will. When this second dimension of the Christ-revelation is obscured (as it is in both the Renaissance culture and in that portion of the Protestant faith which has absorbed the illusions of modern culture) the cultural atmosphere becomes suffused with an air of sentimentality. Thus the Enlightenment regarded liberty and equality, not as regulative principles of justice, but as simple possibilities of history. Liberal Christianity aggravated, rather than mitigated, these illusions by suggesting that love, which appears in history most tragically when it is most perfect, could be a simple historical possibility. Liberal Christianity therefore merely added to the general sentimentality of the age. The outstanding Protestant theologian of the nineteenth century, Albrecht Ritschl, whose influence extended throughout the world, illustrated this defect of liberal Christianity. He could treat of the central theme of Christian faith, namely, that "God was in Christ reconciling the world unto Himself" in a systematic treatment which combined Kantian and Lutheran elements. But the Kantian elements were obviously dominant because Ritschl believed that men needed to be reconciled to God only because of their ignorance. "Insofar as men are regarded as sinners," he wrote, "both in their individual capacity and as a whole, they are objects of redemption and reconciliation, made possible by the love of God. Sin is estimated by God, not as the final purpose of opposition to the known will of God but as ignorance." [2] Thus the whole Biblical doctrine of the seriousness of sin and the necessity of forgiveness is emptied of its meaning and the view of the human situation is altered to conform to the prejudices of the Enlightenment.

[2] Albrecht Ritschl, *Justification and Reconciliation*, p. 384.

The form of interpreting the central revelation of the Christian faith is really the best indication of the ethos of an age. If the two facets of the revelation in Christ are not appreciated, and the figure of Christ is interpreted merely as a symbol and example of human virtue, all that is expressed in Biblical faith from the prophets to the final revelation which emphasizes the continued ambiguity in all historic achievements, is lost. Christianity, in that event, becomes merely another form of "idealism" in and through which men deceive themselves, believing that their actions and lives are as good as the ideals which they are able to entertain.

In individual life this means that the love, which is the core of the Christian "ideal," is regarded as a simple fruit of the human will. It thereby becomes impossible by the very confidence that it is a simple possibility. The "love of Christ," according to the New Testament, is either forgiving or sacrificial love. It therefore depends upon humility and the knowledge of the common involvement of all men in sin on the one hand; and upon "grace" beyond the capacity of anyone's will on the other hand.

In terms of social and political wisdom the destruction of the paradox contained in the concept of a crucified Savior means that there is no understanding of the fact that even the best social structures and schemes of justice may be in contradiction to the "Love of Christ." The elements of self-regard and partial interest are not detected in their pretensions of universal validity. Consequently the enlarging sphere of social obligation and the greater perfection of communications, by which communities are integrated, are falsely interpreted as evidences of "progress"; and the perennial contradictions in life to the felt moral imperative are obscured. We have previously analyzed the curious contradiction between the wisdom of common sense and these illusions. For common sense never doubts that it must deal with the egotism of men on every level of community; but the more sophisticated wisdom is constantly beguiled by the "progressive" elements in the historic situation to imagine that developing technics have permanently eliminated the powerful and persistent factors of self-interest or parochial interest which operate on every level of community in contradiction to the enlarging communities and systems of obligation.

Thus a tolerable solution of modern man's communal problem within terms, created by developing technics and shifting social circumstances, requires that we approach these problems armed by wisdom drawn from two sources. We must have the wisdom of rational discrimination and the sense of a developing historical situation on the one hand. We must, on the other hand, be conscious of the perennial factors which appear in ever new guises. This latter wisdom is, as we have recognized, supplied by "common sense." But common sense is easily beguiled by pretentious and sophisticated wisdom if the pride and self-esteem of man is not continually challenged by a prophetic religious faith which knows that the wise, the mighty, the virtuous and the noble, that in fact all men and all cultures, stand under a more ultimate judgement than any of the judgements which they pass upon themselves and upon each other.

Perhaps the chief cause of illusion in that part of our culture which prides itself upon its reason and its understanding of the flow of history is that it persists in regarding the root of man's self-regard as the force of his immediate needs. It thinks of itself as very realistic if it recognizes the perennial necessities of survival, the hungers and thirst of men; if it knows the economic competitions between groups within a nation, and the economic roots of nationalistic and imperialistic ambitions of the nations. This kind of realism fails to understand the power impulse as distinguished from the economic motive. It is equally blind to the fact that the desire for power and for prestige are curiously compounded. It understands man as a hungry animal; and if it rises to higher levels of realism, it may understand man as a "beast of prey." At the heights of its realism it does not, however, understand that man is most dangerous when he pretends to be God or to have possession of some absolute standard of virtue or wisdom. If modern culture understands the nature of persecution it also misunderstands it because it attributes fanaticism purely to an outmoded religious belief, which a growing intelligence will dissolve. In short, it does not understand man at all as a creature of time who is troubled with visions of the absolute and is torn by the contradictory impulses to subject his finite life to someone or something greater than himself, but also to claim the possession of some unconditioned ground of virtue and wisdom from which he can survey his fellow men and hold them in contempt.

Modern culture does not understand, above all, how closely related the two impulses are, and how inextricably the creativity and destructiveness of men are related, so that the capacity for evil rises with the historic elaborations of his creativity. Therefore resistance to some inclusive value does not reside in some pleasure-seeking "id," which the complexities of civilized life subject to more and more strain; nor in some animal hunger which may be transmuted, satisfied and deflected until it ceases to be dangerous. It is always the whole man who is involved in both creativity and destructiveness, in both self-regard and the sense of obligation to his fellows. It is this whole man who rides the forward march of history and exhibits capacities for both good and evil on every level of culture and civilization.

Therefore it is necessary to draw constantly on the insights of Biblical faith, particularly in an age in which human achievements are great; and illusions threaten to be as great as the achievements. The obvious, and yet so hidden, dilemma of human creativity, must be clarified.

This is why the Hebraic-Christian component of our culture is a necessary tool for the understanding of both our community and of ourselves, and remains perennially relevant even when it is relegated by the contemporary wise men to oblivion. This is true even if conventional forms of faith violate Christianity's deepest insights and become involved in fanaticisms for which a genuine faith ought to be the cure.

But this relevance does not, of course, invalidate the genuine contributions which may be drawn from the culture which had its inception in the Renaissance. Among these contributions the capacity for rational discrimination in the analysis of historical causes and the sense of developing historical opportunities and obligations are most precious.

The partially contrasting virtues and weaknesses of a Christian and a secular culture in estimating both the possibilities and the limits of human striving, and the partially identical illusions of both cultures, operating in the name of either "God" or "reason," have made the achievement of community in the "Christian" world dependent upon the unplanned cooperation of these two facets of a common culture. In some situations the error in the truth of the one facet was corrected by the truth in the error of the other; and on other occasions the weakness of the one was compensated by the virtue of the other. What has emerged in history has, in any case, been better than either component had the wit or wisdom to realize. Modern Western history since the disintegration of the medieval synthesis has, in short, been a dramatic encounter between the Biblical-Hebraic and the Hellenic components of our culture in which the emergence of dynamic factors of a technical civilization gave a new dimension to the ancient encounter.

The dialectical tension between the two components in our culture was rooted in the fact that each was capable of realizing some facts of human existence and tended to be blind to others. The Hebraic saw history as a drama and the Hellenic looked for the structures which underlie the flow of history. The Hebraic was conscious of the organic aspects of human community while the Hellenic discerned the elements of artifact which had been introduced into the community by human contrivance. The Hebraic had a sense of divine providence as ruling over history because it was conscious of the creatureliness of man in the process. Modernized Hellenism was so conscious of the role of man as creator that it became defective in the sense of providence and alternated between an excessive determinism and an excessive voluntarism. It significantly always managed to put the determinism in the service of the voluntarism so that man always appeared to be, or to become, the master of historical destiny. In Marxist or liberal hopes this transformation from ambiguity to mastery was just about to take place. In corrupt Marxism (Stalinism) the claim is made that it has taken place.

The similar corruptions of fanaticism in both piety and rationalism are particularly instructive. They both point to the tendency of finite and creaturely man to think more highly of himself than he ought to think. The problem of community is confused more by these absolutistic pretensions than by the hunger for bread and by the competition for the resources of the earth. The pious try to moderate the pretension by subjecting human pride to divine judgement. The rationalists seek to bring it under critical social scrutiny. Both methods of restraint are necessary, but both methods are also defective. One might claim that it is possible to realize why they are defective from the standpoint of the Christian faith but not from the Hellenic modern standpoint. But this understanding must not be regarded as eliminating the defect.

The chief issue between the two components develops on the issue of the realization of the potentialities of history. The Biblical faith accepts the fact that historical meanings and fulfillments remain fragmentary to the end of history. It even anticipates the growth of both good and evil in history so that the ambiguities of meaning are heightened rather than diminished. Modern rationalism on this issue is not at all Hellenic. It has more confidence in history than the Greek philosophers had. It seeks to bring history to a rationally intelligible conclusion. Invariably these utopian dreams bring new evil into history because the proposed fulfillment of historical potentialities reveals itself to be but the pretension of some class, nation or group that its cherished values have a right to triumph over all competing values.

We must therefore rely upon Biblical faith to encourage the modesty and patience which will prevent present tensions from becoming catastrophic because the contestants, either one or both, are trying to bring history to a premature conclusion.

The preferences of the two components of our culture for the organic qualities of community on the one hand, and for the qualities of artifact on the other, would seem to stand in complete contradiction to their original presuppositions. The one begins by emphasizing the freedom of the self, while the other sees the self as either mind or as a part of nature. The effort to understand the self as a part of nature becomes more and more consistent, as we have seen. Yet this inclination in modern culture does not prevent, but actually encourages the most utopian conceptions of the possibility of community through the volitions of men. On the other hand, the component of the culture which is supposedly based upon an appreciation of the qualities of freedom in the self and of its capacities for dramatic elaborations, develops the most consistently organic forms of togetherness in which the freedom of the person is obscured and in which novelty and new emergences are feared, too consistently feared, as the breeders of anarchy.

A portion of this preference for the organic and the traditional must be attributed simply to that lack of discrimination to which religious faith easily degenerated. But a portion must be attributed to the fact that religion, drawn from the Bible, is as conscious of man's status as a creature as of his eminence as a creator. The concomitant of this knowledge of man's finiteness is faith in an overruling providence which presides over a drama of such proportions that we can not fully discern its intent and meaning, and are certainly incapable of basically altering its meaning. But this religious conservatism is also partly drawn from the fear of man as destroyer of community, that is, the fear of his selfishness. Traditional forms of community are preferred because it is felt that it is better to restrain the ambitions of men by the established patterns of togetherness than to run the danger of anarchy by the removal of traditional habits and restraints. This fear of anarchy proved, as we shall see, to be excessive.

It prevented modern communities from emancipating themselves from the tyranny of the older traditional forms of community. On the other hand, the rationalists of the eighteenth century who imagined that it was only necessary for reason to dissolve traditional loyalties and to substitute the artifacts of man's reason and will for the organic forms, found themselves confronting aggravated forms of ancient evils. They had not sufficiently guarded against perennial dangers to peace and order inherent in human egotism. These facts account in part for the strange contradiction that a faith which ostensibly believes in the freedom and responsibility of the self is used as an ally of conservative politics, while a faith which ostensibly believes man to be subject to nature usually becomes involved in utopian politics which have no appreciation of the limits set to human achievement either by man's finiteness and creatureliness or by his sin.

We must therefore trace the history of how the modern age found a tolerable solution for its problems of order and justice in the context of a technical civilization by correcting the error in the truth of one position by the truth in the error of the other position. We shall trace this history in terms of the development of the political theory of modern democratic states; and the development of the social and economic strategies which perfected justice in the dynamics of a technical society by equalizing power in both the economic and political sphere. We must finally inquire what function each component of our culture serves in the pressing problem of establishing peace, order and justice in the nascent world community.

Chapter 20

ORGANISM AND ARTIFACT IN DEMO-
CRATIC GOVERNMENT

Every human community is both organism and artifact. It is an organism insofar as it is integrated by loyalties, forms of cohesion and hierarchies of authority which have grown unconsciously with a minimum of conscious contrivance. The concept of "organism" is of course only roughly applicable to anything in history because historical developments, even in primitive communities, are never purely unconscious.

The community and its authorities are artifacts insofar as the form of cohesion and the integration of the community have been consciously contrived. The early empires were artifacts rather than organisms insofar as the imperial cohesion, above the level of the city-states which were the components of empire, were contrived by the military and priestly statesmen.

All early civilizations, including our European one until the disintegration of the traditional society of the Middle Ages, were more nearly organisms than artifacts. Kings and their ministers did, of course, consciously manipulate the loyalties which furnished the bonds of community; but no one thought of the possibility of forming a community or even a government purely by an act of the will. The "social contract" theory had not yet been conceived. The principle of legitimacy in dynastic rule was, in a sense, the symbol of the organic quality of traditional communities. It expressed the significance of continuity as a source of authority. The devotion to the principle was by no means simply proof of a lack of "enlightenment." Hereditary continuity was so important for the order of the community because the policy of subjecting the question of succession to the choice of the people or the nobles would have exposed the community to the peril of anarchy. Rome, lacking a stable principle of succession, hastened its doom by the unsolved problem of transmitting the vast imperial authority from generation to generation.

There was, of course, no guarantee that an hereditary monarch would rule justly. In fact, his power was sufficiently absolute and irresponsible to make it quite certain that justice was not a virtue of hereditary monarchy. The preference of all traditional communities for hereditary dynasts is therefore a symbol of the price in injustice which a traditional community was willing to pay for the good order and peace of the community. The whole development toward democratic government in a technical society, which we must trace more carefully, is, in a sense, the story of trying to achieve justice without disturbing the order of the community. The long history of civil strife in modern society proves that the attempt was not always successful.

Naturally the injustices of traditional governments increased when new emergents in the social structure (modern commerce for instance) challenged the "organic" or traditional way of preserving order. Our "modern" age had many beginnings. But in political history it had an obvious beginning in the revolt against traditional authorities, of which monarchial power was most symbolic. The revolt was both inevitable and justified. Unfortunately it created the impression that it was necessary only to substitute the artifacts of order for the organisms of community to establish the desired justice and order. Thereby the permanent significance of the organic factors of community was obscured. An even more grievous miscalculation was that the permanent tension between order and justice was believed to have been eliminated.

The symbol of modern man's belief that both community and government are merely artifacts, that is, the creations of the human will and reason, is the social contract theory, which was propounded by such divergent theorists as the liberal democrat John Locke, the proponent of royal absolutism Thomas Hobbes, and the totalitarian democrat Rousseau. The theory assumed a mythical "state of nature" before the rise of civil society, to which the various theorists attributed contradictory virtues and vices. For Thomas Hobbes the state of nature meant the "war of all against all"; for John Locke it was a state of imperfect order and harmony, suffering from the "inconvenience" of allowing every man to be "a judge in his own case." For Rousseau it was a state of unabridged freedom. None of these presuppositions, of course, remotely resembled the character of primitive society. Indeed the reality of primitive society, of organic communities which developed into more advanced civilizations proves the invalidity of the assumptions underlying the social contract theory. For the community is as primordial as the individual. The social contract theory was merely the expression of the individualism and voluntarism of the rising business community. It was beguiled by its possession of mobile and flexible instruments of power and by the disintegration of traditional society to assume that all men had the power not only to determine their own destiny but the destiny of their communities.

This excessive voluntarism was of course accompanied by a confident rationalism. It was thought that men would only have to exercise their reason to conceive of more just social and political integrations. Both faith and tradition (for religion was obviously a support of tradition) were discredited. Were they not simply the "superstitions" which a more astute intelligence would dissolve?

These uncritical approaches to the past flowered in the French Enlightenment, but they characterized the social viewpoints of modernity from the seventeenth to the nineteenth century. They were motivated by a strong desire for justice within the context of the emerging commercial and industrial community. But they were blind to the contributions which the traditional organs of community made to communal integration, failing to recognize that, even if the price in justice which they exacted was too high, they did serve as organs of integration.

The organs of communal integration which were under criticism and which the modern community was forced to revise in the interest of justice were chiefly three: government, social hierarchy and property. Of these three, the social hierarchy, which provided for integration below the level of obvious government, was not so much an "institution" as a general social phenomenon. Symbolized by traditional aristocracy, it seemed the most useless of the three and its injustices were most obvious. Therefore, the kernel of usefulness for the community in this phenomenon was least apparent. Property furthermore seemed to be chiefly an instrument for making the authority and privilege of this social hierarchy hereditary.

We must postpone for the moment the consideration of the problems occasioned by the phenomena of social hierarchy and property in order to consider the problem of government and the order of the community. Yet it is difficult to separate the three institutions, not only because they are interrelated but because we face the same moral problem in each one of them. They demand an excessive price of injustice for whatever services they perform in communal integration. The injustices of a traditional society were in fact so excessive that the chief victims of its injustice were in revolt against them in the various peasant revolts at the end of the Middle Ages, even before the disintegration of the traditional order set in through the rebellion of the middle classes. The peasants were driven by desperation but they lacked the social power to effect any considerable social change. That change waited upon the class, armed with sufficient social power to effect a radical reconstitution of social forces.

Naturally the religious character of the medieval system and the authority of the Church made the supposition plausible that religion was the primary force of conservatism. Indeed religious authority did reinforce the general conservatism of traditional society. But the accusation does not take into account that both reason and faith were divided upon the issue of the legitimacy of inequality for the sake of integration. Rationalism expressed itself in terms of both Stoic equalitarianism and Aristotelian justifications of inequality. And the protests against medieval institutions in the name of equality and liberty came from both seventeenth-century Christian sectaries and eighteenth-century French philosophers. Each made the mistake of regarding both liberty and equality as simple possibilities of history rather than as regulative principles of justice because both were unconscious of the necessity for social integration of the institutions of government, social hierarchy and property. Naturally the critical attitude toward inequalities was more prevalent in the earlier than in the later period. The mark of this development was the gradual displacement by Aristotelianism of the earlier Stoicism as the rational component of Christian social ethics. For early Christianity the stoic idea of equality was the best social expression of the meaning of love in institutional relations.

Augustine regarded equality as God-ordained. "It is thus," he declared, "that God created man. 'Let him,' He said, 'have dominion over the fish of the sea, and over the fowl of the air . . . and over every creeping thing that creepeth upon the earth.' He did not intend that His rational creature who was made in His image should have dominion over anything but the irrational creation . . . not man over man but man over the beasts. . . . And the righteous men in primitive times were shepherds of cattle rather than kings of men." [1]

[1] St. Augustine: *De Civitate Dei,* XIX, Chapter XV.

This radical equalitarianism in early Christianity was of course balanced by the idea that government, property and social hierarchy were "remedies" for sin. It was understood, in other words, that the egotism of men made these coercive and unequal integrations necessary. The same Augustine could thus accept an extreme form of social hierarchy, slavery, with the excuse that, "It is better to be a slave of men than a slave of sin." The miscalculations of future ages in regard to the inequalities of feudalism are succinctly expressed in that phrase because slavery is more an accentuation of sin than a remedy for it.

This indicated the path by which the Christian faith became the defender of the institutions of the *status quo* rather than their critic from a perspective of prophetic radicalism. This religious reverence is older than Christianity. Religious overtones in the establishment of order were explicit to the point of an idolatrous worship of the monarch in all ancient empires. These empires were created by transferring the religious reverence for the "sacred brotherhood" to the sacred ruler; from the brotherhood of the primitive community to the ruler of the great empire which could not be imaginatively comprehended except through the symbol of the ruler.[2] This idolatrous worship of the ruler will seem irrational to modern men; but it certainly did not err in one direction any more than the social contract theory erred in the other. For in one sense it was merely reverence for established authority and order which was recognized to be beyond the wit and wisdom of any particular generation. It was therefore providentially established. The ruler was believed to have some kinship with the creator of the cosmic order.

This religious attitude toward government made it difficult to realize that a government which did not have the explicit consent of its subjects was bound to be unjust. But the attitude was justified by the fact that government, purely by explicit consent, was, at least in that day, impossible. It

[2] *Cf.* H. E. Frankfort: *Kingship of the Gods.*

may, much to the horror of our simpler idealists, be impossible today, which is why one of the greatest achievements of statecraft was to distinguish between the implicit consent which we give to an established government, if it is fairly tolerable, and a particular government, which is made and unmade by explicit consent. This is the ideal way of uniting the wisdom of traditional with that of voluntaristic societies.

The religious reverence for established order is not created by priests, but it can be manipulated and corrupted by them. It springs up spontaneously wherever men appreciate an order that they could not have created. It is, in short, the chief ingredient of the state's "majesty." Majesty is certainly a more important source of authority than power, though no state can exist without the police power to suppress overt recalcitrance. But the possession of majesty spells the difference between legitimate and illegitimate government, that is, between the government which rules by implicit consent or that which rules by "force and fraud." [3]

The ingredients of majesty are chiefly three: (a) historic prestige, symbolized in the principle of legitimacy in all monarchies; (b) the religious aura, derived either from the sense of the divinity of the monarch or (within Christian terms) his divine ordination to rule; and (c) the moral prestige derived from the justice of his reign. Usurpation does not necessarily destroy this moral prestige of the ruler if his rule is just enough to overcome the original resentment against his conquest and to validate itself by the order achieved in the conquest. Most of the ancient empires were in fact unified by the triumph of one city-state over the others. If there were enough forces of cohesion beside the pure force, the attained unity could validate itself without "force and fraud." Though there may have been some fraud in the manipulation of religious texts by the priests of Heliopolis, Memphis or Babylon for the purpose of proving the God of the regnant city-state to be the supreme God of the world.

---

[3] *Cf.* Guglielmo Ferrero: *Principles of Power.*

The religious element of Western civilization was distinguished markedly in some respects, and less markedly in some others, from that of the ancient pagan empires. The idolatrous worship of the ruler was of course impossible within the rigorous monotheistic framework of Biblical religion. But the religious sanctity claimed for the papal ruler of the whole European culture was regarded by its imperial and other critics as idolatrous long before the Reformation levelled the shocking charge that the Pope was "anti-Christ." The gradation of authority in the medieval system was in fact one of those peculiar historical configurations which may be endlessly justified by rational argument but for which only the unique contingencies of history can account. It represents a quite novel co-operation between priest and soldier in the management of an imperium in which the priest was supreme, though Empire and Church were constant competitors for the primacy of power. The competition was partly responsible for the disintegration of the medieval system, the papacy ultimately requiring the help of the budding nations (chiefly France) as counterweight against the Empire. But the servant became the master of the Papacy, and a long schism resulted (Captivity of Avignon).

But the hazards of political maneuver were certainly not as responsible for the decline of the authority of the Papacy as the mounting resentment against the policy of using the "keys of heaven," excommunication and interdict, to unlock the doors of temporal power.

The devout Dante had expressed the growing resentment against this peculiar mixture of the spiritual and the political long before the Reformation. The universality of this resentment (which incidentally still colors the political life of the Western world) justifies the judgement that the decay of the authority of the medieval papacy was inevitable. Certainly the primary cause of this decay was religious resentment, though it can not be denied that all the reformers and pre-reformers, Huss, Luther, Knox were national heroes; and that the rising nations insinuated nationalistic resentments against imperial rule into the religious protest against the quality of that rule.

It may be significant that competition for political authority made the Church more critical of political power than of the social stratification of society. "Kings have their dominion by perfidy and plunder," said the first great Pope, Gregory I. But it would be unfair to attribute this critical attitude merely to political competition. To do so would miss the point which we are about to elaborate. That is that the Reformation, in its early stages at least, represented retrogression in political morality because of the uncritical reverence which it gave to historically and "providentially" established political authority.

The creative relation of Protestantism to the emerging "free" society rests primarily on its challenge to the keystone of the arch of authority in the medieval structure, the Church. But in terms of the problem which we are now considering: how to relate explicit to implicit consent and how to preserve reverence for order and yet be critical of the authority, which is at the basis of the order, we must admit that the Reformation destroyed, at least in its early phases, the impressive constitutionalism of the medieval Church. This was partly due to the fact that it relaxed the criticism of political institutions upon the basis of their conformity to natural law. This simply meant that order was not subjected to the criterion of its capacity for justice. Norms taken from Scripture were substituted for the natural law, but scriptural norms were frequently capricious. Certainly the Pauline admonition: "Let every soul be subject unto the higher powers. For there is no power but of God: the powers that be are ordained of God," (Romans 13:1) was given a most onesided emphasis in the whole of Reformation thought, and served to make the religious appreciation of providentially established order excessive to the point of prohibiting resistance to any established authority whether good or evil.

Both Luther and Calvin insisted on the duty of obedience even to unjust rulers. This attitude stands in sharp contrast to

Aquinas' justification of tyrannicide. A good deal of political
history was made when John Knox extricated Calvinism
from a too uncritical application of this single word of Scripture, which incidentally, taken alone, disturbs the scriptural
"consensus" by eliminating all the critical words on the injustice of rulers from the prophets to Jesus. "The power in
that place," declared John Knox, "is not to be taken as the
unjust commandments of men but as the just commandments
of God." When asked whether it was right for the people to
judge the justice of the ruler he answered, "and what harm
would a commonwealth receive if the corrupt affections of
ignorant rulers were moderated and bridled by the wisdom
and discretion of Godly subjects?" Thus the camel's nose of
democracy entered the tent of the Reformation for the first
time.

The whole history of Europe might have been different
had it not required three more centuries before Lutheranism,
prompted by Hitler's tyranny, found the same avenue of
escape from the binding force of the Pauline admonition
which Knox had found. It was the simple realization that only
rulers "who are not a terror to good works but to evil"
deserve obedience.

It could not have been scriptural authority alone which
would have created this excessive reverence for the state
(which incidentally was no more sharply defined by Luther
than *Obrigkeit*). All the early Reformers had a great fear of
anarchy, expressed rather hysterically by Luther against the
pathetic peasants who had vainly tried to exploit the new
religious freedom for social ends. The fear of anarchy was
vividly expressed by Tyndale: "It is better," he said, "to
have a tyrant for a king than a shadow . . . for a tyrant,
though he do wrong unto the good, yet he punisheth the evil
and maketh all men obey. . . . A king who is soft as silk
and effeminate . . . shall be more grievous to the realm than
a right tyrant." [4]

---

[4] From *Obedience of a Christian Man,* p. 1528.

Calvin derives the prohibition of resistance even to tyrants from the Scripture, though he does not define the specific source: "If we direct our attention to the word of God," he writes in the *Institutes,* "it will (persuade us) even to submit to the government, not only of those princes who discharge their duties to us with becoming integrity and fidelity, but to all who possess sovereignty, even though they perform none of the duties of their function. For though the Lord testifies that the magistrate is an eminent gift of his liberality, to preserve the safety of men, and prescribes to magistrates themselves the extent of their duties, yet he at the same time declares that, whatever their characters, they have their government only from him; that those who govern for the public good are true specimens and mirrors of his beneficence; and that all who rule in an unjust and tyrannical manner are raised up by him to punish the iniquity of the people; that all possess that sacred majesty with which he invested legitimate authority." [5]

Calvin's pretension in speaking in God's name with such confidence, and his suggestion that unjust rule may be justified as a punishment for the sins of the people, would seem to accentuate indiscriminate reverence for political authority at the precise moment in history where discriminate judgement became most necessary. In short, Luther and Calvin raised religious reverence for political authority to an absurd height. Thus the Reformation in its early stages purged Christian thought of its Catholic discriminations and set it at the opposite pole of the rationalists, who had no reverence for historically evolved integrations of authority at all, and propounded the equally absurd doctrine of the "social contract" which was born of the illusion that each generation had it in its power to make and unmake both communities and governments.

Considerable history was required to close the gap between these two poles and to prove both attitudes, purged of their

[5] John Calvin: *Institutes,* Book IV, Chapter xx, p. 25.

extremism, to be necessary for the creation of a community which would enjoy both stability and justice. The poles of early modernity were, in fact, so far apart that the Catholics may be excused if they ask why it would not be well to consider the disintegration of the medieval synthesis a mistake and seek a return to the original unity. The answer to that question is that it is not possible for modern culture and civilization with all of its vitalities, economic and political and cultural, to find unity under clerical authoritarianism. Not only is the clericalism and the authoritarianism impossible, but the norms by which life was regulated are too inflexible. Whether it was the theory of a "just price" which defined the norm for economic life, or the concept of a "just prince" which outlawed tyranny, or the idea of a "just war" which gave the criteria for legitimate conflict, the standards were in every case too inflexible and simple to define the moral norm in the contingencies of history. The problem of modern culture is to recognize the contingencies but not despair of sensing the norms of justice, though they may not be defined with the precision which medieval "natural law" attempted.

The contradiction between an excessive reverence for authority and an excessive voluntarism, which imagined each generation to have the power to create order and justice in the community by a fiat of its own will, was most successfully overcome in the Calvinism of the seventeenth century.

The right of resistance to unjust government was affirmed by the simple expedient of asserting that the rule of a prince assumed a "covenant" between the ruler and the ruled which was violated by injustice. "It is certain," we read in the memorable anonymous Huguenot tract *Vindiciae Contra Tyrannos,* "that the people require a performance of covenants. The people ask the king whether he will rule justly. He promises he will. Then the people answer, and not before, that they will obey faithfully. The king promises, the which failing to be accomplished, the people are quit of their promises." Thus the idea of a mutual covenant, which could be violated by the injustice of the ruler and was therefore not violated in the first instance by resistance to injustice of the rulers, was born. That idea brushed out the early Reformation idea of a binding covenant of obedience between God and the people, which enjoined obedience, or at least non-resistance, whether the ruler be evil or good. "There is an oath between the king and the people," said the Scottish Calvinist constitutionalist Samuel Rutherford, in his memorable *Lex, Rex,* "laid on by a reciprocation of hands, mutual civil obligations, of the king to the people and the people to the king." Rutherford simply expanded the opening, first proposed by John Knox to stop the fateful influence of Romans 13. "If any cast off the nature of a king and become a tyrant," he declared simply, "his office is not from God." It would be interesting to examine how much wisdom of this later Calvinism was acquired by historical experience, and how the certainties about the God-ordained quality of all government evaporated in the conflict of Protestants with Catholic monarchs.

However, the real achievement of later Calvinism was in distinguishing between the fact of government, which is not in the competence of any generation to create out of hand, and a particular government, which rests upon explicit consent. "It is not in men's free will to have government or no government," declared Sam Rutherford, "or to obey or not to obey the acts of the court of nature which is God's court. But we must distinguish between the power of government, and the power of government by magistracy . . . the latter the people must measure ounce by ounce-weights, no more and no less." Providentially ordained government and political order neither ordains monarchy nor any one particular monarch. "The essence of government is kept safe in aristocracy or democracy," declared Rutherford, "though there be no kings." To the question, "whether this man or that man be crowned King," Rutherford answered "the people have the power" to determine.

Thus a balance was reached between proper reverence for

the ordinance of government and affirmation of the principle of consent by which particular governments are made and unmade; between the conception of the community as an organism and as an artifact; between the factors which are beyond the power, and those within the power of a given generation. This balance is also creative of a government with a maximum of stability and a maximum of justice. The former created by traditional forces and the latter by the workings of a democratic order in which the people measure out "ounce by ounce-weights" the power which they wish to entrust to a particular ruler.

It is this balance which has made constitutional monarchy so serviceable an instrument of democracy in the healthier West European states long after the institution of monarchy was relegated to the scrap heap of history by the rationalistic idealists of the eighteenth century. The monarchy, shorn of its power, proved to be a very good symbol of the continuities of order and authority beyond the majesty of any particular governments.

Our own nation has achieved stability without the use of this symbol, though we are frequently embarrassed by the fact that the symbolic head of the entire nation is also a party leader, subject to the changing estimates of party loyalties. Perhaps it is this defect in a symbol for the "organic" aspects of government which makes us so hysterical in our insistence that there shall be no disloyalty to our government. For one of the great achievements of democracy was certainly to have incorporated resistance to a particular government into the very structure of government itself. This does not of course preclude revolution whenever the tradition of government in a nation becomes so discredited by the actions of particular governments that the resentments, which generate revolutions, are aroused. But on the whole the democracies which had modified the power of the monarchy to some extent before the twentieth century were able to preserve the monarchial symbol for democratic purposes. Monarchies with absolutistic pretension, or vestigial remnants of absolution, on the other hand, perished in the First World War. Even constitutional monarchies, in which the monarch connived with totalitarian parties, succumbed in the Second World War.

If there is to be an ideal fusion of freedom with stability, of justice with order, and of democratic experimentation with tradition, it is of course necessary that the symbols of stability should not be used as weapons of the parties of privilege to preserve a traditional privilege against the will of the majority. If the symbol is to remain untarnished as a symbol of the unity of the community above party conflict and of the continuing majesty of its government, any party in the community must have the confidence that it may, upon attaining a majority for its conception of justice, be able to speak through the royal symbol. This is to say that it achieves the right to speak for the whole community, though it is only a majority of the community. There must also be a corresponding respect by the majority of the rights of the minority. Otherwise a frustrated minority may become desperate and defy this attempt at national unity.

In British history it is significant that constitutional monarchy which Edmund Burke extolled so eloquently as an instrument of justice in countering the illusions of the French Revolution [6] actually had more power in his day to frustrate the will of the majority than a rising democracy found sufferable. The monarchy was gradually shorn of its power, not by revolution but by organic historical processes, that is to say, by the gradual extension of the logic inherent in the democratic idea. This process in British history was not complete until a very recent day when George V refused to create enough Peers to provide a conservative majority in the House of Lords for the purpose of defeating the ruling government.

In our own nation the Constitution takes the place of the monarchy as the symbol of stability and continuing majesty of government. Though it does not have the advantages of combining flexibility with inflexibility, it is significant that there are evidences of an organic growth of

[6] Edmund Burke: *Reflections on the Revolution in France.*

extended democracy upon it. The most significant of these is the relegation of the Electoral College to powerlessness. It had been prompted by the fear of the founding fathers of the unmediated expression of the popular will, which proved to be unfounded. Perhaps the development of the party structures and party conventions, also not anticipated in the Constitution, hastened the relegation of the Electoral College to the status of an archaic remnant. The fear of the founding fathers of the divisiveness of "factions," i.e., parties, also proved to be unfounded.

It should be added that the institution of constitutional monarchy was itself a product of the "providential" force in history which it came to symbolize. It was not what the monarchists intended nor what the anti-monarchist democrats intended. But it incorporated a political wisdom, higher than the intentions of either party. It is thus a perfect illustration of the way that truth may come out of the competition of contrasting errors. In this case the truth was a fusion of the factors of stability and those of freedom and justice. If constitutional monarchy is a potent, though not a solitary, symbol of the wisdom which combines stability with freedom, we may assume that the nations of Western Europe, which have retained this type of monarchial institution, have some measure of this wisdom. They also required a considerable measure of historical good fortune to escape the hazards incident upon the disintegration of a traditional society.

But whatever their several merits, it can not be denied that Britain is the most exemplary exponent of the wisdom which combines reverence for historical integrations of community and authority with a rational and voluntaristic discrimination of the factors and forces which make for freedom and justice in the complexities of a technical society. Britain was able to absorb the bourgeois revolution into an essentially traditional society, to pour the new wine into the old wine skins without bursting them. It was able after that achievement to absorb the second democratic movement of the industrial workers, and to return to the conditions of a modified welfare state when the panacea of the socialization of property proved inadequate in overcoming the collective poverty of a war-impoverished nation and when it proved to be unnecessary in view of the measures of justice which had been accomplished without socialization.

Such a measure of stability and freedom to experiment points to real treasuries of political wisdom. If we compare the British achievements with those of France and Germany, for instance, it may not be too hazardous to suggest that these two nations may be inferior because one was formed politically by Luther's extravagant reverence for political authority and the other is the product of the illusions of the Enlightenment and of Rousseauistic romanticism. In either case, the one or the other ingredient of the compound of reverence for history and rational discrimination was lacking.

George Santayana pays eloquent tribute to the British genius for establishing liberty within the framework of stability. "The slow co-operation of free men, this liberty in democracy," he declares, "is wholly English. In its personal basis, its reserve, its tenacity, its empiricism, its public spirit and in the assurance of its own rightness it deserves to be called English, to whatever countries it may spread." [7]

The wisdom which combines the two approaches runs from Ireton through Edmund Burke to Winston Churchill. Ireton preferred the "rights of Englishmen" to the "rights of man." That phrase incorporates an awareness that rationally conceived "rights" are not very secure, even if defined as "inalienable," if they have not been acknowledged in the living community; and that the inordinancy of the ambitions of fellow men, which imperils our rights, are checked with more effect by historical habit than by appeals to reason. For each party is so intransigent in its claims precisely because it regards them as "rational."

The capacity to absorb the ferment of democratic justice

[7] George Santayana: *Character and Opinion in the United States,* p. 195.

without bursting the wineskins of a traditional society may be partly due to the peculiar history of sectarian Christianity in England. The "Schwaermer," the Anabaptist of the Continent, projected wholly perfectionist and fantastic goals for society. They were defeated by Protestant and Catholic conservatives and left no deposit in the life and thought of the Continent. All the radical sects on the left wing of Cromwell's army were addicted to almost as fantastic perfectionism as the Anabaptists. They were also defeated. But their life and thought left a deposit which became the basis for subsequent democratic developments. Perhaps the difference was that while their ideas and ideals were extremist and perfectionist, they did not cease to be relevant. They provided the counterweight of criticism of established authority to the traditional reverence for authority.

Richard Hooker, at the turn from the sixteenth to the seventeenth century, was able to mix this democratic ferment with the old wine with a balance which was superior even to that of the later Calvinists. He thus became the most expressive symbol of English political philosophy, the reflective exponent of a compromise between Protestant and Catholic forces, unreflectively achieved under Queen Elizabeth, and the potent source of the balanced thought which prevented the restoration after Cromwell's adventure from being a mere return to the past.

Hooker's political genius was based on his awareness of the relation of implicit to explicit consent. He knew that government without consent means tyranny. But he also knew that the principle of the "consent of the governed" as propounded by the Christian, as later by the rationalistic, idealists was too simply conceived to do justice to the implicit consent which accrues to relatively just governments through historical achievement. "Laws there are not, which public approbation has not made so," he declared. But he also knew that assent is frequently indirect rather than direct. "In many things," he continued, "assent is given, they that give it, not imagining that they do so because the manner of their giving is not apparent." [8] It is particularly important to justify the inheritance of good laws from previous generations. For, argued Hooker, "The act of public society, done five hundred years ago, standeth as theirs who are presently of the same society, because corporations are immortal."

It is a tribute to Hooker's genius and to his representative character in British political thought, that both John Locke and Edmund Burke were indebted to him.

Immediately the issue solved by Hooker and the later Calvinists is how to relate the freedom and justice of a democratic society to the organic stabilities of a more traditional society. This requires that new and more adequate equilibria of power be substituted for the disbalances which created injustice. It also requires replacing too conventional acceptance of traditional authority with discriminate judgement about the actual consequences of given policies in the life of the community.

But more ultimately considered, this political problem is merely a version of the more general problem of how man is to be aware of his status as both creator and creature in history. If he forgets that he is a creature and imagines himself purely a creator, he will lack reverence for the achievements of the past, which are beyond his competence, and for the mysterious providence under which an order has been established which blesses his life. Heedless of past achievements and unable to profit by past lessons, he will gaily build new societies only to find them subject to worse corruptions than the traditional ones. Thus the dreams of the seventeenth-century Christian sectaries culminated in Cromwell's dictatorship; the dreams of the French Encyclopedists culminated in Napoleon's adventures and despotism; and the Marxist dreams turned into the nightmare of Stalinism.

These miscalculations resulted from the failure to take account of the persistent impulses of self-interest which would express themselves in new historical configurations. It was

[8] Richard Hooker: *Laws of Ecclesiastical Polity.*

also due to the fact that past injustices had obscured the positive contribution of traditional societies in restraining self-interest by historically established norms and by setting limits to the inordinate ambitions of men.

On the other hand, if man does not acknowledge his status as creator, his freedom over the historical flux, his right and duty to challenge the inherited traditions of the community, his obligation to exercise discriminate judgement in rearranging or reconstructing any scheme of togetherness which has been faulty in providing justice, he will merely become the victim of the past which accentuates its vices when it is studiedly preserved into the present.

He will have an undue reverence which will be particularly obnoxious in a civilization in which the emergence of new factors and dynamics makes the extension and the preservation of justice dependent upon discriminate judgement.

Freedom over the traditions of the past and discriminate judgement in weighing the relative factors and forces which effect the establishment of community and the attainment of justice become particularly important in the extension of community to global dimensions, the task which now confronts mankind, and in organizing the economic relations below the level of the minimal integration of the community. This latter problem we have suggested as related to the problem of government, but not to be identified with it. We must now consider it more specifically.

Chapter 21

PROPERTY, SOCIAL HIERARCHY AND THE PROBLEM OF JUSTICE

We have provisionally considered both property and social stratification as instruments, with government, of the integration of the community but have dismissed them provisionally in order to center our attention upon the problem of government and justice. We must now study these "institutions" more carefully, both in their relatedness and separately. The definition of "institution" is correct for property; but it is dubious for describing the hierarchy of authority and the consequent social stratification below the level of government which characterizes all forms of communal integration. These phenomena are not so much institutions as aspects of the communal life. If we define them as "below the level of government," we can do this only tentatively. For all subordination of life to leadership in the various activities of the community is in a sense "government," though pluralistic and democratic communities have understood how to create independent centers of authority without relating them to state authority. The establishment of grades of authority inevitably leads to social stratification because grades of privilege invariably are related to grades of authority and power. Property is related to this stratification because it is the primary instrument for transmitting authority and privilege from generation to generation. It is this function of property which makes the institution morally so ambiguous. For property, as the consequence of mixing our labor with nature (John Locke) and property as the right of inheriting power and privilege, are certainly in different categories of moral legitimacy.

But the fact is that not only property, but the two institutions of property and social stratification are in the same position of moral ambiguity. Both are necessary instruments of justice and order, and yet both are fruitful of injustice. Both have, no less than government, grown up organically in traditional civilizations in the sense that they were unconscious adaptations to the needs of justice and order. Both were, even as government, productive of injustice. The injustice is inevitable because the economic and other privileges attendant upon special function tended to be in excess of the necessities of the function performed. Both institutions continued for millenia until the dissolution of the medieval order in Western Europe. The revolts against both of them by both the radical Christians and the radical secular idealists of the seventeenth and eighteenth centuries tended to be indiscriminate. This lack of discrimination expressed itself in the notion that liberty and equality were simple possibilities in history.

We therefore have the task in a mobile and technically efficient society to come to terms with the necessities which have created both phenomena, for these necessities are indeed perennial; but to apply the regulative principles of liberty and equality so that they will be more effective than in the older organic societies but will not be regarded as simple possibilities as the radical rebels against a traditional society regarded them. In performing this task we must be aware that the detailed adjustments between the necessities of subordination and leadership and the principles of equality and liberty are the product of historical growth and of adjustment to highly contingent power realities.

A preliminary word must be said about the economic and political situation in traditional civilization which generated

the resentments expressed in so vehement a protest. It was a
Christian civilization which suffered and nourished the social
inequalities of feudal civilization. This culture was well aware
that the principles of equality and liberty were regulative. Yet
it was more, rather than less, complacent about them than
it was about government, though the latter had a higher moral
legitimacy, being more necessary to the order of the community. We have previously noted that political competition
between the Church and the political authorities may have
been the cause of this more rigorous criticism. But the religious imagination easily accepts a *status quo* as normative
and tries merely to perfect the moral realities of the structure by personal love in individual relations. Therefore, the
Medieval Church was not peculiar in its policy of accepting
the hierarchical structure of medieval society. However it
accentuated its vices by sanctifying its inequalities in terms
of its principles of "natural law." The inequalities seemed
to correspond exactly to the view of Aristotle and to the
patriarchal social organization enshrined in the Old Testament. It is significant however that the Medieval Church did
not have the ethical insight of Hebrew prophetism, which
castigated the injustice of the rulers of Israel so rigorously.
Of course, the Christian was encouraged to be loving within
and beyond the requirements of justice as established by the
status quo. This counsel produced the sentimentalities of the
"lady bountiful," who issued from the castle periodically to
give succour to the poor. On a much higher level it also
created the tradition of *noblesse oblige* which has permanently influenced the ethos of the European aristocracy and
given it a more humane outlook than that of the new commercial and industrial owners. These failures and accomplishments are significant for an understanding of the relation
of love, the keystone and core of Christian morality, to the
realities of social justice. The fact that love was frequently
used to cover up and to excuse social injustice has given the
very word "charity" a bad connotation in the lexicon of
modernity. It proves indeed that love in its purest form may
not be as immediately relevant as either equality or liberty to

the issue of establishing justice within the social structures and traditions of the community. But if love means wanting the welfare of the neighbor, it can never be irrelevant to any social situation. If love is defined exclusively in terms of attitudes which can express themselves only in personal relations, as it is frequently defined by Christians (and incidentally more consistently so by Protestants than by Catholics), it becomes irrelevant to any situation in which structures of justice must become instruments of love. Furthermore, love may easily be corrupted, so that a powerful man will use benevolence in personal relations as a substitute of granting justice in the basic organization of life. For in benevolence he displays his power with his goodness while justice challenges his power as incompatible with goodness. These facts are withheld from the wise but they are known by the "simple," particularly if they should be the victims of the "benevolence" of the powerful. Resentment against these hypocrisies are the root of the laboring man's objection to "paternalism." These corruptions can not however obscure the fact that it is always possible for the love or the self-love of individuals to perfect or to spoil even the most ideal structure of justice. Though nothing could redeem slavery, or serfdom for that matter, as a structure of justice, yet this does not change the fact that it was a matter of life or death on occasion whether a slave or serf had a benevolent or cruel master.

Medieval Christianity, in short, contributed to the social resentments which engulfed the social structure of feudalism by its complacency about social inequality. But in this, as in the instance of government, the Reformation initially worsened the situation. Luther was certainly as indiscriminate in dealing with the social desires of the peasants as he was in exalting political authority. This distinction had the fantastic effect of making suffering and sacrificial love the norm for the poor victim of injustice, while encouraging the beneficiaries of injustice to a rather cruel suppression in the name of order. "You will not bear that any one inflict evil and injustice upon you . . . But want to be free and suffer only freedom and complete justice," wrote Luther to the revolting peasants. He argued with them that their resistance to injustice was not in conformity with their "rights" as Christians, for Christ had enjoined complete non-resistance in the Sermon on the Mount. In other words he made a perfectionist ethic completely irrelevant to the struggle for justice. Samuel Rutherford corrected the logic of this perfectionism a century later with the simple affirmation: "Resistance is in the children of God an innocent act of self-preservation, no less than is patient suffering." Luther's admonition of non-resistance for the poor peasants was in striking contrast to his intemperate advice to the princes to beat down the peasant rebellion: "Stab, hit, kill here whoever you can," he said, "for nothing can be more poisonous, deadly and devilish than a revolutionary . . . It does not help the peasants that they claim Genesis I and II that all things were created free and common and that all were equally baptised. For in the New Testament Moses counts for nothing, but there stands our Master Christ and casts us with body and possessions under Caesar's and the worldly law, when he says 'give unto Caesar the things that are Caesar's.' " [1]

This rather violent dualism which gives the feudal lord the benefit of an ethic of order bereft of a sense of justice, and enforces an ethic of love upon the poor peasant equally bereft of a demand for justice was, of course, part of the radical dualism implied in the doctrine of the "two realms." In the history of social thought it is significant only in revealing how rigorously the early Reformation attempted to preserve the medieval structure despite, or probably because, it challenged the keystone of its arch of authority. In the history of Christianity it is significant because it reveals a permanent embarrassment of Christian thought in making the final insights into the destiny of the individual relevant to the problems of ordering the life of the community with tolerable justice. Luther was as wrong in making love completely irrelevant to the issues of justice as subsequently

[1] Martin Luther: *Werke Gesammtousgabe Weimar,* Vol. 18, p. 361.

liberal Christianity was in holding love to be a simple historical and social possibility.

If Luther accentuated the problem of establishing justice within the organic and traditional hierarchies of the community, the general tendency upon the dissolution of the medieval culture was to condemn these hierarchies completely because they violated the law of love and the principles of liberty and equality.

The radical Christian sects, the Anabaptists of the sixteenth century against whom Luther fulminated, the left-wing sectaries of Cromwell's army in the seventeenth century, and the philosophers of pre-revolutionary France were of one voice in their moral condemnation of the hierarchical structure of medieval society, and in their belief that freedom and equality were simple historical possibilities. They have therefore created an ethos in modern culture which does not know how to come to terms with the facts and the moral necessities involved in the organic growth of social hierarchies.

"Men and women," declared the Leveller leader John Lilburne, "are by nature equal and alike in power, dignity, authority and majesty, none of them having by nature any authority or dominion or magisterial power, one over and above the other. Neither have they or can exercise any but merely by institution or donation, that is to say by mutual agreement and consent, given, derived or assumed for the good benefit and comfort of each other and not for the hurt, damage or mischief of any." [2]

The embryo of the later social contract theory of community is obviously in this reasoning. It is a Christian version of Rousseau's dictum that "Men are born free but are now everywhere in chains." These rebels against traditional social hierarchies were right in condemning the injustices of a feudal order. They were wrong in supposing that it would be possible to organize society without a social hierarchy.

Edmund Burke spoke eloquently about the effects of this rigorous equalitarianism in the French Revolution. They were

[2] John Lilburne: *Free Man's Freedom Vindicated*, 1646.

identical in his opinion with the devastation wrought by a cruel conqueror. "Acting as conquerors," he wrote, "they have imitated the policy of the harshest of that harsh race . . . to produce general poverty to put up their properties for auction; to crush their princes, nobles and pontiffs; to lay low everything that had lifted its head above the level, or which could serve to combine or rally a people in their distresses. . . . They have made France free in the same manner in which those sincere friends of the rights of mankind, the Romans, had freed Greece, Macedon and other nations." [3]

This observation by one who resisted the abstract dogmas of the idealists because he had discerned the wisdom in the organic developments of history, astutely describes the devastating effect upon a community of the dogmas of idealistic revolutionists. They "lay low everything that has lifted up his head." In other words, they destroy the organic integrations of community in the fierce resolve to conform the order of the community to standards of justice.

The Russian Revolution must be regarded as a kind of second chapter of the French Revolution, which logically completed some issues toward which the French Revolution had vague or ambiguous attitudes. It had exactly the same effect upon society. In both cases the inequalities which developed in the new society, grown upon the debris left by the destruction of the old society, proved to be more insufferable than those of the old because the balances of power were even more defective than those of the traditional society. (Igor Gouzenko gives a devastating account of the moral realities embodied in the new Russian oligarchy in his *Fall of a Titan*.)

If we take Luther's complete rejection of the relevancy of the pinnacles of the Christian ethic of love to any social situation, involving permanent structures, on the one hand, and, on the other, the conviction of liberal Christianity that love is a simple norm for communal integration and the similar conviction of the French, and subsequently of the

[3] Edmund Burke: *Reflections on the Revolution in France*, E. P. Dutton Edition, p. 179.

Russian Revolution, that liberty or equality, either or both, are simply attainable norms for society, we have the moral predicament of Western Christian civilization about the integration of its communities in a nutshell. Its norms taken not as ultimately regulative, but as immediately relevant, destroy community by levelling all those organic forms of integration by which a community organizes its life. On the other hand, an unreflective and complacent attitude toward these forms of social hierarchy causes their injustices to reach monstrous proportions.

We have been tentatively tolerant toward the vehemence expressed in revolutionary resentments because we believed that resentments against injustice were justified, as indeed they were. But we failed to recognize the fact that these resentments generated quite untenable social philosophies, blind to the problem of social integration. These philosophies preserved nihilistic social policies long after the original revolutionary vehemence had abated. This miscalculation contributed to the original tolerance of the "liberal" world to the excesses of the Russian Revolution. Was it not destroying injustices about which all "liberals" had a sensitive conscience; and would it not begin to be creative after it had broken all the eggs which must be broken to make an omelette?

These miscalculations are understandable enough. But meanwhile there are some very obtrusive evidences of the perennial nature of these social hierarchies in our daily life which we might have heeded with more astuteness had we not been blinded by dogmatic presuppositions about the demands of "nature," of "reason" and of "love."

Beginning with the family, we know of integrations of the community in which power and competence are the levers of authority to subordinate some men to others. Conservatives have generally derived explicit analogies from the authority of the father in order to justify monarchy. John Locke spent most of his polemic fire upon this analogy in his *Two Essays on Civil Government*. But the conservatives were certainly in closer accord with history than the social contract theorists who posited a wholly mythical "state of nature." The family is indeed the embryo of all social integration. Love and power are more coordinate in its organization than in any other. One might sentimentally define our whole social problem as an effort to reconstitute the co-ordination of love and power in the larger communities which obtained in the family. In this sense the various myths of the "Fall" as identical with the rise of civilization are expressive.

Of course the family does not perfectly co-ordinate power and love. Modern women had to wait upon the independent economic power given them by a technical civilization before they could challenge the unjust dominance of the male in traditional society.

Most children feel the power of the parents to be unjust when they reach the rebellion of adolescence. They may be right or wrong in their several rebellions, depending upon the character of their parents. But they are usually more right than their parents can realize in suspecting that power impulses have been subtly compounded with love in the motives of their parents, and that the justice which their parents mete out is least sufferable if the parents are wholly unconscious of this mixture of motives.

Above the level of the family we meet the pattern of integration and co-ordination of life through subordination on every hand; schools with more than one teacher have a "principal"; and school systems with more than one school have a "superintendent"; churches are supervised by a bishop. The extreme congregational polity of sectarian Churches, which is the counterpart in the religious community of the libertarianism and equalitarianism of the modern age, was modified by experience; and the modification was obscured by giving the effective bishops the title of "superintendent." The industrial life of the nation is integrated from factory foreman to superintendent, to manager to owner. We must speak about the significance of the authority of the owner presently though it is relevant immediately to observe that the owner is not so potent and the manager more potent than Marxist theory assumed.

In every sphere of life this integration of the community through social hierarchy proved necessary and inevitable, however much the Christian conscience, in either its traditional or secularized variety, protested against it. And in every case these hierarchies of authority tended to be unjust, power and authority tending to arrogate more privilege to itself than its functions warranted. Thus the criticisms which frequently resulted in the abolitions seemed to be justified. But the abolitions were never justified.

If we have gained a tolerable justice in modern society despite these confusions, it is because the wisdom proceeding from common experience and from the welter of social competitions has been wiser than that of either the conservatives who justified both social hierarchy and its unjust privileges, and the radicals who sought to abolish both. To justify this thesis it will be necessary to examine two correlations which we have presented rather uncritically: the correlations between liberty and equality and between property and social hierarchy.

In both seventeenth-century English sectarianism and in eighteenth-century rationalism there was a confused identification between liberty and equality, and an equally confused supposition that the primary cause of inequality was property. In England the "Levellers" and "Diggers" were equally libertarian and equalitarian. But it was the Digger leader Gerrard Winstanley who anticipated modern Marxism in calling for a socialization of property. Unlike Marx, he attributed property to government rather than attributing the rise of government to the motive of safeguarding property, which was the thesis in Marx's thought. "The oppression of kingly governments has made this age to desire commonwealth government," he wrote, "and the removal of kings, for the spirit of light in man loves freedom and hates bondage." [4] But the purpose of commonwealth government was the res-

---

[4] Gerrard Winstanley: *The Law of Freedom on a Platform; or True Magistracy Restored.*

toration of a supposedly primeval common ownership. "When the earth becomes a common treasury again as it must, the enmity of all lands will cease. For no one shall dare to seek dominion over others; neither shall any dare to kill another or desire more of the earth than another." [5]

Winstanley in his more orthodox moods ascribed the beginning of evil to the rise of "particular love," to supplant the "universal love" of primitive innocency. But as a pre-Marxist (a development which even non-Marxists hail as progress in reason) he attributes sin to property, and hopes that the abolition of an institution will change the character of men. The whole modern radical error of attributing injustice to the social institutions, which were the main instruments of inequality and domination, is contained as a seed in Winstanley's thought.

The French Revolution was notoriously ambiguous toward the problem of property. The Jacobins attempted to cover this confusion by the expedient of dispossessing the enemies of the Revolution and conferring the property upon the "patriots." Equalitarianism was associated with communism in the thought of the most rigorous equalitarians. Malby, for instance, believed that equality was one of "nature's" laws. "You will easily see," he declared, "how important it is to study the natural law . . . the law of equality among men. . . . Without such study morality without certain principles would run the risk of erring at every step." The discovery of the transcendent principle of justice and equality in "nature" was of course characteristic of all of the thought of the Enlightenment, and we find an echo of it in our Declaration of Independence.

The rigorously collectivist and equalitarian tendencies of the Revolution, having been lost in the ambiguities of the early Revolution, tried to gain a triumph and were defeated in the Paris Commune. This attempt and defeat inspired Marx's resolutions and expectations. Why was the Revo-

---

[5] *True Levellers Standard Advanced,* 1649.

lution in France so ambiguous? In answering this question, we shall come upon many of the secrets of the wisdom of history, correcting the explicit wisdom and the attendant foolishness of men. For through the lack of the expected correlation between liberty and equality it was possible for modern society to elaborate a communal justice with a tolerable equality and liberty which was better than the justice of traditional society, and which negated the abstract notions of the idealists who upset the old order for good cause; but with mistaken notions about the perennial factors in the anatomy of the community.

The vague identification of liberty and equality in both seventeenth-century sectarianism and the French Enlightenment undoubtedly derived from the eschatalogical views of the sectaries and the Enlightenment's views of "nature." Both the kingdom of God and "nature" were supposed to present the norms of equality and liberty. The similarity of the norms is eloquent testimony of the Christian inheritance in the conceptions of those who ostensibly defied and despised this inheritance. The two norms were vaguely identified because it was believed that an elimination of traditional political coercions automatically would make for equality. That was the physiocratic theory which Adam Smith was to elaborate and upon which our "free enterprise" is founded. Property was vaguely identified with inequality, but not consistently so. This lack of consistency was undoubtedly due to the composition of the revolutionary forces of the seventeenth and eighteenth centuries. They consisted of peasants and commercial classes in the first instance, and of commercial classes and industrial workers in its later stages. Of these three, the middle classes were the only ones who possessed property. Moreover, they possessed a very dynamic form of property, which was soon to prove a more potent social power than landed property. That left only the agrarian and the industrial poor who had ideological reasons for believing property to be the chief cause of injustice; and among the agrarian poor there were a small number of free-holders who had a more personal attachment to their property in the soil than any of the bourgeoisie. This is why the Marxist dogma was too slow in taking root, and why it could take root only in decadent feudal societies of Asia where the monstrous injustices, too tardily corrected, could create the revolutionary resentments which would persuade a community to adopt even implausible creeds in its desperation. The middle classes which were originally ambiguously involved in the attack upon the traditional order came, in time, to be the most assiduous defenders of the rights of property, and the class which was most blind to the abuses of economic power.

These same middle classes were convinced that equality and liberty were not only compatible, but that equality flowed from liberty, that is, from the liberty to exercise one's own initiative without traditional restraints.

One of the most ironic facts in modern history is that the middle classes which elaborated modern culture first supported liberty under the illusion that it would make for equality, and subsequently supported the idea because they were convinced that it would not. For they had meanwhile secured their equality with the aristocracy; and they were not anxious to share it with the industrial workers, who incidentally had no such potent force as dynamic property to enforce their demands for equality. Thus the middle classes were as assiduous in protecting their liberty against the political power dominated by the poor as they were rigorous in establishing it against the political power dominated by the aristocrats. In the one case, it was done to achieve equal justice and in the other case to prevent more equal justice (particularly by that body of rigorous libertarians who opposed the "welfare state").

This is how the civil war began between the two classes, the bourgeoisie and industrial workers, who were once comrades-in-arms in a common struggle against an aristocratic feudal society. This is how the tension between liberty and equality as norms of justice became apparent.

The original chapter in this war, which almost wrecked the whole of Western society, seemed wholly to justify the Marxist creed by which the industrial workers ultimately became armed. Industrialism in its earlier stages certainly seemed to justify the Marxist polemic against "capitalism." Economic freedom did not make for equality and justice. The theorists had neglected to observe that the market place, that alleged equalizer of everything, would not be capable of an equal bargain for two bargainers of unequal power, the employer and worker, for instance. The boasted "enlightened self-interest" of the utilitarians proved to be an equally frail reed for justice to rely upon. For self-interest proved itself too powerful to bow to the persuasion of enlightenment. The inequalities of an agrarian society became dynamic. Social realities seemed to justify even Marxist catastrophism according to which the bourgeois civilization, boasting of "liberty and equality," would hasten the "class struggle" to a climax of injustice and would brush out all the poetic veils for injustice which a feudal society cultivated, thus leaving the "cash Nexus" open and exposed, and curing the victims of social injustice of their long illusions.

What happened to change this grim picture and expectation? Why has the Marxist creed, designed for the ripe and over-ripe period of "capitalism," failed to take root there and has been relevant instead to the decadent feudal societies, particularly in Asia?

What happened was an analogy of the organic adaptations of traditional societies within the new conditions of a technical society. Social forces not too conscious of themselves, or at least not armed with explicit philosophies, took immediate actions to fend off particular forms of injustice. The workers were individually weak in bargaining with the employer. They could redress some of the balance by collective action. Thus the trade unions were born and nourished by the workers, while the intellectuals elaborated schemes of redemption which were to prove ultimately to be the root of modern tyranny. The workers never acquired the social power of the middle classes, even when skilled and even when acting collectively. A theory was never developed which would determine just how much privilege would be justified by special social function or power or for the purpose of providing incentives for the performance of function. But the steps which were taken to prevent inordinate inequalities of privilege from arising—chiefly by preventing inordinate disbalances of power from developing—proved adequate to save modern society from revolution and disintegration. It saved at least the healthiest members of modern civilization. Among those less healthy it is significant that a typically bourgeois nation (France) and one with remnants of traditional feudal injustice (Italy) are most exposed to the perils of revolution because in them either agrarian or industrial poor have become desperate. The flexible instruments of justice, designed for equilibrating power, do not seem to work in their case. It became apparent, incidentally, that an exact definition of how much injustice may be allowed for the integration of society is not as important as an "open" situation in which the hope for improvement of one's lot is never snuffed out.

Ultimately, of course, the workers became aware that equalization of economic power was not enough to establish justice. The class that manipulated political power and set the rules for the game had an undue advantage. The workers therefore organized political as well as economic power. Despite the fact that the commercial classes were established in the seats of political power, the political liberty which they had established was serviceable to other classes.

In Europe the industrial workers have their own parties, informed by a quasi-Marxist creed. But in our own nation the absence of any rigorous Marxist movement has not prevented a comparable party alignment between those classes who are interested in qualifying economic by political power in the interest of justice and security and those who resist the encroachment of political authority upon the economic sphere because they possess either enough property or personal skill to enjoy security and dislike any control upon their initiative.

In any case, both political power and economic power have been sufficiently balanced to prevent grave injustice. The process has been accomplished by exploiting the political freedom beyond the ideological intent in the motives of the first proponents of liberty. This effect in the field of social and economic life is analogous to the establishment of liberty in the cultural and religious sphere. It is enjoyed by all, though the original proponents of religious liberty were less interested in liberty as such than in their own emancipation from oppressive majorities. In either case, a free society derives general profit from the interested desires of particular groups, each group leaving a deposit of virtue in the community beyond its intentions and interests. The health and justice of the community is preserved, not so much by the discriminate judgement of the whole community as by the effect of free criticism in moderating the pretensions of every group and by the weight of competing power in balancing power which might become inordinate and oppressive. Democracy in short is not a method which is effective only among virtuous men. It is a method which prevents interested men from following their interests to the detriment of the community. There must of course be a minimal inclination for justice to furnish a base of community. For if groups and individuals merely pursue their interests without a measure of self-restraint, no political restraint, short of a tyrannical and oppressive one, could preserve the unity of the community. Hobbes' proposals for order through despotism are mistaken in assuming a consistency of self-interest which is not apparent in human history. Men do not follow their own interests consistently in defiance of the community. They do however interpret the interests of the community with a reason tainted by considerations of their own interests.

All modern nations are engaged in political debate on the question how much or how little economic life shall be regulated. There is no "ideal" solution for this issue. It will probably remain inconclusive for a long while, both because the contestants are fairly equal in strength and because the consequences from their proposals are ambiguous. Complete economic liberty obviously makes for injustice because forces in the economic process itself lead to centralization of power. Healthy free societies have therefore used the broadly based political power (universal suffrage) to equalize the inequalities of economic power, to establish minimal standards of security and justice, and to assure the community some services which the market does not find it profitable to supply. These are the general and minimal accomplishments of the "welfare state" which develop in healthy nations, whether their original orientation was "capitalistic" or "socialistic." The development confounds the Marxist theory which regards government as merely the "executive committee" of the property holders.

Thus the development of the trade unions and the growth of the welfare state have negated the historical "logic" which, according to the Marxists, made a climax of injustice and revolution inevitable in a technical civilization.

These effects are so desirable that one might well ask why it would not be right to increase the consistency of the logic which produced these effects. But such a view does not consider the genuine virtue in the philosophy of a free economy. The proponents of "free enterprise" guaranteed that equality would flow inevitably from the release of all economic vitalities. They were wrong. But they were not wrong in Adam Smith's contention that we must secure the assistance of our fellow men by "engaging their self-interest rather than their benevolence." A free economy may have been in danger of substituting the "law of supply and demand" for the moral law. But it has meanwhile released energies for production which no moral or political control of economic activity ever released. It has, in short, harnessed rather than suppressed self-interest. It has created a vast system of mutual services through a competition of interests. The claim that it has done this perfectly is ideologically tainted and must be resisted. But it can not be denied that the market place furnishes for the complexities of modern trade and for the mutual services of highly specialized skills, a counterpart of the unconscious adjustments to community which made traditional society organic.

Therefore every effort to restrict freedom in the interest

of justice has its limits, even as the effort to secure justice from the effects of freedom is limited.

There is a certain danger in modern democracies that the balance of political forces and the limits of the proposals for justice of each party may create a "dead center," making further progress impossible. But ideally we have merely approached a situation in Western political history in which we have discovered, by tortuous experience, that liberty and equality are strictly compatible only in the heart of perfect love. They are partly contradictory in the political order. For politics is an effort to establish tolerable community, the sinfulness of men presupposed. The tension between competing interests makes authority, contradicting equality, necessary. The interests of the "rulers" make this authority dangerous to justice. The sentimentalities of the Enlightenment about liberty and equality were the consequence of its errors about human nature.

We have, even now, failed to solve theoretically the problem how much privilege special function requires; and how much power is necessary to maintain order. We have however reached moderately satisfactory practical solutions of these problems, not by disinterested intelligence but by the balance of interested wisdom. We know that the integration of community requires not only the authority of government but various subordinate authorities in economic life. We know that authority means power; and that power usually arrogates more privilege to itself than a pure wisdom or conscience could justify. We have learned how to moderate these excesses by balancing power as much as possible. But we realize that the balancing of power can not reach a consistency which would destroy the integration of the community. For the community is integrated by centers of authority which defy the abstract principle of equality.

These discoveries of common experience have refuted the presuppositions of the Enlightenment to which we in America are still consciously committed. They have justified Luther's definition of the political or civic realm as an "empire of sin to restrain sin." It was a real insight which Luther tended to discredit by his lack of discrimination. It is an insight without which modern idealists will forever try to rid communities of the instruments of community, government, hierarchy of authority and property because these produce by-products of injustice, but fail to recognize that they are also instruments of justice and order. The recognition of the moral ambiguities of these instruments is tantamount to the discovery why the "kingdom of God" is relevant to every historic situation but can never be realized in history, and why the love which creates community must be tentatively violated to give the community the bones of authority for the flesh of its brotherhood.

Perhaps it is necessary to add that we in America have achieved a tolerable solution for these problems in actual experience without penetrating to the heart of the mystery of community because of some very favorable circumstances. The wide and open continent, the wealth and productiveness of our industry and the shattering of the class distinctions and resentments of the European society mitigated the class struggle and made for equality at the most strategic place: equality of opportunity, and provided for a sufficiently generous social fund to permit a faulty distribution of the fund without resentment. For when everyone is gaining in wealth or welfare, the questions of justice are not asked too anxiously, and injustices in distribution of privileges are not the cause of vehement resentments.

As a nation, we therefore belong to the healthier nations of the Western world who have reached a tolerable solution of the problem of justice within the conditions set by a dynamic civilization. But the favorable circumstances which aided us in finding practical solutions prevented us from discovering the principles which underlie such a solution.

This fact is rather unfortunate in view of the power which we have in the process of integrating an embryo world community. To this problem we must now devote our attention.

Chapter 22

THE INTEGRATION OF THE WORLD COMMUNITY

The United Nations is not exactly the "Parliament of Mankind and Federation of the World" which the nineteenth century fondly believed to be the "one far-off divine event, to which the whole creation moves." It is nevertheless a symbol of what was true in the illusions of the previous century. It shows how man's communal problem develops toward global proportions. The ambiguities of the United Nations however refute the error in these hopes. The hopes erroneously implied that historical development would, in a sense, guarantee the solution of problems, the dimensions of which were constantly extended.

The most vivid proof that this was an error is given by two contemporary facts which were not at all anticipated. The one is the attempt of communism to organize the whole world upon the basis of its utopian vision. The other is the development of atomic weapons which, in a breathlessly brief time, has confronted us with the dread possibilities of destruction through the hydrogen bomb. The one development has divided the world into two camps. The other has filled the enmity between the two with the awful possibility of mutual annihilation. Both developments are reminders that every historical advance is fraught with possibilities of good and evil. Human history would seem to remain ambiguous, if not to its end, then at least to the present moment.

Thus we face the problem of integrating the world community under unanticipated hazards. For the fulfillment of our task it is obvious that we require all the instruments of rational discrimination which our various social and historical sciences are able to develop.

The social conditions of community have shifted so rapidly and the factors to be taken into consideration are so endlessly varied that it would seem that the primary necessity is a development of all the social and political sciences with a particular view of overcoming the "cultural lag." This favorite diagnosis for all our ills seems to have acquired new relevance today. Must we not help people to meet the new situations which they confront by measures appropriate to the situation? Must we not establish educational programs to impress upon the new generation the responsibilities and perils of "one world"? Must we not help Americans, living in a paradise of luxury in comparison with world standards, to recognize the problems of peoples emerging from a primitive economy and possibly from colonial tutelage? Must we not, as our sensitive spirits insist, make technical instruments and skills available to them to overcome their poverty? Having done that, must we not be wise enough to send cultural anthropologists along with our technicians in recognition of the fact that "raising living standards" is not a simple procedure? It involves breaking the mold of organic societies and exposing communities to the peril of social disintegration.

In all these problems a greater knowledge of all the factors involved and a larger perspective upon the total situation is certainly a primary necessity for the kind of statesmanship which will guide the nations toward a political and moral integration.

But perhaps this is another instance in which the presuppositions, from the standpoint of which we gather the facts, are as important as the diligence and honesty with which we try to ascertain the facts.

The most diligent elaboration of social and political skills seems not to have challenged the basic presuppositions of our culture in regard to the problem which we confront. That presupposition is that the forces of history are tractable if we only amass sufficient insight and skill to manage them; that even the most complex problems may be solved if we approach them with sufficient knowledge and resolution. In short, we approach them as potential managers of our own and other people's destiny. It has seemingly not dawned upon us that we have only limited competence in deflecting historical destinies in the drama of history in which we are creatures as well as creators and in which we meet competitive creators who have contrasting ideas of our common destiny.

The immediate consequence of these exaggerated notions of man's competence as an historical creator is that our idealists project all kinds of programs for integrating the world community purely by artifact and conscious contrivance. Our realists follow contrasting, but essentially similar pretentious, schemes of community. The one dream of world government; the other would establish the supremacy of our nation in the world community purely by the affirmation of our technical power.

Both the idealists and the realists propose to solve the problems of the world community by a display of wisdom or of power, by an extension of the artifacts of community and by disregard of the organic factors. Both tend to disregard the possibility of unpredictable emergences in the drama of history. This disregard of the organic growths of the past and of the unpredictable emergences of the future, this emphasis on artifact and contrivance would seem to be plausible enough at first blush. Every extension of community does indeed imply a greater reliance on artifact and less reliance on organic factors.

The nascent world community certainly possesses few organic factors of cohesion. It lacks a common language and a common culture. The common element in its diverse moral systems is probably the single idea that order is to be preferred to chaos. Its means of communication are growing, but they have not grown enough to establish the sense of an integral community. Economic interdependence is as frequently the cause of friction as of accord. The world community is bereft of not only those organic factors which are closest to "nature," but also organic historical factors such as memories of a comradeship in meeting a common danger.

It is however significant that this factor is being supplied in each half of a divided world by the enmity between the two halves. There is of course no prospect of peace in these new historical factors on both sides. For the integration of each power bloc increases the tension between the two. But before dismissing this possibility of integration, we must examine the historical forces at work more carefully. They may offer more hope than the explicit contrivances of world community. There are indications that these historical factors are certainly more potent in forming community in the so-called "free" world than all the constitutional arrangements, except as the latter serve the community whose unity has been forged by the fires of present emergencies. The organization of the free world is an historic product with absolutely unforeseen perils and promises. It exists through the organization of various *ad hoc* defensive arrangements under the aegis of the United Nations. The United Nations itself can not of course be a final security against the war between the two blocs. It was organized on the basis of the idea of unanimity between the great powers. This idea is expressed in the right of the veto of the great powers. This idea betrays, on the one hand, the illusions of the past decade that the free world could establish community with communism. The intransigeance of this political movement was not correctly estimated. But the veto right has another justification beside the one furnished by this illusion. It is based upon a shrewd insight which the idealists who would abolish the veto do not understand. This insight is that the world community is not sufficiently integrated to permit a majority to be victorious over a minority in the councils of the nations. For in that case the minority, having the power and the inclination, would merely challenge the majority by the arbitrament of war. The grant of the right of veto is based upon the understanding that the world community has not yet reached a degree of integration in which minorities trust majorities. Yet this trust is a basic requirement of the constitutional instruments of which we are so fond.

Thus the United Nations, incapable of serving its original purposes, serves the very necessary end of integrating the world as far as present realities permit. On the one hand, it is a minimal bridge across the chasm between Russia and the West. On the other hand, it furnishes the meeting ground for the free nations, the aegis for its various *ad hoc* arrangements for defensive communities; and an assembly of peoples in which world opinion serves to check the policies of the most powerful nations in the alliance. These are quite important and yet unintended services to the process of integration. It is one of the interesting revelations of the charm of historical surprises that all these factors of cohesion would probably not have had a chance to become established if the framers of the original United Nations charter had not been beguiled from their justified fears by an unjustified hope.

The loyalties and mutual trusts which are forming in these *ad hoc* arrangements such as "NATO" are certainly more potent than any possible explicit contractual commitments, though as the loyalties grow, they will presumably avail themselves of more adequate institutional arrangements.

In addition to these nascent forms of "social tissue" in the form of mutual trusts and loyalties, the free world is being integrated by another "organic" factor, which is less obviously moral but no less necessary. That is the integration through differentiation of authority, chiefly by power. A hierarchy of power and authority has been furnished for the world community by historical "accidents," chiefly the wholly unanticipated rise of American power and the sudden transformation of an isolationist nation, content with continental security, to the hegemonous power among the free nations. It goes without saying that the American leadership has not been established by explicit consent, though it must deserve the implicit consent of the community to survive. It is also obvious that the preponderance of American power is as valuable for the unity of the free world as it is dangerous to justice. In this, the situation does not differ very much from the creative and perilous factors in all such hegemonous situations in past imperial integrations. Perhaps the Greek city-states could not achieve unity because Athens and Sparta were too equally balanced in power. About the lack of apprenticeship of our nation for these great responsibilities and about other peculiar rather than perennial hazards in this American possession of preponderant power, we must speak presently. At present, it is necessary merely to call attention to the fact that the integration of at least half of the world community has proceeded through forces and factors which were less under the conscious control of men than our philosophies would find tolerable. Yet they have been provisionally more successful that the more obvious artifacts.

All this integration leaves us, of course, with the two embattled power blocs and the peril of atomic destruction through a possible conflict between them. If we are to escape disaster, both sides would have to be sufficiently aware of this peril to be more than ordinarily hesitant to take any step which would lead to general conflict. If we are to escape unification of the world through tyrannical power, the loose organization of the free world would have to outlast the monolithic unity of the tyrannical world, and it would also have to be more successful than communism in bidding for the loyalties of the non-committed nations. In that case the present growths might yet contribute to the ultimate integration of the world community. Such an eventuality would of course be possible only if the tyrannical power, having served the purpose of providing the danger which prompted the free nations to integrate their efforts and communities, would gradually lose its power to challenge the world. It is not probable that it will cease to exist as a potent secular religion. But it could well continue to exist without the power to challenge the world.

Such a loss of historical dynamic is not unprecedented. Mohammedanism was once a dynamic politico-religious movement. It has not ceased to exist, but it now lacks the power to challenge any established unity. The hoped for loss of historical dynamism of the now so powerful a movement could come about through the disillusionment of the world in the truth of the communist dogma. There are so many facts of experience which refute the dogma that there is some hope that the dogma will not always hold its sway over the conscience and consciousness of men. The other cause for hope is that there are no instruments or inclinations in its dogmas and strategies for the accommodation of divergent interests, without which it is not possible to integrate a great alliance of power. According to its simple creed, every divergence of interest or conviction seems to be a threat of treason to the basic loyalty. In the long run, the Russian dominated alliance is therefore likely to disintegrate.

Naturally many hazards must be overcome for the culmination of this solution of our world problems. Of these, two deserve special mention. The one hazard is the attractive power of the communist creed in the non-technical civilizations, chiefly in Asia. The other is the dubious endowment of our own nation for the leadership which historical events have thrust upon us in this world crisis. Both hazards deserve mention because they are both related to the theme of the relation of organic factors in community building to the contrivances of statecraft.

Communism is found attractive by the Asian nations for exactly the same reasons that the revolutionary creeds succeeded in France of the eighteenth century and Russia in the twentieth century. The social facts and resentments of a dying feudal structure, based in an agrarian economy, correspond more nearly to the Marxist diagnosis than any of the facts of the technical world, particularly after that world has corrected the original injustices of its economic and political life. The injustices of such a world are the obvious consequences of the disbalances of power in the traditional structure. They are naturally attributed to the character of that structure. It does not occur to anyone that he may be dealing with perennial factors which might be aggravated under the disbalances of a contrived revolutionary social system. The illusions from which Asia suffers are therefore almost identical to those, from which it required Western civilization generations to be emancipated.

Furthermore, the modern Asian nations have an additional reason for their illusions. The first impact of the European technically equipped nations upon them was "imperialistic." They were reduced in that encounter to colonial status, to political and economic dependence. They cherish profound resentments against this dependence which are effective now even if the injustices remain only as memories, the independence of many having been won. It is therefore easy for the communist overlords to present European civilization as "imperialistic" and to derive the imperialism from the "capitalism" for the imagination of the Asian world. It is even possible to hide the new imperialistic impulses of Russian hegemony. For according to the communist creed, Russia is but the holy land of an emancipating political faith. All these illusions are possible; and the resulting embarrassment to us is aggravated by the fact that the Western system of justice preserves liberties which are not as dear as we imagine to peoples who were buried until recently in the organic cohesions of a feudal society. Furthermore, the delicate balance of power by which justice is preserved and extended in modern technical societies is the product of a long history of trial and error. It is therefore probably beyond the competence, as it is certainly beyond the comprehension, of these awakened peoples. In short, our "way of life" does not have the persuasive power which we attribute to it. It is perfectly possible for the nations of Asia to slip from the tyranny of the older social forms to the new tyranny under the illusion that the new system is better, and not worse. We must therefore expect many a defeat in Asia before the tragic facts, gradually disclosed to the Western world in the past decades of experience, are revealed to the Asian nations. Every defeat increases the danger of a desperate defensive gesture by the defeated party, a gesture which might start the atomic conflict which it is so necessary to avoid. It can easily be understood why European nations have come to the conclusion that the danger of stumbling into the war is greater on our side than on the side of communism. We must admit that communism is not primarily a military movement. It avails itself of revolutionary pressures and conspiratorial technic in the first instance though it is not adverse to the use of military weapons when it can do so without risk of a general war. It certainly will not wittingly begin such a war so long as its other methods and weapons continue in their present success.

An American must speak with regret of the other great hazard to the success of an undertaking requiring great coolness as the whole world negotiates its differences on the edge of the abyss of atomic destruction. For that hazard is the lack in our own nation of those qualities and competencies, required for the word leadership which historical destiny has thrust upon us. Certainly the rise of America to world leadership is as surprising an eventuality as the atomic age itself. American world leadership was not quite unanticipated. Alexis de Tocqueville writing in 1835 had this remarkable prescient prophecy about both America and Russia:

"There are at the present time two great nations in the world, which started from different points, but seem to tend towards the same end. I allude to the Russians and the Americans. Both of them have grown up unnoticed; and while the attention of mankind was directed elsewhere, they have suddenly placed themselves in the front rank among the nations, and the world learned their existence and their greatness at almost the same time.

"All other nations seem to have nearly reached their natural limits, and they have only to maintain their power; but these are still in the act of growth. All others have stopped, or continue to advance with extreme difficulty; these alone are proceeding with ease and celerity along a path to which no limit can be perceived. The American struggles against the obstacles that nature opposes to him; the adversaries of the Russian are men. The former combats the wilderness and savage life; the latter civilization with all its arms. The conquests of the American are therefore gained by the plowshare; those of the Russian by the sword. The Anglo-American relies upon personal interest to accomplish his ends and gives free scope to the unguided strength and common sense of the people; the Russian centers all the authority of society in a single arm. The principal instrument of the former is freedom; of the latter, servitude. Their starting point is different and their courses are not the same; yet each of them seems marked out by the will of Heaven to sway the destinies of half the globe." [1]

Our most obvious deficiencies do not arise from our lack of apprenticeship for so great a task, though it would have been fortunate if responsibilities of such enormity had not been thrust upon us so soon after we were thrown out of the cradle of our continental security and bidden to negotiate the tricky currents of world politics. Our deficiencies are also not due, in the first instance, to our pride of power. All powerful individuals and nations have exhibited a like corruption. Our friends have given us credit for the virtue of having achieved so great an eminence without having lusted for it. We are in the unusual position, in fact, of having been very reluctant to acknowledge both the power and the responsibilities which we now bear. This virtue is of course not a clear gain. For the absence of lust for power grants no immunity against pride in its possession. We may, in fact, aggravate that pride by the pretension that we do not have it. But sensible men are usually patient with these corruptions, as they were patient with the arrogance of kings

[1] Alexis de Tocqueville: *Democracy in America,* Vol. I, p. 434.

of old. The international community of course lacks the traditions by which the arrogance of kings was veiled and transfigured in the imagination of their subjects. These traditions probably would not avail in any event to hide the vices of collective kings.

Yet these unique deficiencies of inexperience and perennial vices of the corruption of power are not our chief problem— or the world's chief problem with us. The chief problem arises from our inclination to accentuate all the errors and illusions of Western civilization in regard to man's mastery of historical destiny. We are tempted by various factors in our history to the error of imagining historical destiny to be under the dominion of man. Only yesterday we seemed in complete control of our own destiny within the limits of our continental security. We are not yet accustomed to the fact that we are more powerless in our larger world scene in the day of our seeming omnipotence than we were in the days of our innocent impotence. The power which gives us such eminence on the world scene is drawn from our technical competence and our economic abundance. Its possession therefore leaves us unconscious of the loyalties and trusts, the allegiances and habits of adherence which are compounded in the larger communal integrations. We are, essentially, children of the Enlightenment. The ideas of the Enlightenment seemed to achieve special relevance in our history because our nation came into being by the covenant of our Constitution. This fact obscured the organic factors which entered into the forming of our nation: the comradeship in arms against a common foe, the common language and culture, the propinquity of a virgin continent. It is therefore not surprising that we should believe communities to be the fruit of simple contrivances of the human will. These convictions make us impatient with historical frustrations and unprepared for the experience of defeat. It is not surprising that our European allies suspect us of heedlessness and desperation in moments of frustration, and are afraid that our desperation because of disappointments, particularly in Asia, may tempt us into taking the fateful steps which lead to a global war. These fears are incidentally responsible for the threats to our alliance with our European allies. The show of our power can not remedy the weakness in our alliance, for power, though necessary, can not supplant the mutual trust which must be the primary cement of political cohesion. Our impatience thus tends to destroy organic growths of community which are very precious because they are beyond conscious contrivance. Our moral weaknesses are aggravated by the fact that our idealists are not as active in resisting our impatience and pride as in projecting more ideal constitutional arrangements for world community which must remain irrelevant to our present emergencies. For these constitutional instruments can only perfect that which the slow processes of common experience have formed.

The immediate issue between ourselves and our allies is the question of "co-existence" with communism. Despite the fact that we dread the alternative of war as much as they, we do not seem really to believe in the possibility of co-existence. Our lack of confidence is prompted partly by our belief that communism will always have the same power and venom as it now displays. We might well grant that the venom compounded of power lusts and human self-deceptions will remain consistent. But the power may not be consistently menacing for reasons previously considered. In any event, our attitude reveals a pretension of omniscience toward the future. This is almost as grievous a mistake as the pretension of omnipotence.

A wise statesmanship naturally rests upon a modest disinclination to penetrate, or to seem to penetrate, the veil of the future any further than immediate foresight makes necessary. It is better in fact for the statesman to be completely sceptical about the meaning of history and to regard its drama as a "series of emergencies" than to have too confident a philosophy of history. The statesmanlike slogan should be "sufficient unto the day are the evils thereof." That slogan is particularly appropriate in a day in which the evil of tomorrow might be atomic destruction. It goes without saying that the resistance to the spread of tyranny by all appropriate measures is a necessary part of such statesmanship. Naturally, the world will, despite the perils of war, finally choose this dread alternative if it were the only means of escape from slavery. At least, that part of the world which has known and cherishes freedom would make such a choice. And it is idle for idealists to persuade that part of the freedom loving world that slavery might be preferable to death and that there are prospects of the gradual relaxation of its terror.

Winston Churchill of all contemporary statesmen is the most perfect embodiment of such wisdom. His attitudes reveal that his modesty in regard to man's capacity to foresee the future is not incompatible with rigorous action in averting present dangers. The same man who seeks to persuade to give "co-existence a good try" is the man who warned our heedless statesmen a decade ago not to trust communist intention too naively.[2]

Mr. Churchill's embodiment of this wisdom is significant for many reasons. We have assumed such wisdom to be the final fruit of a Biblical faith. But Mr. Churchill is not an explicitly pious man though a wartime colleague of his has testified that Churchill's religion consists primarily of "a strong sense of providence." Thus it is uncertain from what source Mr. Churchill has drawn his wisdom, though it must be confessed that, though highly individual, it also expresses the typical reactions of a whole European culture.

The "common sense" of the European nations, especially as contrasted with our own seeming heedlessness, may well be the fruit of long experience rather than specifically Christian insights. We have previously observed the coincidence between the wisdom of common sense and the characteristic insights of Biblical faith. That coincidence is due to their common acceptance of the fragmentary and inconclusive

---

[2] There are welcome signs that our American President, Mr. Eisenhower, shares Churchill's attitude toward world problems to a greater extent than the nation as a whole and more than seemed at first apparent.

nature of the various themes and dramas which fill the human story. We have all learned to accept this fragmentariness for our individual life, whether it leads to despair or the tremendous adventure of faith, that our fragmentary lives and projects are ultimately purged and completed in a divine design beyond our comprehension. But what has been accepted by individual selves does not readily lend itself to transference to the collective national self, which is bound to find the idea irksome, that it is powerless either to discern, or to fulfill what it discerns, as the true end of history. In the case of our nation, this temptation is particularly great because our power is very great, our experience with the frustration of history is limited, and our culture is informed by strains of perfectionist and utopian illusions stemming from the Enlightenment on the one hand and from sectarian Christianity on the other.

Thus we are in danger of bringing human history to a premature conclusion (its "end" as "finis") because we imagine that we have discerned the true end of history ("end" as final purpose). A touch of irony is added to this situation because we imagine the defeat of communism to be history's true end, and we have forgotten that some of the evils of communism are derived from the fact that it regarded "capitalism" as the final form of evil and therefore proposed to grasp the *summum bonum* of history by the destruction of capitalism. It is certainly significant that so much evil is born of these frantic graspings after the final end of history.

The idea of a brotherly world community is certainly more legitimate as the goal of history than either of these conceptions of fulfillment through victory over a hated foe. But it is certainly significant that two less attractive alternatives are more probable than this ideal. The one is global destruction through atomic conflict. This alternative is not really as probable as those would persuade us who believe the dread possibility might scare the nascent world community into virtue, if not into existence. But it remains a possibility. The other alternative is a period of development in which destructive conflict will be avoided, but in which no neat world order will be achieved. This alternative is, of all possibilities, most probable. It would not change the international situation from the status of partial order and partial anarchy of the past centuries very radically. It would merely heighten the perils of anarchy and increase the potency of community. If we are patient enough we could cultivate the gradually growing organic factors of world community and perfect them at opportune moments by the constitutional contrivances which always express and perfect what the forces of life and togetherness have established.

Our nation will be able to contribute to these developments, as it is purged of its illusions by the experiences of history. It will be purged as surely as old men have accepted the limits of human striving more definitely than young men. It is natural that young men and young nations should be concerned primarily to extend the limits of human power and explore the resources in every human potentiality. It is as natural for old men and nations to be persuaded by frustrations and common experiences that there are limits for both individuals and nations, as indeed for all human striving. When the fragmentariness of all human existence, both individual and collective, is fully realized, and human creativity is content to operate within this fragmentariness, it achieves a new possibility of creating without the threat of disaster. We can only hope that we will be mercifully saved from the fate of bringing our own and a very great common enterprise to a premature and violent conclusion so that we may have the chance of being purged of our illusions and, in a more modest mood, dedicate our great energies and virtues to the building of a tolerable world community.

Chapter 23

INDIVIDUAL AND COLLECTIVE DES-
TINIES IN THE CONTEMPORARY
SITUATION

The engagement of sensitive individuals, or for that matter of any individuals, in the perplexities and perils of nations, cultures, and even of the whole enterprise of civilization, which we discussed in the previous chapter, does not annul any private hopes or ambitions or simplify the drama of any individual life. Our contemporary situation is therefore a vivid reminder of the fact that while history constantly enlarges the scope of the collective drama which becomes the basis of all individual destinies, it does not obviate any of the problems which the single self faces in its involvement in, and transcendence over, its collective destinies.

The individual may become involved in responsibilities for the security of a world-wide community; and the perennial fear of death may appear in the new dimension of the fear of mutual annihilation through atomic destruction. But these wider responsibilities and more terrible dangers do not change the situation of the self essentially. It still has hopes and fears, fulfillments and frustrations, which are partly related to, and are partly independent of, the collective drama. It still faces the grandeur and the misery of its existence. Its grandeur or

dignity is still derived from its ability to transcend the temporal flux and to touch the fringes of the eternal. Its misery
is still compounded of both "death and sin," that is, of both
the essential brevity of a life concerned with such ultimate
matters; and of the evil into which it falls by attempting to
avoid or obscure the brevity and insignificance of its life.
In the words of Augustine, it "falls into sin, which it could
avoid, by attempting to escape death which it can not avoid."
Even if the collective fulfillments of the meaning of life,
promised to this generation, had not proved to be illusory,
any individual, living at any particular locus of the sweep
of history, would have been justified in the poignant cry of
the Fourth Ezra: "What doth it profit us that ages of fulfillment are promised them (our posterity) whereas we perish
so miserably in futility?"

Even the most perfect community can not overcome the
fragmentary nature of the self's life or still its uneasy conscience, either because it did not conform to the community's
standards or because it failed to rise above them sufficiently.
It is bound to suffer from the latter form of uneasiness because it always has some source of norms and standards higher
than those of the community. Furthermore, even the most
impressive collective enterprise can not obscure the weakness
and impotence of the single self which "brings its years to
an end like a tale that is told."

Modern culture, in addition to the difficulties in comprehending the nature of human selfhood previously discussed,
finds it practically impossible to conceive a frame of meaning
which will do justice to both the private and the collective
drama in which human beings are involved. The reason obviously is that it tries to comprehend them both in terms of
some fairly simple scheme of rational intelligibility. And the
dramas are so disparate and incommensurate in some of their
dimensions that either the one or the other is unduly subordinated to the other. Every system of intelligibility must
begin with a starting point and have a terminus of meaning.
Lacking a frame of meaning which is high and broad enough

to comprehend both the pathos of individual existence and the meaning of the total human enterprise, the culture is forced to treat the historical drama in terms which make either the individual or the collective enterprise the keystone of meaning. In the one case, history is interpreted as the story of the gradual emergence of the individual from every collective enterprise to become a self-justifying existence. In the other case, history is regarded as the record of the community's gradual triumph over the recalcitrant individual. In both cases the freedom of man is not sufficiently appreciated, particularly the freedom to pursue particular, as against common, or universal, ends. Therefore the historical drama is falsely presented in terms of moral progress, whether individual liberty or social harmony is regarded as the moral norm.

For reasons previously discussed, the individualistic interpretation was most popular in the liberal society created by the commercial classes, while the agrarian classes were more given to the traditional organic sense of community, and the industrial workers were attracted by the newer Marxist-inspired collectivism. But the individualism of bourgeois culture could not prevent the emergence of subordinate interpretations which gave meaning to the drama in terms of subordinating the individual to the community. Sometimes this was done by promising the individual fulfillment for his fragmentary life in the community. Sometimes it was done by pretentious scientists who imagined themselves the master of historical destiny and regarded ordinary mortals as merely the stuff of history which would have to be "managed" toward "socially approved ends."

But these subordinate and tentative collectivist solutions of the problem have not changed the dominant note of individualism in bourgeois life. This individualistic creed imagined the individual self capable of creating communities by an act of the will, and justified the communities merely in terms of their support of the individual. The individualism of the liberal society was prompted by a moral error; and the technical developments of modern civilization served to support the error. The moral error was the notion that individuals could be self-justifying ends. Immanuel Kant gave the error classical expression in his dictum: "So act as to make humanity, whether in thine own person or in that of another, in every case as the end withal and never as a means."

The precept compounded a typically modern error with a classical Christian truth. The truth is that individuals are of transcendent worth and that no individual may legitimately use another merely as an instrument of his ends. Even this truth must be qualified sufficiently, however, to permit social integration. It is true ultimately, but in the social dimension individuals must make use of each other. The error which is compounded with this truth is succinctly expressed in the Kantian phrase: "Whether in thine own person or in another." For that phrase reveals the incapacity of the Enlightenment to think "existentially" and therefore to perceive that the same individual who must guard against using others as means to his ends can not make himself his own end.

The self is so great and so small that its greatness can not be contained in its smallness. It can only realize itself by endlessly being drawn out of itself into larger ends. The community may provisionally be that larger end. But it can not be so ultimately. For the community is, though broader than the individual, also much closer to the necessities of nature than it. The individual must have a higher end than the community.

The moral error contained in the Kantian precept was aggravated by the technical developments which created first a commercial and then an industrial society. The former emancipated the individual from the bonds of an organic society and the latter created forms of urban togetherness which did not necessarily provide the self with community. In them the individual required an explicit act of the will, to be delivered from preoccupation with himself. Such an act of the will is not an impossibility, but it is beyond the moral competence of ordinary mortals. The forces of cohesion in an organic society are serviceable, not only in providing for restraints upon the self-will of men, but in drawing individuals out of the narrow prison of their self-concern. The spiritual health of a peasant mother compared with the malaise from which sophisticated cosmopolitans suffer will illustrate the point.

The isolated individual, lost in an anonymous mass, was rather a sorry fulfillment of the hopes of the nineteenth century. His situation was too untenable to be long maintained. It was challenged by overt forms of collectivism and by the further technical developments which added mass communication to other technical forms of cohesion so that the individual, even in a liberal society, was pressed into standards of conformity which left him even less private room for his uniqueness than was enjoyed by the peasants of traditional communities.

These inadvertent forms of totalitarianism, which engulfed the individual in communities, which were ostensibly devoted to his freedom, were not as significant, however, as the more explicit disavowals of individual liberty and worship of the community which grew on liberal soil, inspired by the untenable position of the self-justified individual. Long before the more explicitly collectivist religio-political movements of Nazism and communism arose, the national loyalty tended to assume religious dimensions in a community which had only recently celebrated the emancipation of the individual. The nationalism of the France of Napoleon in relation to the revolution which preceded it is a vivid exemplar of the tendency.

The tendency reached its climax in the two totalitarian movements of contemporary history, Nazism and communism. Each had its own social causes related to the chaos of national communities of technical civilization. But both gained some of their momentum because of the spiritual embarrassment of the individual in a technical society. Nazism, inspired by a decadent form of romanticism, persuaded, beguiled and forced individuals of a very advanced Western community to renounce their individual dignity and freedom for the sake of establishing the simple communal cohesion of a primitive society.

Communism, as an economic-political creed, is based upon the theory that the institution of property is the root of all social evil and that therefore its abolition would usher in an ideal social harmony. Marxism as a religio-moral creed is based upon the illusion that the social solidarity of primitive society expresses the "social essence" of man, from which he has been "alienated" by the rise of civilization. This typically romantic theory contains only one half of the truth.

The individual is indeed endangered in his "social essence" by the emancipation from the "primeval we" (Kunkel) which represents the birth of civilization. But he also comes to his full state by that emancipation. The communist collectivism which tries to make the community (in this case something allegedly more universal than the national community) into the source and end for individual existence would have been intolerable even if it had not degenerated into an overt tyranny. For Marxism, without the corruption of "Stalinism," would yet have expressed the tyranny of Rousseau's "General will" which was supposed to provide for a fulfillment of every particular will but which betrayed the obtuseness of the whole romantic movement to both the perils and dignity of the unique individual will.

The communities created by these forms of collectivism were indeed as free as primitive communities of the friction created by the competition between particular and parochial interests which characterizes the complex life of advanced communities; but they were also bereft of all the richness and variety of the harmonies and disharmonies of civilized life. In short, it was even more intolerable to force the individual to find the final end of his existence in the community (whether conceived in nationalistic or pseudo-international terms) than to persuade him to regard his life as a self-justifying end.

The war between these untenable collectivist and individualistic solutions of the problem of the individual has engrossed our generation and has led to consequences of tragic proportions. The war was prompted by many social causes which do not concern us here. But in terms of the basic problem of the relation of the individual to the community and to the total historical drama, with which we are now concerned, the two errors were caused by the fact that each creed was blind to one of the two dimensions of human selfhood. Both understood either the social dimension or the transcendent dimension of the human self. But neither creed understood that the self must both be related to a community and become progressively related to a more and more inclusive historical process; but must also have the freedom to transcend every social process, to seek after unique fulfillments of its own, to consider the plight of its frustrations which no communal activity can overcome, and to inquire after the meaning of its existence in terms which are finally irrelevant to any sense of meaning which the community may have.

The contrast between collectivist and individualistic elaborations of the same "liberal" creed of the nineteenth century is dramatically illustrated in the misunderstandings between Auguste Comte and John Stuart Mill. Their philosophy seemed so similar that Mill at first assumed their conclusions to be identical. He made very complimentary references to Comte. But he gradually qualified and then withdrew his appreciations as he came to realize that Comte's philosophy tended toward totalitarianism in complete contrast to Mill's libertarianism. Mill's philosophy was certainly more tenable than that of Comte. But Mill was blind to the creative aspects of community, and Comte was blind to the dimension of transcendence of the individual over the community. It was not possible to contain both dimensions within a simple system of rational intelligibility.

The fate of the individual in Western civilization has fortunately not been completely determined by the strife between, and the inadequacies of, these warring creeds. The

relatively tolerable condition of individual existence has been
due in part to the richness of the culture which armed the
individual with the competence and inclination to stand his
ground against the community and which endowed him with
possibilities of scientific and artistic creativity in which he
could fulfill his life. It has been due in part to the remnants
of a Christian-Biblical faith which the force of modern "secularism" was powerless to destroy and which endowed him with
both a source of authority which could persuade him to defy
the community with a resolute "we must obey God rather
than man," and with a sense of meaning which made him
independent of the structures of meaning which the community constructed for him.

We have previously analyzed the unique affirmation of
mystery and meaning which characterizes Biblical faith. We
must now consider the resources of that faith for the solution of the problem of the individual and the community.
This is a problem because any system of rational intelligibility
which seeks to comprehend the disparate and incommensurate
entities of the individual and the community into one system of coherence is tempted to make either one or the
other unduly subordinate to the other. A system broad
enough to provide a frame of meaning for the collective
drama is not high enough to give significance to the indeterminate possibilities of both good and evil of individual
life. A system which, on the other hand, takes cognizance of
the indeterminate possibilities of self-transcendence of the
individual easily degenerates into a mystical affirmation of
ultimates and universals which rob both the individual and
the collective drama of any specific meaning.

Biblical faith combines a sense of mystery with specific
meaning. It asserts that the divine mystery of creation and of
the judgement sensed by the individual in the height of his
self-consciousness has been clarified by a specific historical
drama; that in the life, death and resurrection of Christ we
have the key to the mercy and love of God whom we have
previously known as the power of creation and as ultimate
judge. This is the "light that shineth in darkness." This is

the key to the mystery which does not however transmute mystery into rational intelligibility. It merely relates the ultimate mystery to the mystery of the human drama so that the one makes sense out of the other. Naturally, this key must be accepted "by faith." There is no way of convincing the mind to accept the key by proving it to be the necessary logical consequence of an analysis of structures and coherences. For we are dealing with a realm of freedom and mystery beyond all structures except the patterns and themes of history.

The frame of meaning established by Biblical faith is able to give meaning to both the individual and the collective dramas of history. The God who created the world has the power of a higher majesty than that of the nations. "He bringeth the princes to naught," declares the prophet Isaiah, "and maketh the judges of the earth as vanity." But the majesty of His mercy and love is one with the majesty of His power. The Christian faith is primarily the acceptance of a divine mercy, of the assurance that the variance between the human and the divine Will has been overcome by the divine mercy. The divine mercy proceeds from the same love which is the criterion of judgements for every individual life. This love is the norm which establishes a frame of meaning for the individual. It makes the dignity of human freedom comprehensible because it establishes an environment above the obvious structures of nature for that freedom. But it also discerns that there is misery in this dignity; that there is both the power and inclination of self-concern in the same freedom which is the basis of human creativity.

There is, in short, in the key of meaning to the ultimate mystery a center for historical meaning as well. That is the significance of Christ as both human and divine. And the historical meaning, which is established, is broad enough for the whole historical drama, high enough to contain the freedom of the individual and realistic enough to discern the corruptions of freedom in human history.

If the individual rises above the courts and judgements of the community to appeal to a more ultimate judgement

("With me it is a very small thing that I should be judged of men; yea I judge not mine own self, for I know nothing by myself; he that judgeth me is the Lord," declares St. Paul), he faces a judgement more, rather than less, severe than the judgements of the community. He is judged by the norm of the love of the neighbor. The neighbor may be some fellow man whom the community does not recognize. But he may also represent the members of the community which is passing the judgements upon his conduct. The ultimate judgements which are interpreted by the key of the Christ revelation can, in short, never be socially irrelevant. They can not prompt the individual to defy the community for the sake of his own "pursuit of happiness"; nor do they prompt him to flee the collective enterprises and perplexities of men to escape into some realm of "eternal bliss." The believer is indeed promised the "peace of God which passeth understanding." It passes understanding, however, precisely because it is a peace which contains the pains and sorrows of suffering love. For the believer is challenged to become engaged in the sorrows and sufferings of the world. He worships a God whose peace is not some supernal equanimity of detachment. It is the peace of the triumph of the Cross.

The fact that the frame of meaning provided by the Christian faith clarifies the collective and the individual dimensions of the human drama and that it discerns the possibilities of both good and evil in it, that it therefore gives the basis for a tolerable solution of the problem of the individual and the community for which modern culture could find no satisfying solution, may justify the faith by inference. But we face the interesting situation upon which we dwelt in another context—that this faith may be justified but can not be established by inference. No analysis of the inadequacies of alternatives can persuade the believer to believe that Christ is the key to the ultimate mystery and to the meaning of his own life.

The adventure of faith must remain an adventure, however much it may be supported by inferential evidence. The individual has a freedom and loneliness of freedom which make all social correlations and processes inadequate bases of meaning. In addition he faces the contradiction between this greatness and the brevity of his life. He is so great and yet so small. He may be "fearfully and wonderfully made," but that does not save him from "bringing his years to an end like a tale that is told." To these perplexities one more must be added. Partly consciously and partly unconsciously he complicates his problem by abortive efforts to solve it through the man's assertion of his strength or wisdom or virtue. Yet every effort to hide or to deny the fragmentary character of his life increases the pain and sorrow of life. This situation may drive some men to despair and may prompt others to embrace Christ as the key to the mystery. But the alternatives which seek to give meaning to human existence by correlating the individual and the collective dramas, or by equating man's freedom with his mind, or by deriving the evil in him from the inertias of "nature," are obviously inadequate to satisfy anyone who is inclined to look honestly at the antinomies and tragedies of human existence.

In this post-Christian era, in which a scientific culture is preoccupied with systems of coherence and seeks to reduce these systems to simpler and simpler proportions, it would be idle to speculate on the possibility of many people, particularly "representative people," finding their way back to a faith which doubly offends the pride of man. It offends the pride of perennial man by convicting him of a lack of virtue on which he relies for his self-respect. And it offends the pride of modern man by convicting his rational faculty of inadequacy both in guaranteeing his virtue and in making sense out of the strange drama of his existence.

The thesis that the Christian faith offers an adequate frame of meaning for the comprehension of both the individual and the collective drama and for an understanding of the relation between the two, does not imply that every problem of the relation of the individual to the community is solved by such a faith. The gradual gain by the individual of a tolerable security against the community and of a tolerable freedom to develop his own uniqueness was frequently won in

the teeth of religious opposition; and there was good reason
for resisting the unqualified claims of the individual, at least
provisionally. For on both the religious and the moral level
it was necessary to do justice to the social and transcendent
dimensions of selfhood before a satisfactory solution of the
individual and the community could be achieved. The experience of God can not be coerced or even induced by the
community, whether political or ecclesiastical. In that sense,
religion is "what man does with his solitariness" (Whitehead);
and the Reformation is justified in insisting on "evangelical"
liberty for the individual, that is, for the right to appropriate
the divine pardon upon contrition, without the mediation
of church or priest. But private religious experience may be
a capricious "wish fulfillment." It requires the discipline
of the community of believers. Christianity, in common with
Judaism, is, moreover, dependent upon the norm of an historical revelation.

Thus even the Reformation, despite its principle of the
"priesthood of all believers," did not abolish or diminish the
significance of the Church while limiting its authority in the
ultimate sphere and denying it the competence to give and
to withhold forgiveness in God's name.

When the Catholic Church speaks of liberty, it is thinking
of the liberty of the person to seek his "eternal end" beyond
the temporal and immediate ends of the political order. This
acknowledgement of an end, transcendent to the purposes
and projects of the political community, marks the radical
difference between an authoritarian religious community and
a totalitarian political community. The difference in establishing the humanity of the person is tremendous and not
sufficiently appreciated by modern anti-authoritarians. It must
be appreciated even though it is recognized that an authoritarian religion may be too blind to the pinnacle of individual
uniqueness in the religious life and to the inability of any
religious community guaranteeing the repentance, trust, and
new life, which is the mark of a genuine encounter between
the self and God according to Biblical faith.

We face the same difficulties on the moral as on the re-

ligious level, and in the realm of "civil" as well as in the
realm of "evangelical" liberty. The Reformation was so
polemical in its protests against ecclesiastical authority, and
Luther was so preoccupied with his theory of the "two realms"
that the Lutheran Reformation, at least, tended to deny any
relevance between "evangelical" and "civil" liberty. For the
"earthly" realm of civil life was under the control of "the
sword, the law, chains and courts" and nothing was supposedly known in it of "forgiveness, pardon and mercy."

Later Calvinism, of course, drew other conclusions. John
Milton's spiritual services to the democratic idea was based
primarily upon his Christian conviction that God had given
the person a transcendent worth and related him to a transcendent authority which the state must honor. Significantly,
he used the text which for Luther meant the rigorous separation of the two realms: "Give unto Caesar the things that
are Caesar's; and to God the things that are God's," to draw
different conclusions and to claim liberty of conscience from
the political community. "My conscience I have from God,"
declared Milton, "and therefore I can not submit it to Caesar."
A free society could not have been created without this conviction. It prompted the individual to defy the community
on crucial issues of conscience. It also finally persuaded the
political community to have some reverence for the sanctity
of the individual conscience. This self-limitation of the
state in approaching the conscience of the individual has come
to be one of the chief marks of distinction between an open
society and a totalitarian one. Yet the conscience of the individual is not as infallible as the strict libertarians imply.
It is not even infallible when it is ostensibly informed by a
genuine desire to submit to a higher divine judgement. Therefore even the most democratic states have learned to insist
on certain standards of common decency and public order
even against the dictates of religiously inspired conscience.
Furthermore, the most effective opposition to tyrants in recent
decades has come not so much from isolated individuals, but
from individuals whose conscience was formed by political,
scientific, cultural, and religious communities. There is, in

short, no dimension of existence in which the individual is purely an individual and is not in need of either material or spiritual and moral support from some community. This is one of many reasons why the cherished civil freedom of open communities is meant for its subordinate communities as much as for individuals. We may conclude that the higher the level of consciousness, the more unique the individual becomes, in which case the religious level is the most genuinely individual. But we must understand that even on this level (about which Luther observed that men face the fear of death alone) the solitary soul is in need of both sympathy and instruction from its fellows.

These complexities offer some explanation for the slow and tortuous progress of Christian communities toward an adequate solution of the problem of relating the individual to the community without endangering the integrity of the one or the good order of the other.

But it is not only because the testimony of Christian faith recognizes the ambiguities of life that the path was tortuous and the progress slow. Another reason was that with religious faith alone, without the support of the competence and creativity with which cultural disciplines endow the individual, he can not maintain himself against the immense weight of communal authority. He requires two, and not one, weapons in his armor. He must have the weapon of religiously inspired self-respect against the pretensions of the community, but he must also have the critical competence to arrive at conclusions independent of the decrees of custom and the authority of traditions; and he must have creative resources in the arts and crafts, in science and in culture to make his own unique contributions to the life of the community. These resources are not supplied by any faith but by the disciplines of culture. It is therefore idle to attribute the self-respect and integrity of the individual in an open society to either the one or the other of the two sources of his independence. The independence which is derived from artistic or scientific competence has been honored and guarded by modern democratic communities with less reluctance as communities belatedly discovered that the community would ultimately benefit from activities of individuals in which it had no immediate interest and which it was tempted to regard as a threat to its obvious interests and order. The technological competence of modern communities rests upon the pursuits of pure science, developed by the inquisitiveness, the ingenuity and the creativity of individuals who were not prompted by any immediate communal purpose. The richness and variety of a culture, ultimately beneficial to the community, depend upon a freedom of the artists to pursue goals not immediately beneficial to the community. The Nazis benefited from a technology which was itself parasitic on the purer sciences which had been developed in freedom. Even a democratic society like our own may find to its sorrow that a too frantic effort to enlist the scientists for the defensive purposes of atomic wars may imperil the advances in nuclear physics on which the competence in the construction of atomic weapons depends.

If the security of the conscience of the individual against the perils of communal oppression remains a perpetual problem in even "open" societies, the community has a contrasting problem of appropriating the dictates of the individual's conscience for its own good order and health. This is a problem because the conscience of the individual frequently, if not usually, functions in terms which are irrelevant to the ends of the community. The reason for this irrelevance can be easily stated. The individual, when considering a moral problem ultimately, finds every form of self-assertion to be suspect before the judgement seat of conscience. The community, on the other hand, must establish some kind of harmony and justice within its own boundaries by encouraging an equilibrium of power among competitive forms of self-interest. And when the community's relationship to other communities is weighed (the national community being the chief modern exemplar of the most powerful community), the question always arises whether the willingness to sacrifice self-interest for the general good, which is the final norm for the individual, is really a possibility for the nation. For the force of alter-egoism in powerful communities is such that the high-

est possibility would seem to be that they find a point of concurrence between their own and a more universal interest.
It is significant, at least, that it is not generally expected of
nations that they subordinate their interests to the community of mankind. The highest desideratum seems to be
a sufficiently prudent self-interest to prompt actions which
will ultimately, though not necessarily immediately, benefit
both the limited and the universal community.

This conflict between individual and social morality is not
caused, as some critics would claim, by the Christian error
of proposing an impossible norm for both the individual
and the community, the norm of sacrificial love as exempli-
fied in the Cross of Christ. The problem would not be solved
even if a more possible norm would be set first for the
individual, but most definitely for the community. The fact
is that the revelation of the "Cross of Christ" does not super-
impose, but merely clarifies, the truth about man's situation
when ultimately considered. The situation which is clarified
by the Christian faith can be validated by common experience. It is that the self is bound to destroy itself by seeking
itself too narrowly, that it must forget itself to realize itself,
but that this self-forgetfulness can not be induced by the
calculation that a more ultimate form of self-realization will
flow from the forgetfulness. The ethic of the Cross therefore
clarifies, but does not create, a norm which is given by the
very constitution of selfhood. It is this constitution which
prevents the self from ever finding virtue or happiness or self-
realization by seeking them too directly or insistently. It is
this constitution of selfhood which makes "grace," including
common grace, a more effective instrument of redemption
than prudence. This is so clear that even a culture which
glorifies prudence manages to give an inadvertent honor to
heroes and martyrs, to brave men and those who were heedless
of their interests. Thus the final paradox of human selfhood
shines through even in cultures which have no way of
appreciating any wisdom of life above the level of prudence.

The conflict between the conscience of the individual and
the community must not be abolished, for it is a source

of wisdom and grace for both the individual and the community. But it can be prevented from becoming a source of confusion in the moral and religious life of mankind by clarifying some facts about both the individual and the community which both Christians and rationalistic forms of perfectionism have obscured.

The obvious fact about the individual is that no one completely fulfills the norm which is given in the very constitution of selfhood. Everyone is involved in the sin of grasping after self-realization too immediately and too clamantly. We are thus involved in, even if we do not consciously recognize the validity of, the law of love. We may not recognize this contradiction between our acceptance of the law and our inevitable betrayal of it, except when we consider ourselves ultimately, that is in prayer. In that experience we become aware of the fact that "there is a law in my members which wars against the law that is in my mind." We know that the "love of Christ" is not a simple possibility for us. It is, on the one hand, the revelation of ultimate possibilities and, on the other hand, the revelation of a divine mercy which understands us in the inevitable contradiction in which even the most perfect life is involved. When this fact is clearly understood about the individual self, one of the main sources of confusion about the demands of individual conscience and political morality is removed. For even a very sensitive Christian understands that the community is forced to deal with precisely these residual self-interests of even the most perfect men. It must harness, deflect, balance and beguile these various competitive interests for the sake of a tolerable harmony and justice.

Orthodox Christianity, whether Protestant or Catholic, may have been involved in various errors of obscurantism or literalism, and may have been blind to social complexities which a scientific culture has explored. But it has been a source of wisdom to the community as long as it preserved the Biblical estimate of the capacity for both love and self-love of the self which both modern secularism and liberal Protestantism have obscured.

The wisdom drawn from this Biblical account of selfhood is not only relevant to the elaboration of a political morality which both protects the self in its dignity and protects the community against the self-regard of the self. It is relevant to social relations in even such an intimate group as the family. A loving mother will deal wisely with a rebellious adolescent child if she understands that the rebellion is an inevitable assertion of the child's ego but also a natural reaction to the power impulses in the love of even the most loving parents. Furthermore, the mother will not allow the "sacrifices" of her love to be the occasion for encouraging heedlessness toward the right of others in her children. The mother of more than one child will soon discover, moreover, that a calculus of justice is a necessary instrument of even the most disinterested love. In this way the ultimate dimension of the ethical life must be related to the proximate ends of a tolerable peace and justice.

The organization of these proximate ends naturally requires an astute estimate of the interests and rights which are in competition with each other and of the probable consequences of any given course of action. Therefore intellectual disciplines are increasingly necessary instruments of social morality, the more intricate social relations become. But no intellectual analysis can eliminate the ultimate paradox between prudence and "grace," between justice and love, in the moral life of man. That paradox consists in the fact that heedless love is at once the fulfillment and the negation of justice; and that mercy and forgiveness are at once the fulfillment and negation of punitive justice.

The social relations within a community can be ordered more wisely if the individual is known in terms of both his capacity for love and for self-love. The ethic of the community (in the contemporary instance, the national community) in its relation to other communities can be estimated wisely only if it is understood in what sense the community, as such, has a "conscience" or moral sense. It obviously does not have a conscience in the full sense in which the individual possesses it. It lacks such a conscience because it has a more developed organ of will (the state) than of the further self-transcendence which is tantamount to conscience. The moral sense of the community is constituted of its traditions plus the competitive ideas of its various citizens as individuals about what the conduct of the community should be. The force of alter-egoism colors the moral testimonies of these individuals in such a way that they frequently define the right conduct for the nation in selfish terms, partly because that conduct would be unselfish for them and partly because the conduct would be a collective expression for an unconscious and suppressed individual self-regard. All these complexities, together with the confusion of counsel within the nation about its collective actions, make it inevitable that the moral sense of the community should be at a lower level than that of the individual; and that a wise self-interest which can find the point of concurrence between a particular and a general interest, should represent the *summum bonum* of the community rather than sacrificial love. It must be observed however that if the conscience of individuals within the community does not operate to concern life within it with the welfare of life outside of it, the collective self-concern of the nation will express itself in narrower and more self-defeating terms. That is why love can not be declared irrelevant even for the life of the community (chiefly the modern nation) and why the individual conscience must be concerned with the conduct of the community even if its dictates in their purest form are not directly relevant.

It is partly because individuals set higher goals than the community is able to realize that we have the problem of utopianism in modern culture. But this problem is partly due to the very structure of human selfhood. Not only for the community but for himself the individual persists in entertaining ideals which are beyond his capacities. "Our reach is beyond our grasp," declares Browning, "or what's a heaven for?" The hope of heaven and the modern man's hope of a heaven on earth are obviously expressions of the same inner necessities of selfhood. The human drama in both its individual and collective terms constantly sets tangents of mean-

ing which remain unfulfilled in the limits of nature-history.
The Renaissance culture began with the supposition that the
extravagance of human hopes was the cause of human ills.
"You have set your ladders into heaven," declared Cosimo de
Medici, the harbinger of modern culture. "We will not
strive so high or fall so low."

It must be regarded as an ironic refutation of Cosimo's
prescription for virtue that one part of the Renaissance culture consistently moderated the "reach" so that it would not
be beyond the "grasp" of man; and that strategy, consistently
applied, ended in Nazi cruelty. Nazism significantly prided
itself upon having disavowed Anglo-Saxon "hypocrisy" which
may be defined as the pretension of having a grasp equal to
the reach. The other part of the culture built more absurd
"ladders to heaven" than the Christians whom Cosimo criticized. And these ladders to heaven proved an even greater
source of confusion than either the Christian ones or the
Nazi disavowal of every kind of moral or religious ladder.
These contradictory developments prove that the relation of
the reach to the grasp is an unsolved problem of man's
existence.

The answer of Biblical faith to this problem has long since
been discarded even by some Christians, and regarded as
completely irrelevant by moderns. The Christians (and the
Jews for that matter) found the idea of the "resurrection of
the body" so irrational that they fled ιο the Hellenic conception of the "immortality of the soul," though the immortality conceived by Plato was certainly not of the self, and
it annulled man's collective history as well as his unique
selfhood.

We must remember that all hopes and ideas conceived
from within the temporal process of a system of meaning
which transcends the temporal flux, are "irrational." At least
they are not simply rational. With this presupposition we
may well approach the Biblical hope afresh to see whether
it may give us a keystone to the arch for the understanding
of human selfhood.

The Christian hope is derived from the Christian revelation of the meaning in the divine mystery. That revelation is centered in the crucifixion and resurrection of Christ. Confidence that the crucified Savior was "raised again" is the very basis of the faith which gathered the first believing community. Yet honest scholarship must admit that the resurrection is not as well attested as an historical event as the crucifixion. There is the question whether the experience of the "living Lord" was not the private experience of his disciples and was later justified and made more vivid by the story of the empty tomb. If this be true, it is significant for the very quality of the Christian faith in boldly asserting that there is a realm of meaning, transcending nature-history and defined by the purposes of the God who has a freedom beyond the coherences of nature, in which the crucified Savior is alive and "sitteth at the right hand of God." He is apprehended not only as a specific individual whose life has power beyond the grave, but as the key to the ultimate mystery of God and history. Naturally this whole revelatory drama presupposes, and would not be thinkable without, the Hebraic-Messianic hope of the resurrection in the Messianic age.

Before this hope is dismissed as utterly incredible, it would be well to recognize that it brings to a climax one of the basic characteristics of the Biblical faith, namely, its lack of logical coherence and its consequent "empirical" superiority in comprehending facts which can not be brought into logical coherence. The facts about the self which the idea of the resurrection clarifies, are all important for the understanding of the antinomies of the human self. They are: (A) The self in its final freedom transcends the conditions of nature-time and can not be fulfilled within them. (B) The self has a unity between this freedom of the spirit and the organism of its body and soul, which makes the emancipation of an immortal soul from a mortal body unthinkable. Therefore the ultimate hope is expressed in the idea of a transfigured body. "It is sown a natural body, it is raised a spiritual body," declares St. Paul (I Corinthians 15:44). Thus the unthinkable idea of the resurrection of the body guards and supports the

unthinkable but directly experienced idea of the unity of the
self as animal organism and as free spirit. (C) The freedom
of the self is not merely a dignity which must be asserted
in defiance of death. It contains a corruption of self-concern
which is revealed to be ultimately culpable, even though it may
be justified in immediate instances. Therefore the death and
resurrection of Christ is felt to be symbolic of the dying of
the self to its narrow self, that it may truly live. "I am crucified with Christ; nevertheless I live," declared St. Paul. This
emancipation from self and the revelation of a divine mercy
which understands that the emancipation is never complete,
is a more primary assurance of the "kerygma" than the hope
of the resurrection. The creed ends with three affirmations in
a significant order: "I believe in . . . the forgiveness of sins:
the resurrection of the body: and the life everlasting." Completion of the human story without the forgiveness of sin would
be unthinkable. The Gospel, in short, both guards the dignity
of the self which transcends death and recognizes the misery
of the self, which faces the problem of sin, as well as the fact
of death. The tendency to disregard this part of the Gospel
invariably reduces the Christian faith to the affirmation of the
"spiritual" character of man against the threat of death.

(D) The resurrection of the individual is incredibly related
to a "general" resurrection which completes the whole human
story, and which is associated with the "coming again" of the
suffering Savior in triumph "with great power and glory."
This hope implies that the antinomies of history will express
themselves to the end but are not able finally to overcome the
meaning of human existence. The antinomies are not caused
by the inertia of nature against the freedom of spirit. They
are therefore not overcome by man's gradual triumph over
nature. They grow with that triumph so that the most explicit evil, the "anti-Christ," appears just at the end of history. One need hardly analyze our current perplexities and
the perils of tyranny and atomic destruction to prove that
this incredible hope for the end of history is more in accord
with actual experience than the alternative hopes which have
beguiled, and then disappointed, past generations.

A concluding word must be said about the intimate relation between the hope of the fulfillment of individual selfhood with the hope for the fulfillment of the whole historical
drama. How incredible and how valid this combination of
hopes is! It is valid precisely because the individual self is
grounded in a collective history as surely as it is based in a
physical organism. Its fulfillment is not possible without the
fulfillment of the whole drama, yet the fulfillment of the
total drama offers no adequate completion of meaning for the
unique individual. One is reminded in this instance of the
many humble souls of either pathetic or noble proportions.
Historians may fit the lives of the thinkers and the statesmen of history into some kind of correlation which endows
their lives with meaning. But what is to be done about the
humble spirits who do not rise to the height to be fitted into
these correlations and schemes of meaning? And for that matter what is to be done with these same statesmen and philosophers insofar as they are anxious individuals rather than
great thinkers and doers? How, in other words, can we bring
the whole human story, including all the relevant and irrelevant individual dramas, into some scheme of intelligibility
without obscuring and denying the richness and variety of
the drama? The hope of the forgiveness of sins and life
everlasting is thus a fitting climax of the faith that there is a
meaning to the story beyond our understanding of its meaning because it is grounded in a power and purpose beyond
our comprehension, though not irrelevant to all our fragmentary meanings. It is the final venture in modesty for the
mysterious human self, which understands itself more completely if it understands that there are heights and depths
of human selfhood which are beyond any system of rational
intelligibility, but not beyond the comprehension of faith and
hope.

The question about interpreting human selfhood and its
dramas within either a framework of rational intelligibility
or a framework of meaning and mystery, which is the question between modern culture and faiths which are rooted in
the Bible, can be briefly summarized. There are directly

experienced realities in the realm of selfhood which point beyond any system of rational intelligibility to mystery, and they create a sense of meaning and mystery in which the one penetrates the other. Such realities or "facts" are the freedom and responsibility of the self, its sin and guilt, the unity of its freedom and its physical organism, and the variegated dramas and dialogues of which it is capable. These facts can not be contained in a system of rational intelligibility because there are no causal sequences and coherences which could contain the facts.

The systems proposed by classical or modern philosophers or scientists invariably deny or obscure some directly experienced facts for the sake of the coherence of the system. The facts point beyond themselves to a realm of mystery. But pure mystery destroys meaning as surely as pure intelligibility. The genius of Biblical faith is that it discerns by faith, glimpses of meaning in the ultimate mystery ("the light that shineth in darkness") which furnish the keys to the understanding of directly experienced realities. The fragmentariness and brevity of life, united to its dignity, is a mystery which is made meaningful by the promise of a fulfillment which is beyond the capacity of man. His sin and guilt are intolerable burdens without forgiveness which is available to those who acknowledge rather than hide the ultimate predicament of man. The dramas of man's history can be explained by discerning various patterns in history, but they are too multifarious to fit into any of these patterns. They can be fitted into a framework of meaning only if the meaning has a penumbra of mystery. The mystery consists of a power and a love beyond our comprehension which overrules these various historical dramas. The relation of the creative power to the redemptive love is also a mystery without the apprehension of which the whole of history falls into meaninglessness.

The hope that both the individual and the total drama of life will end in "the forgiveness of sins: the resurrection of the body: and the life everlasting," is thus the natural fruit of the faith that there is a height and depth of reality in God in which the individual in his uniqueness and freedom has a reality which the coherences of nature and reason do not assure him, and in which the endless dramatic variations of his collective life also have significance ultimately.

The Biblical faith makes the affirmation not only about the divine life which assures significance to selfhood and its dramas, but it also insists that the God who is powerful enough to bring the fragmentary dialogues and dramas to a conclusion also has a power of love which is able to overcome the recalcitrance of human sin.

There is no way of making either this faith or this hope "rational" by analyzing the coherences of nature and of reason. Efforts to do so inevitably result in some form of very attenuated philosophy and religion in which some of the experienced incoherences of life are obscured by the philosophically established coherences. One may only validate such a faith inferentially by calling attention to the fact that it answers the ultimate problems of the human self, which also has an incredible but directly experienced freedom, unity of freedom and finiteness and the capacity to elaborate endless dramas which do not fit into any pattern of nature and reason.

The fact that the individual feels his life to be fragmentary, despite its fulfillments in the community and in the historical process, proves that the self has a dimension which does not fit into any historical correlations. The divine power and love which gives this freedom meaning must be apprehended by faith. The reality of this power can be proved inferentially in the sense that any meaning which is imparted to life, purely in terms of the historical flux, can be proved to be a too simple meaning.

The fact that the self's freedom is involved in the contradiction of self-love is established by any careful observation of human history. But the self does not acknowledge itself to be implicated in this contradiction except in an encounter with the God who stands above all the historical judgements.

The self is involved in, and creates, various historical dramas which are known to have meaning. But the meaning which is ascribed to them is usually too simple if the frame of meaning consists merely of the correlations which may be charted by historical observation. Certainly the idea of progress which was the regulative religious idea of the past decades is an inadequate principle of meaning for the realities of an age which faces the dangers of atomic wars.

The unity of the self in its freedom and its natural and historical structure certainly invalidates all hopes of heaven which rest upon the idea that an immortal "soul" or mind may escape a mortal body. Thus the Biblical faith and hope, which gives meaning to human existence, may be proved inferentially to be true, or to be more in accord with experienced facts than alternative faith and hopes. But these inferences can not force the self to commit itself to them. The Biblical faith must remain a commitment of the self rather than a conclusion of its mind. Only such a commitment can do justice to the self's freedom and its discontinuity with the coherences and structures of the temporal world. The commitment is not possible without the prerequisite of repentance because the darkness about the meaning of its existence is due not so much to the finiteness of the self's mind as to pretensions of its heart. It is because men "became vain in their imaginations, and their foolish heart was darkened" (Romans 1:21) that they found such great difficulty in recognizing the true Author and end of their existence and the Divine Judge of the actions.

The dramas of history contain many facts and sequences which must be rationally correlated. But the frame of meaning in which these facts and sequences are discerned must be apprehended by faith because it touches the realm of mystery beyond rational comprehension. The ultimate question always remains whether the mystery is so absolute as to annul the meaning of the historical drama or whether there is a key of meaning in the mystery, a "light that shineth in darkness," which clarifies, rather than annuls, all the strange and variegated dramas of human history.

INDEX

Agape, 31 f., 95
"Love of Christ," 156
America,
    influence of Enlightenment on, 212-213
    problem of "co-existence" with East, 213-214
Amos, 83
Anaxagoras, 82
Anthropology, 14, 42
Anthropomorphism, 81
Anxiety, 21-22
Aquinas, Thomas, 101, 102
Aristotle, 4, 5, 48-49, 75-76, 82, 83-84
    in the Middle Ages, 101, 104
    Philia, 31
    reason, 3
    slavery, 150
Asia, 209-210
Atomic weapons, 202
Augustine, 99 ff., 167-168, 218

Bacon, Francis, 104, 114
Balzac, 42
Barth, Karl, 108
Benedict, Ruth, 132 n.
Benevolence, 185 f.
Bennett, J. W., 15
Bergson, H., 17 n.
Biblical Faith, 71, 224 ff.
Biography, 47, 48
"Bondage of the Will," 18
Bowers, Claude, 54
Bradley, F. H., 62, 122
Briffault, R., 150
Buber, M., 88
Bultmann, R., 97
Burckhardt, J., 47
Burke, E., 149, 177, 189
Burrow, Trigant, 142 n.

Calvin, John, 173
Catholic Church, 55-57, 102 f., 185 ff.

and authority of kings, 171
as force of conservatism, 167 f., 170
on liberty, 228 f.
Chamberlain, Neville, 47
Christ, 224 ff.
    anti-Christ, 239
    ethic of cross of, 232 f.
    love of, no simple possibility, 233 ff.
    resurrection and selfhood, 237 ff.
Churchill, Winston, 43, 47-48, 214
Classes, 36, 151 f.
    struggle of, 194 ff.
Clutton-Brock, 109
Collingwood, R. G., 57-58
Communism, 42, 125, 202, 208 f., 222
    illusion of community with, 205
    its "messianism," 63
    "Marxist-Leninist Science," 124
    not principally a military movement, 210
Community, 38 f., 148 ff.
    authoritarian, 228
    British, 40
    conscience of, 235 f.
    covenant, 92
    Hegel on, 35
    Jewish, 40
    open, 230 f.
    relation of individual to, 220 f.
    resistance to tyranny, 230
    symbols of, 177
    totalitarian, 221 ff.
    types of, 219
    world, 203 ff., 219
Comte, A., 42, 120
    relation to J. S. Mill, 223
Conant, James B., 114
Condorcet, 119, 150
Congress of Industrial Organizations, 46

243